ZA 315?   Y0-CCW-609

St. Clair, Guy, 1940-

Total quality management in
information services

DATE DUE

DEMCO 38-297

Total Quality Management in Information Services

Other titles in this series include:

Entrepreneurial Librarianship: The Key to Effective Information Services Management

Customer Service in the Information Environment

Power and Influence: Enhancing Information Services within the Organization

Corporate Memory: Information Management in the Electronic Age

Human Resources Strategies in Information Services Management

Total Quality Management in Information Services

Guy St Clair

BOWKER
SAUR

London • Melbourne • Munich • New Providence, New Jersey

British Library Cataloguing in Publication Data
A catalogue record for this book is available from the British Library

Library of Congress Cataloging-in-Publication Data
St. Clair, Guy, 1940-
    Total quality management in information services/Guy St Clair.
        p.   cm.
    Includes index.
    ISBN 1-85739-039-3 (hardback : alk. paper)
    1. Information services—Management. 2. Total quality management.
I. Title.
ZA3157.S23   1996
025.52'068—dc20   96-43536
                                                                    CIP

Published by Bowker-Saur,
Maypole House,
Maypole Road,
East Grinstead,
West Sussex RH19 1HU, UK
Tel: +44(0)1342 330100 Fax: +44(0)1342 330191
E-mail: lis@bowker-saur.co.uk
Internet Website: http://www.bowker-saur.co.uk/service

ISBN 1-85739-039-3

Cover design by Juan Hayward
Typesetting by GCS, Leighton Buzzard.
Printed on acid-free paper
Printed and bound in Great Britain by Antony Rowe Ltd, Chippenham

The author

Guy St Clair is the president of *InfoManage*/SMR International, a management consulting, training and publishing company with offices in New York. The company's clients include major chemical, pharmaceutical and engineering firms, and information organizations connected with the federal government, medicine, the arts, professional associations and the academic community. In the information services field, *InfoManage*/SMR International is also known as the publisher of *InfoManage: The International Management Newsletter for the Information Services Professional* and *The One-Person Library: A Newsletter for Librarians and Management*. Guy St Clair is a past president of the Special Libraries Association (1991–1992) and an active member and participant in the Information Futures Institute. An alumnus of the University of Virginia (BA), with his graduate work at the University of Illinois (MSLS), Guy St Clair lives in New York City.

Dedicated To Andrew Berner
and to Miriam A. Drake,
who has greatly influenced
my thinking in matters relating
quality management to information services

Introduction to the series

A broader management perspective for information services

For several years – decades, it seems – librarians and other information services professionals have lamented the fact that there is not enough emphasis on management in their training. They learn their subjects, and librarians especially connect very early on in their training to the concepts of service and the organization of information. Management skills, however, are frequently neglected or given minimal attention, and many information services professionals find themselves working in the corporate environment, research and technology organizations, government information units, or community/public administration organizations where management skills are needed. Much of what they need they learn on the job; other approaches, such as continuing education programs, are utilized by those who have the initiative to recognize that they must do something to educate themselves to be managers. Some of it works and some of it does not.

Bowker-Saur's *Information Management Series*, for which I serve as Series Editor, seeks to address this need in the information services community. For this series (and indeed, since the entire field of information management is strongly predicted by many to be going in this direction), the concept of information services is being defined very broadly. The time has come, it seems to me, to recognize that the various constituent units of our society concerned with information have many of the same goals and objectives, and, not surprisingly, many of the same concerns. The practice of management is one of these, and for our purposes it does not matter if the reader is employed as an information manager, information provider, information specialist, or indeed, as an information counsellor (as these information workers have been described by one of the leaders of business and industry). In fact, it does not matter whether the reader is employed in information technology, telecommunications, traditional librarianship, records management, corporate or organizational archives, the information brokerage field, publishing, consulting, or any of the myriad branches of information services (including service to the information community and the many vendors who make up that branch of the profession). These new titles on the management of information services have been chosen specifically for their value to all who are part of this community of information workers.

Although much work is being done in these various disciplines, little of it concentrates on management, and that which is done generally concentrates on one or another of the specific subgroups of the field. This series seeks to unite management concepts throughout information services, and whereas some of the titles will be directed to a specific group, most will be broad-based and will attempt to address issues of concern to all information services employees. For example, one book in the series deals with entrepreneurial librarianship, which would seem to be limited to the library profession but in fact offers information and guidance to anyone working in the information services field who is willing to incorporate entrepreneurial thinking into his or her work. Another title looks at corporate memory from the perspective of data and records management, and would seem to be limited to those who are practicing the discipline of records management. In fact, the book has been specifically structured to be of value to anyone who is working in the information services field, that 'umbrella' concept of information services described above.

As we attempt to bring general management practices into the realm of information services, it will be pointed out that the practice of management is addressed within the organizations or communities that employ information workers. This is true, and certainly in the corporate world (and, arguably, in the public and academic library communities as well), there are plenty of occasions for information services employees to participate in management training as provided in-house. There is nothing wrong with that approach and in many organizations it works very well, but the training does not proceed from an information services point of view, thus forcing the information worker to adapt, as best he or she can, the management practices of the organization to the management practices needed for the best provision of information services. The titles of the Bowker-Saur *Information Services Management Series* will enable the information worker to relate *information* management to *organizational* management, thus putting the information worker (especially the information executive) in a position of considerable strength in the organization or community where he or she is employed. By understanding management principles (admittedly, as frequently 'borrowed' from the general practice of management) and relating them to the way the information services unit is organized, not only does the information services employee position him or herself for the better provision of information services, but the entire information services unit is positioned as a respectable participant in organizational or community operations.

This last point perhaps needs some elaboration, for it should be made clear that the books in the series are not intended exclusively for the corporate or specialized information services field. It is our intention to provide useful management criteria for all kinds of information services, including those connected to public, academic or other publicly supported libraries. Our basic thesis is that quality management leads to quality services, regardless of whether the information services activity is privately or publicly funded, whether it is connected with a private research or public government agency, or indeed, whether it is a temporary information unit or whether it is part of a permanently funded and staffed operation. Writing for this series will be authors who, I am sure, will challenge some of the usual barriers to effective management practices in this or that type of library or information services unit, and certainly there will be librarians, records managers, archivists and others who will be able to relate some of their management practices in such a way that CIOs and computer services managers will benefit from the telling. In other words, our attempt here is to clear away the usual preconceptions about management within the various branches of information services, to do away with the concept of 'well-that-might-work-for-you-but-it-won't-work-for-me' kind of thinking. We can no longer afford to fight turf battles about whether or not management is 'appropriate' in one or other of the various subunits of information provision. What we must do, and what the *Information Services Management Series* expects to do, is to bring together the best of all of us, and to share our management expertise so that we all benefit.

Guy St Clair
Series Editor

Contents

Foreword

'Core assessment planning', 'long-term operating infrastructure', 'strategic customer-oriented centralization initiatives' – it seems as if every new business book and every article in a professional journal touts a trendy, jargon-laden business concept or management technique. Professionals who care about their organizations, colleagues and clients cannot help becoming confused and overwhelmed, because professionals who care are always on the lookout for new tools that will help them do their jobs. So they must continually ask themselves, 'Which new management concepts are worthwhile investments of time? Which are merely the latest business fads?'

Guy St Clair has seized on a concept that represents a worthwhile investment for all management professionals. Of course, total quality management isn't a totally new concept. As the author points out in the introduction, TQM was 'the management war cry of the eighties'. And for some people it has become yesterday's news. But total quality management is a noteworthy methodology for many reasons, chief among them being that it focuses on customers' needs, which is precisely where the focus in management belongs. It doesn't matter whether a professional works in a corporate, academic or government environment: serving the customer is the manager's life work. This is a simple idea (the best ones usually are), and it has been said many times before. But it cannot be said too often because the focus on the customer is too easily lost amid the hectic pace and the competing demands for accountability in today's work environments.

Total quality management reasserts that the manager is primarily accountable to the customer. It then works backward from the customer's perspective to achieve a continuous improvement in processes that directly benefit an organization's clients.

Guy St Clair's thoughts on TQM make his book a worthwhile read for any management professional in any type of work environment. The author's greatest triumphs, however, are his practical suggestions on the best ways to weave quality management techniques into the day-to-day practices of the information professional. He suggests, for example, that the best way to bring TQM to information services is to 'lessen the emphasis on process and put the emphasis on analysis'. This is a modification that engages the information professional's judgment and tradition of intellectualism.

The author provides a complete and clearly defined course on TQM for any type or size of information services organization. He leads the reader through the most important concepts and shows how they apply to the professional's goals. He then offers a step-by-step guide for developing, implementing and benchmarking a TQM plan.

As with the other titles in this series, *Total Quality Management in Information Services* demonstrates Guy St Clair's editorial excellence. As always, he shows a deft hand in the organization, depth and clarity of his material. The professional who invests time in it will be rewarded with new tools that will enhance not only his or her provision of services, but also the role of the information services organization within the larger organization or community it serves.

So, the next time you are confronted with such fashionable but overblown concepts as 'fundamental strategy propositions' or 'value-based marketing mechanisms', you can be assured that your time is better spent with the proven ideas and techniques embodied in the book in your hands.

Joseph J. Fitzsimmons
Retired President, CEO and Chairman of UMI,
a Bell & Howell Company

Introduction

'Total quality management means quality service'

Few subjects generate as much controversy in the library and information services profession as quality management. Why this should be the case in a discipline in which quality management – as accepted by all practitioners – is the basis upon which it is built is something of a mystery. Such 'essentials' of quality management as an emphasis on customer service, accurate measurement, continuous improvement, work relationships based on trust and teamwork, when added to a desire for quality services and the support and enthusiasm of senior organizational management,* would seem to be as fundamental to the successful management of an information services facility as they would be to the management of any entity. Surely any library, records management unit, archive, computer services department, or any of the other types of organizational entities concerned with the delivery of information services, products or consultations, could benefit from the practice of quality management principles.

However, there is much resistance in the information services field to the use of the 'quality' approach to management. Why we cannot come to grips with this difficult phenomenon is a subject which might be worth pursuing in a more scientific and empirical manner one day. For the present, though, we can be satisfied with a more modest approach. If we want to attempt to understand why information services practitioners shy away from engaging in formal quality management activities, we must remember that in practically all organizations in which information services units have been developed and established, the management and delivery of information is usually relegated to a less-than-essential role in

---

*It should be noted that these four 'essentials', as identified by Michael Barrier in a famous essay (1992), and the others, which I identified and first wrote about in my book on customer service, will be repeatedly referred to in this work, to the extent that they might be considered to be a sort of running theme or pattern in this book.

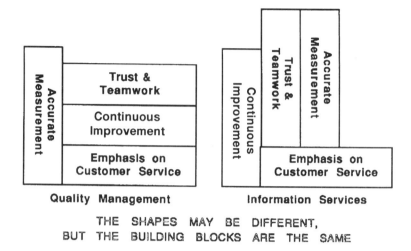

THE SHAPES MAY BE DIFFERENT,
BUT THE BUILDING BLOCKS ARE THE SAME

the organizational framework. Having been so positioned (or perceived as being so positioned), the information services unit is thus not taken very 'seriously' in the management operations of the organization or community (if we are speaking of public information-delivery facilities, such as a public library, say, or a governing authority's vital statistics department). The further result is that the *management* of that unit is not taken very 'seriously', and we have a situation in which all stakeholders in that unit's operation – senior organizational managers who have authority over its operations, the customers who come to it for information products, services, and consultations, and even its own managers and employees – have difficulty seeing the management of the unit in quality terms. In fact, for many of these stakeholders the very fact that the information unit is a service facility and not a production department means that it exists in a sort of operational 'free zone', not expected to bring in any sort of return on the organizational or community investment and certainly not to be managed with any emphasis on management criteria that look towards a return on investment. Consequently, these information services units are undermanaged, often to the extent that any management or performance evaluation is casual and extremely 'loose' (in terms of what is expected of other departments and units), and the notion of bringing anything as sophisticated as quality management into the operation is not only not of interest, it is rejected out of hand as being 'inappropriate', 'not related to what we do', or – typically – 'too business-oriented' for a library or information services function.

Of course such a description is a vast oversimplification, but pieces of it come forward in practically every discussion one has with information services managers. Regardless of the type of operation under discussion, there is almost always a 'reason' why quality management principles won't 'fit', and while much of the argument in favor of adhering to quality principles will be listened to respectfully, there is usually resistance. In their useful compilation of articles on quality management in the library community (especially with respect to academic libraries), Susan Jurow and Susan B. Barnard (1993) identified four barriers which prevent the adoption of total quality management in libraries, and reference to their analysis is appropriate here:

1. **Vocabulary.** Librarians are uncomfortable with the use of terms and concepts affiliated with business and the marketplace. Librarians are not engaged in "business" and, in the minds of many librarians, the linking of "business" concepts and methodologies with the "scholarly" and erudite environment of the profession of librarianship demeans librarianship.
2. **Commitment.** Not limited to librarianship, a lack of commitment often dooms a quality process. The energy, resources, and, particularly, the time required for the successful realization of results from a quality initiative are simply not always available, and the managers of some libraries are of the opinion that they cannot "afford" to invest in the organization and implementation of a quality program.
3. **Process.** Librarians are "impatient with process and eager for closure", so there is often a disinclination to invest in a process – such as TQM – that concentrates more on systematic analysis and less on the "quick fix". Librarians are accustomed to solving problems – their clients' and their own – quickly. A quality initiative with its promise of success far down the road is distinctly unappealing.
4. **Professionalism.** Often based more on ignorance or cultural inexperience as much as anything else, librarians as professionals have difficulty with some components of the quality management "culture". Professionals are "mystified by, if not fearful of, the consequences of what they think could mean turning over their services and practices, which are based on tradition, standards, and respected bodies of knowledge, to the uninformed whims of customers." (Jurow and Barnard, 1993, pp. 5-6).

To stop here, though, implies that this is an 'either/or' situation, and that the information services manager must either attempt to apply total quality management (and/or its many variations) in the information setting and relinquish professionalism, or avoid the move to quality management and retain professionalism. What a simplistic approach! The picture should not be painted so bleakly, for there is much in quality management that fits with the goals and objectives of sophisticated library and information services management. In fact, one place to begin (which hopefully will come through as another of the themes of this book) is to look at the best practices of library and information services management and match them to the best features of TQM. For example, if an impediment to the adoption of TQM for librarians is say, their preference for the 'quick fix' and their avoidance of process and analysis, perhaps the best way to bring TQM to librarianship is to lessen the emphasis on process and put it on analysis, incorporating into the analysis the professional judgment and intellectual consideration that librarians' 'tradition, standards, and respected bodies of knowledge' have imbued them with. It may not be pure TQM, but a distinctive characteristic of any quality approach to management is that no one formula is going to work in every situation. If this is so, then what is wrong with adapting TQM to information services management, rather than the other way round? The answer is of course that there is nothing wrong with this approach, and it is what must be done if TQM is to be successfully applied in the information environment.

Why total quality management in information services?

One reason why this book has been written is frankly and candidly proselytical: it is a direct and blatant attempt to persuade those who have management responsibility for the delivery of information services and products in their organizations and communities to look to the inclusion of quality management practices in their work. It truly does not matter what kind of operation it is, whether it is a library, records management unit, or other type of information delivery function, and the size of the operation is similarly irrelevant. It is my strong belief that the accepted principles of quality management can be as effective in a one-person operation as they are in a multistaffed information facility: the difference is merely one of focus (and the smaller the operation, the greater the chances of success, simply because the staff responsible for direct delivery of information services are closer to the customer, but this point can and will be argued). Regardless of the size of the operation or the type of information facility, quality management principles can and should be part of the management structure.

Nevertheless, there are other reasons for initiating a quality program, and it doesn't matter whether the program is self-directed (that is, originates within the information unit itself) or mandated from a higher administrative authority. The primary reason, of course, has to be information delivery from the customer's point of view. In all service delivery operations today we hear much about 'the authority of the customer', but most of us who are involved in actually delivering those services have some difficulty giving that concept its due. We are uncomfortable with having someone else – even if it is the customer for whom our operation exists – drive the delivery of that service. But in information services we simply cannot step back from the authority of the customer because, with very few exceptions, the services we provide and the information we deliver can be obtained elsewhere. The world today is one of competition, and for every information function (except for unique materials and the information contained within them) the customer who comes to us could go somewhere else if he or she chose to.

Yet there is more to it than simply meeting the needs of customers. Of course, this is why the information services unit exists in the first place, but another piece of the picture that must be considered, particularly from a managerial point of view, is the place of the unit in the organizational structure. Again, the framework of the structure of the organization doesn't matter: its senior managers may have decided to operate under a traditional hierarchical management framework, or have gone for the more modern flattened management structure, or even moved into the almost avant garde web management structure that is beginning to be seen in some organizations. Regardless of the parent company or authority's management structure, the information services unit requires a role of some prominence and a quality management program ensures that position. Why? Because it sends a message to the decision makers (and the resource-allocation authorities, if they are not one and the same) that the information unit is one in which the business of management is taken seriously. This is, of course, very much a matter of perception, but in the eyes of the people who matter, who have influence in the organization or the community. Once these people are convinced, the role of the unit is considerably enhanced.

However, competition for the customer's business and enhancing our unit's role in the organization or community are not really the reasons we look to quality management: we do it because it's the right thing to do. Regardless of the arrangement under which the information unit is supported, as information services managers we have a responsibility to provide the best information delivery that we can. It is part of the contract – sometimes only implicit and not specifically articulated – that we and our staffs have with the governing authority with senior management responsibility for the support of the information services unit. And, of course, with the information customers themselves, who are presumably part of the organization or community for which that authority also has senior management responsibility.

As is discussed in Chapter Three, information services management is founded on the principles of planning, organizing, leading and controlling. We do these things because we are part of a greater system, to which it is assumed we are going to give the *best* that we can give in terms of products, services or other outputs, from the system over which we ourselves have managerial authority. But we cannot give our best if there is no firm definition of what 'the best' is. We thus find ourselves seeking measurement tools, calling forth all kinds of schemes and mechanisms so that we can tell those who need to know that we are doing a good job.

In librarianship, for example, we have traditionally relied on usage statistics to judge how good our services are; but, as the current debate about effectiveness measures surely indicates, in this new era in which we are blessed with enabling technology that we can use to create information marketing systems, we do ourselves and our organizations a major disservice if we do not use these tools to identify and quantify just how effective our services are. Such worthwhile programs as specifically profiled selective dissemination of information (SDI) systems, routinized customer follow-up systems and the like, can provide data that can be manipulated and reformatted and analyzed to provide us with much information about the quality of the services we are providing. These and other mechanisms, whether they are loosely organized 'quality assurance' programs built on some external framework, or a formalized TQM system built according to the tenets of the most famous of the quality systems, or a codified system built to match the ISO 9000 standards now required for quality certification in some countries, can be used to demonstrate to senior management, community leaders, customers and staff that the information services operation is being operated as well as it can be. This is not a bad position for any manager to be in.

Is it relevant?

There are, of course, those who contend that quality management schemes are no longer appropriate. As with many management trends, quality management initiatives (and particularly TQM) are often denigrated and derided.

Yes, TQM was the management war cry of the 1980s, and in some environments it has become an object of scorn in the 1990s. As the new century approaches, TQM is for many just one more management attempt to impose standardization on industries and services that get along just fine without it. For these skeptics, the less said about total quality management, quality assurance, 'quality circles' and the like, the better. These and similar attempts to codify quality, they would have us believe, are passé. They are no longer part of the scene for librarians and other information services managers, even for those who attempted to incorporate them into their management programs, and they probably never were.

These skeptics, however, couldn't be more wrong. If there were ever a time when management standards are needed for libraries and other information-related operations, it is now, and if there is a better set of guidelines than those that make up the quality management framework, I haven't learned about it yet. Certainly nothing we've tried in library/ information services management rings as true, or offers so much potential for success, as the quality focus. Yes, the management world at large has ventured beyond TQM and moved into such replications as benchmarking, the 'fifth discipline' of the learning organization, and process re-engineering, but each of these methodologies, especially when applied to the delivery of information through a library or other information services operation, is basically a piece of or closely related to what TQM has been doing all along. And, yes, there are the deliciously rewarding anecdotal methods we use for effectiveness measures (simply because we have no other methods, at least not yet, for that tricky task), but here again there is a built-in weakness to the approach, because there is no factual and objective underpinning from which the conclusions have been drawn. It is nice to hear how 'important' the information unit is, and the anecdotal presentations make us all feel good, but just *why* is it so important? What effect does that information services unit have on the organization or community of which it is a part?

Quality management helps provide the answers. The more we think about the *function* of librarianship or other information services management, and the more we study quality management and its goals, the more apparent it becomes that it is the pursuit of quality that leads to success in information delivery. Just the very seeking after quality predisposes those with managerial responsibility towards the achievement of organizational or community objectives, with respect to library and information services management.

This assertion can be demonstrated by describing the basics of quality management in information management alluded to earlier. Library and information services managers might argue some of the specifics, but from the point of view of the library/information services operation's role in the organization or community, the value of these particular fundamental attributes cannot be refuted: the emphasis on the customer in the information delivery transaction; continuous improvement and the continuous seeking after new and better ways of doing what has to be done; measurement (including both quantitative measures and, as noted above, effectiveness measures); and the value of trust and teamwork within the organizational or community framework.

Beyond these, however, in the library/information services community two other quality management characteristics point the way:

1. **Desire for quality.** In order for libraries and other information services operations to offer quality products, services and consultations to their identified customers, there must be an honest desire on the part of the service providers to provide that quality. As librarianship and most other information services disciplines seem to be predicated on the 'service ethos', so to speak, it seems slightly churlish to bring the subject up. But there are many people working in libraries or other information units who do not particularly like what they are doing, who are not particularly concerned about the level of service they provide, and who do not like their customers and patrons very much. Until these staff members have been converted to a true service ethos, and are not simply paying lip service to it because it is expected, a quality management effort is a futile exercise. Information

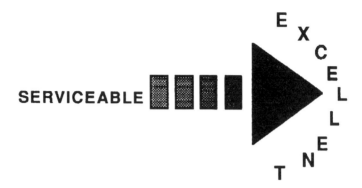

services managers must recognize that not all their staff will be as committed to quality information delivery as they are, and they must earnestly devise and implement initiatives to match expected quality with delivered quality.

2. **Enthusiasm and support of senior management.** Regardless of the type of library or other information unit, no quality effort can even begin to succeed without the commitment of senior management. Sadly, however, this characteristic for success is closely related to that mentioned above, for many library/information services managers have been promoted from within and may be the same uncommitted information workers who advance up the managerial hierarchy by virtue of their bureaucratic tenacity, and not because of their excellence as professional information delivery staff. These are the managers who are quick to dismiss TQM and similar activities as 'too much trouble', who, when required to institute quality programs, malign them as a 'waste of time' but condescendingly go along with them, because they have been mandated. Such a quality management program will end in dismal failure at all levels.

From a more positive perspective, however, it should be noted that there are those library/information services managers who have embarked on quality programs with great success because they recognized that such an undertaking would result in a better service for the users and easier management for them. There are many communities, organizations and businesses providing true quality management in the delivery of information services because their managers had the interest and the vision to understand just how good the operation could be, and they recognized that a quality management program would enable them to achieve that vision of goodness. Whether the impetus came from above or from the manager himself or herself, it was seized upon as an opportunity and not seen as yet another try at good management to be struggled with without enthusiasm. In fact, those information services managers who took the initiative and proceeded with a quality program could not have done it without the support and enthusiasm of their own managers, and they made it their business to have that support and enthusiasm in place before they committed themselves to the process.

For those information services managers who are still struggling, still seeking the best methodology for moving their operations from the mere serviceable to the excellent, it is worth looking at quality management programs. The concept is not dead yet (just walking through the 'Management' section of any large bookstore will demonstrate that), and if we take the best characteristics of quality management and link them to benchmarking, business process re-engineering, systems thinking and other management methodologies, we are likely to come up with a customized practice that can lead to real benefits for the organizations and communities of which our information operations are a part. So, in response to those who think that TQM as a management tool is dead, I refer them to the many organizations where quality management makes a difference. It is a management tool that is very much alive and will remain so, simply because, when given its due (and supported by all information stakeholders), quality management *works.*

How well it works has come to my attention through much observation and study, but as much as anything else through the many interactions I have with people who talk to me about these things. The development of the ideas put forward in this book has come about over many years and through the influence of many different people. It is appropriate to acknowledge some of these colleagues and friends who are so encouraging in the work I do.

Andrew Berner, my business associate and close friend, understands my thinking and spends many hours in delightful conversation with me about these matters. In addition, I am indebted to Andrew for the graphics that illustrate these books. Miriam A. Drake is a professional manager in the information services discipline whom I respect greatly, and our many conversations on the subject of quality management, growing out of her own successful experiences, continue to provide me with much stimulation and intelligent provocation. Mimi Drake collaborated with me on an important chapter for this book and contributed the case study of the quality initiative implemented at her institution. Like Andrew Berner, Mimi Drake is a good friend as well as an esteemed professional colleague, and to the two of them I dedicate this book and thank them for their work with me over these many years.

As I developed these ideas about quality management in the information services community, I also had good conversations with and received much support from several other people. Beth Duston, my good friend and strategic partner in many projects, knows and understands my thinking about quality management and supports me as I attempt to encourage information services practitioners to incorporate these methodologies into their work. David R. Bender, Joseph J. Fitzsimmons, Robert E. Frye, Kenneth Megill, Mary Park, Thomas Pellizzi, Ruth Seidman and Ann Wolpert have all provided useful and stimulating conversation. Barbara M. Spiegelman kindly spoke with me about her work at Westinghouse, and I was then permitted to incorporate many of her ideas into this text; I appreciate her willingness to share her experience with me. The members of the Information Futures Institute, at the semiannual meetings coordinated by my good friend Bernard Vavrek, are continually discussing these subjects in a broader context and I am grateful to them for~ their fellowship and exhilarating conversation. Ann Lawes, Evelin Morgenstern, and Marisa Urgo have spent many hours talking with me about these subjects and I greatly respect their opinions and their ideas. Finally, both my sons are in fields of work wherein they are expected to understand management principles and use them, and I find myself often in conversation with Gil and Austin St Clair in these matters, conversations which are rewarding for all three of us. I can state sincerely and without exaggeration that all of these people have much influence in my life as I work on these subjects, and I thank them for their continued interest in this work, and for sharing their thoughts with me.

At Bowker Saur, too, I am supported in much of this effort, especially as we begin to build this series beyond my own writings. Linda Hajdukiewicz and Geraldine Turpie, and others on the editorial staff at Maypole House, are invaluable colleagues. They are steadfast in their kindness, they offer very good and very practical advice, and I appreciate all that they do for me and for the work that we are attempting to do together.

A technical point should be made. Although direct quotations from the literature are given, there are many occasions where I refer to people who have been interviewed in two of the publications produced by our company. *InfoManage: The International Management Newsletter for the Information Services Professional* has a monthly feature called 'The Information Interview', in which a prominent leader in the information services field describes his or her work and some facet of that work which is relevant to the subject under discussion. *The One-Person Library: A Newsletter for Librarians and Managers* also includes occasional 'profiles'. For both of these newsletters, I am responsible for interviewing these people and for writing the articles. Therefore, for many references to particular people, or discussions of their ideas, there are no formal citations, as the information was gleaned in the interview or profile. Obviously, however, if the interview or profile is quoted directly, it is so cited. In both cases I am grateful to these people for allowing me to interview them, and for contributing both to our newsletters and to this book by sharing with me their insights about the management of information services.

References

Barrier, Michael. 'Small firms put quality first.' *Nation's Business* 80 (5), May, 1992.

Jurow, Susan and Barnard, Susan B., eds. *Integrating Total Quality Management in a Library Setting*. New York: Haworth Press, 1993.

Part 1

Quality and Information Services

Chapter One

The information services environment

Within the library and information services discipline there has long been tension between the professional staff who deliver the information products, services and consultations, and others in the general management community. For many information services practitioners, management as a scientific discipline was too often connected with business and the pursuit of wealth, and was rejected as compromising the 'pure' and untainted delivery of information. For these people the noble pursuit of information for its own sake, with no questions asked of the customer, seemed almost ideal. During the last half of the twentieth century this attitude has been taken to its extreme, most notably in the public library field, where the librarians – as the arbiters of information delivery – would show the users how to find the information, even teach them, as part of their educational role, how to use the different tools and resources that would enable them to find the information, but would take no responsibility for the quality of the information delivered and most certainly would not enquire about how it was to be used.

Despite the fact that the very act of enquiring makes the information interview a more productive one, and enables the professional to make a wiser choice about what types of materials and information to direct the customer to, issues relating to privacy and the individual customer's 'right to know' became far more important than the librarian's need for complete information about the information quest. And although this situation would seem to suggest that the authority of the customer was indeed being given full consideration in the information transaction, it actually meant that the librarian was doing two things. First, the librarian was putting himself or herself in a position to pass judgment on what information the user should receive (becoming, as it were, a 'moral' arbiter, a critical and judgmental mediator, in the information delivery transaction). More seriously, the information services worker was relieving himself or herself of professional accountability: if he or she didn't know how the information would be used, the librarian could not be liable for the quality of the information transferred and was not going to be held accountable if the customer did not get what he or she needed (and was not responsible if the information was used in some way that brought harm to society).

This is a harsh indictment, and thankfully it reflects the way things were, not the way things are. Information services management has changed in the last decade or so, and information is now expected to be delivered with serious attention to such issues as the quality of delivery, the level of service, the role of the customer and accountability and responsibility on the part of the people delivering the information.

Among information services workers it is generally agreed that specialized librarianship is driving these changes in information delivery. In this branch of information services, in which information materials and information delivery are provided for the exclusive use and 'private advantage' of the organization that supports the library financially, the focus has always been slightly different from that of other types of librarianship (Ashworth 1979, p. 6). With the introduction of enabling technology into the information process, as well as changes in what might be called the philosophy of information delivery, that focus and that difference have been considerably enhanced. In special libraries the attention is directed to the customer, the recipient of the information. Whereas in other branches of librarianship such service has been the stated goal of academic librarians, public librarians and school librarians, in fact the authority of the customer is often compromised by rules, regulations and other barriers, erected not to prevent the exchange of information but to ensure that the exchange fits into the librarians' carefully defined limits of what the service should be.

On the other hand, special (or specialist) librarianship is part of the competitive capitalist system. It was Ed Strable who used this phrase to distinguish the special library from other libraries, and even though times have changed considerably since he came up with the idea, it is still a valid distinction (Strable 1980, p. 216). A large percentage of special libraries – perhaps half – are to be found in the for-profit sector, and those which are not so affiliated are found in research organizations, in government, museums, trade associations and all organizations that use or produce specialized information and in which the use of that information, and hence the authority of the customer, cannot be compromised. The function of all specialized libraries is to provide the customer with the information product, service or consultation that he or she is seeking. The specialized library does not exist to show the customer *how it find* the information: it exists to *provide* the information. This is the primary difference that has always existed between specialized librarianship and all other types, but it is a line of separation that is quickly being eroded.

Sometimes, however, the customer really does want to learn *how* to find the information, rather than having the professional do it for him. In

I ... **Is a resource**

N

F ... **has value**

O

R ...**can be managed**

M

A ...**should be available**
      to the broadest
T   **possible audience**

I

O ...**should be organized**
      to meet the needs of
N   **the user**

this case, the information services transaction becomes simply a question of choice, as is discussed later, and defining the authority of the customer becomes a matter of determining what the customer wants, what his choice in the matter is. Does the customer choose to be shown how to find the information? Or does he choose to have the information provided to him? This is what is meant by the 'authority of the customer', regardless of the discipline or industry in which the transaction is taking place.

What we are seeing is, in my opinion, a movement in librarianship and information services that is very much influenced by management objectives brought from other fields of study. The synergy in much of this can be found in the emerging discipline of information resources management (IRM), and just as it includes specific direction for information services managers as they seek to establish information policies for the organizations and communities where they are employed (as described in *Entrepreneurial Librarianship*, another of the books in this series), so it can provide useful direction as an information services operation moves toward quality management. With its emphasis on the information customer, its empowering and decentralizing management structure, its integration of *all* information as its primary task, and its commitment to automation and electronic data transfer, IRM looks at information in management terms that fit very smoothly into a quality initiative.

THREE PATHS TO SUCCESS FOR THE INFORMATION SERVICES MANAGER

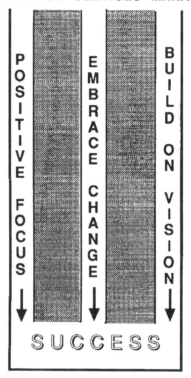

P
O
S
I
T
I
V
E

F
O
C
U
S
↓

E
M
B
R
A
C
E

C
H
A
N
G
E
↓

B
U
I
L
D

O
N

V
I
S
I
O
N
↓

SUCCESS

Kenneth Megill has been doing much of the important work in this field, and he has identified several principles of IRM. Megill's list can provide a basic philosophy for how a library, records management unit, archives operation or other information delivery function is managed. With these principles as a foundation the information unit is well on its way to the successful achievement of the organization or community's information mission:

- Information is a resource. Like other resources it has value and can be managed

- Information gains value with use

- Since information gains value with use, it should be available to the broadest possible audience

- Information should be organized to meet the needs of the user; organizations should be organized around the flow of information

- Work will be fundamentally transformed if: information is managed as a resource; information is organized for dissemination; work is organized around information flow (Megill 1994, p. 5).

In describing the management of information services in today's highly competitive and fast-moving environment, it is necessary, in addition to thinking about the values inherent in the IRM approach, to give some attention to what are being referred to as 'shifting paradigms', that important management and societal concept that Joel Barker (1993) identified a few years ago which has had such an important impact on the way those of us who are involved in management do our work. Whether we want to or not, to succeed in the future in information services we must think about change and change management, and how change is required to ensure success in our professional futures.

If the management of librarianship and information services can be moved into a positive framework that builds on the inevitable and desirable attributes of change, which recognizes that the paradigms of information delivery shift as society changes, then that successful future is assured (Ferriero and Wilding 1991, p. 2). If we cannot do so, or refuse to do so, that future is not going to happen. Or it will happen with other professions and other disciplines becoming information providers, and those who are today defined as information providers will be left behind. We have the choice, and how we make our decisions, which path we choose, is what determines whether we will be here in the future.

There are three paths information services managers can take to achieve success, both now and in the future. The first is to move away from the negative, 'how-bad-things-are' approach to information services, to change our perspective to focus on positive and optimistic thinking. The second is to begin to think about changes in information services and society – to 'shift' the paradigms – to a point of view which recognizes that change is both inevitable and desirable. The third is to work towards the future from a perspective that builds on a vision of library and information services in the twenty-first century and a future that we as the information experts will lead our customers to. That future will require us to work with the information customers, the managers and decision makers (and those with resource allocation authority) in our organizations and communities, as well as with all other information stakeholders, but this is not a problem, for it is going to be a future in which both we *and* they will delight in the collaborative and cooperative role we each will play in the achievement of this future success in information services.

Information services practitioners are now working in a field that requires –even demands – a great deal of forethought and planning. We are also working in a field that now demands a considerable amount of advocacy from those who support us, and part of what we do with quality management is to ensure that support from those who must provide the resources we need to do our work. Advocacy for information services is no longer an isolated phenomenon, and in seeking power and influence in the organizations and communities with which the information services operations are affiliated, the value of a successful quality management program cannot be underestimated.

Positive management

In attempting to find a balanced perspective for the management of information services, a positive, more optimistic approach is called for, because much of what is perceived about information management by our customers is thought of as negative, tiresome, and not forward-looking – not *modern*. If we are going to be effective in the delivery of information services, we must move our customers from that old-fashioned perspective to one that truly reflects the positive effects of information delivery, that makes them confident about the products, services and consultations we will provide for them. How do we do this? And how can positive management be related to the work we do as information services providers?

To answer these questions we must begin with a somewhat personal interpretation. For me, positive management has to be considered in terms that relate to the success of information delivery, based on a clear understanding of the mission of the organization or community that employs us and connected to the library/information services unit's own mission and that of its employees. It means that we concentrate on the needs of the information customer (and not on the bureaucratic and institutionalized rules that we have devised for our own and our unit's convenience), and especially that we and all the other information delivery staff in the organization take a proactive, creative, positive approach to the delivery of information services and products. We do not whine, we do not complain, and the phrase 'we don't do that here' is not part of our departmental language. Above all, we bring enthusiasm to the information delivery process.

It is this enthusiasm that defines for us the positive construct in management terms. In the modern service-oriented information facility, in which the foundations of the operation are based as much on quality of service as on the content of the information delivered to the customers, enthusiasm is key. Information workers and their managers must understand that the delivery of information products and services is an exciting, rewarding and ever-changing process, and they must always be (or position themselves to be perceived as being) delighted to be participating in that process. In this respect, a rather neat analogy can be made with those working in the hotel business, and while to some of us it might appear to be something of a 'reach' to think of customer services in the hospitality industry and to connect this with customer care in information services, there really is no difference. For one hotel manager, customer service is rather neatly summarized as problem solving. 'Look', he says, 'when you manage a service operation, your customer comes to you with a problem. However you define it, it's a problem, at least for the customer. Our job is to take that problem and to give that customer a solution, *to fix things*.' This concept neatly sums up what information services providers do: they *fix things* for the information customers, and when their customers leave them their lives have been changed, hopefully for the better and hopefully with some enthusiasm and delight on the information provider's part. That, I think, is what we mean by positive management.

The shifting paradigms

From this perspective, then, we can think about those shifting paradigms. Joel Barker is the management specialist who is generally given the credit for encouraging us to think about the paradigms – the models – on which our management practices are built, and it was Barker, in the late 1980s and early 1990s, who organized a number of books and presentations that brought his concept so dramatically to life. Simply put, Barker is suggesting that the models and patterns that affect our management decision making are shifting, and that many of the decisions we make as managers will be faulty unless we recognize these pattern shifts and build them into our decisions. For library and information services workers the almost unreal developments in information delivery mechanisms and the speed with which these are occurring provide a perfect example. For the graduate student attempting to learn how to manage a library or other information services operation, a concentration on what is fondly referred to as 'the art of the book' is an anachronism. Although it might be pleasant for a book-loving individual to take such a course as an elective, unless he or she plans to manage a specifically book-oriented collection, the information gleaned from such a course will be pretty meaningless. Indeed, that student will not learn about management in such a course, will not learn about such things as personnel issues or financial management, and certainly will not learn about customer service. In the library and information services field the paradigm has shifted, and that student – and his or her faculty advisers – must move in a different direction if he or she is going to be prepared to be a manager in library and information services work.

So, when we talk about 'shifting paradigms', we are talking about looking at the different perspectives required for management success these days, and there are few professions where the shifts are as dramatic as they are in library and information services. Look, for example, at the changes that have come about in the three areas just mentioned.

When we think about personnel issues we have to give special consideration to the role of the librarian or other information provider, and to be prepared as managers to deal with the different work that we and our employees are expected to perform nowadays, and for how different that work is from what we did in the past. For example, in a popular magazine article about downsizing, the point was made that all companies, in fact, are not downsizing. Many jobs, according to the article, go begging because workers do not have the required skills. Librarians, though, are perceived as having the skills if they can adopt new work habits and procedures:

> Technology changes work – and not everyone who has mastered the old work will succeed at the new. Two years ago, Air Products and Chemicals Inc. decided that paying librarians to look up facts is a waste of money. Instead, it wants teams of librarians like Stacy Hach, 33, to function as consultants, using computers to pull together analyses for scientists and market researchers. "This is way beyond what would be the original skills of librarians", says Hach's boss, Bill Townsend. "Librarians are moving toward a two-tier pay scale", Townsend says, "with those who can analyze information earning much more than those who shelve books". (Levinson 1996, p. 43).

Unfortunately, the quotation conveys the abysmal ignorance some people have about what librarians do (for not many professional librarians think of themselves as book shelvers), but the basic idea behind the quotation is a valid one. The librarian or information services provider who wants to succeed in what is very much a global information environment must be more than simply a provider of facts. New responsibilities and management expectations include the *analysis* and *interpretation* of information, as well as its delivery. The paradigm has shifted. The librarian of the twenty-first century, and even of the late twentieth century, is a far different creature from the librarian of previous times.

The paradigms have also shifted when we talk about financial management, about how libraries and information services are supported. There was a time when a library director, for example, went to the responsible funding authority and, through the presentation of a carefully prepared budget request, asked for the resources to manage the library for the upcoming budget period. Not any more. Today's library manager knows that resource allocation is based on the value of the services the library provides, and that value is determined by the *effectiveness* of the services in the lives of the information customers. The library or other information services unit is judged to be a good one if its services are of value to its users. The determination of that value is established by the information customers themselves, and not by the library's director or the resource allocation authority. The paradigm has shifted.

This shifting paradigm leads, of course, to the third example, for there are few areas of our library and information services work that have changed more than our attitudes to customer service. We now recognize explicitly what had been only implicitly acknowledged in the past (and that more frequently in the breach than in the observance): that the reason for our existence is to provide the customers with the information they need. This is a far cry from the days when the librarian or information services provider was the moral 'arbiter' in the information sphere, when *we* decided what the *user* needed. The customer service paradigm has indeed shifted, and we have adjusted our management approach to incorporate this.

To these three shifting paradigms must, in my opinion, be added another critical change that is taking place in the delivery of information: the adding of value in the information transaction, and the fact that added value is now expected in the work that information services practitioners undertake to do.

Adding value simply means doing more, going beyond the simple solution to the customer's problem. With respect to value, of course, we know that when the information customer leaves with what he or she came for, there is already some value built into it. The *added* value comes into the transaction when the information provider goes beyond the basic response and offers further information that will enhance, or indeed have some impact on, the enquirer's use of that information. In these situations the information provider has given the customer what he or she needed, but recognizing that the usefulness of the information provided is conditioned by the *additional* information, seeks to provide the additional information as well. In doing so, he or she is adding value to the information transaction.

That's the simple version. As information services managers and their staffs assume more and more responsibility in the successful achievement of their organizations' goals, the concept of added value takes on new significance in the information services function. Stephen Abram, for example, who is Director of Corporate and News Information at Micromedia Limited in Toronto, suggests that specialized librarians understand the concept of added value 'at a deeper level'. 'As information professionals', Abram says, 'we offer a service based on our professional skills and knowledge, and we are adding value when we transform the relationship of the customer with respect to the information that person requires'.

Abram suggests that if we aren't transforming information as it passes through our operation in order to make it *more* useful, *better* understood and *more easily* put to work as knowledge, then we aren't adding value and we are not fulfilling our potential. 'You have added value', he says, 'when your client is "different" for having used your service – when that person is more *knowledgeable* and *decision-empowered*'. This is what

Abram calls 'transformational librarianship' (Abram 1996, p. 5).

Certainly it makes sense, from a managerial perspective, to seek added value. When added value is pursued in all other operations in the community or enterprise in which information services workers are employed, we can expect it to be sought in information delivery as well. In our new information environment it is expected: it is no longer an 'add-on'.

Inevitable and desirable change

As far as the future of information services is concerned, we don't have a crystal ball and we can't say that we know what's going to be happening in the twenty-first century, particularly since, in the information services discipline, change is so drastic and so fast. But we do have a pretty clear picture of what is happening at the end of the twentieth century, and some of the things we're observing now are germane to what will be happening in the next century.

For one thing – and this is going to be exactly the same in the next century – information services management is characterized by *change*. As we engage in the critical process of strategic planning for information services, we recognize – and it is a recognition that is finding a growing acceptance with all information workers –that change is both *inevitable* and *desirable*. In this context, of course, specialized librarians and their organizations are in the forefront: in fact, with respect to the methodologies of information delivery, this last decade of the twentieth century might well be called the age of specialized librarianship, for information services practitioners of all kinds are now attempting to do what special librarians have been doing all along, that is, doing everything they can to devise, create or otherwise initiate practices that will give their customers the highest levels of information delivery they can provide.

The concept of inevitable and desirable change was articulated by David S. Ferriero and Thomas L. Wilding, who in 1991 wrote a very important paper on the use of the environmental scan in strategic planning for information services, and who posited that strategic planning, unlike other planning models, 'assumes that change is desirable and inevitable'. It assumes, they wrote, that 'organizations exist in a dynamic relationship with their environments, and that for an organization to thrive, it must be in a constant state of change in order to maintain a high degree of relevance'. This assumption, of course, puts strategic management in direct opposition with those planning models that assume the continuation of the organization in much the same shape and structure as at present. Strategic planning, Ferriero and Wilding argue, assumes that an organization must undergo dramatic and sometimes even drastic transformation on a 'somewhat regular cycle' in order to ensure organizational success, however defined (Ferriero and Wilding 1991, pp. 2–3).

Put that concept in library and information services terms and what do you have? An almost overwhelming contradiction, it seems to me, about how these operational units were managed in the past and for which – and of this there can be no doubt – there is no place in the future. The dynamic library or information services operation must from now on embrace change, not only as inevitable but as the desirable element of its management that will bring it to success in the future.

These are all conditions and concepts that we must think about if we are going to be effective information services providers, if we are going to understand and excel at information delivery in a global information services arena (as we will be expected to do), and we must pull them into the work we do. For example, in today's information services environment, the delivery of information products, services and consultations depends as much on the provider's ability to access remote information sources as on education, background and local conditions. So, while this new information environment puts new pressures on us, the globalization of information also offers unparalleled opportunities and challenges, not only in terms of how better information services can be provided, but in the management and organizational or community spheres as well.

This phrase, 'organization *or* community', is of particular importance in this context, for although much of this thinking has developed from the specialist libraries community, it has now been firmly established that the ideas and concepts put forward can be applied effectively and appropriately to public, academic and even school librarianship if the information practitioners are willing to think about their communities in organizational terms. They also relate to all areas of information services management, regardless of the type of information services unit that has been structured.

What is being suggested, then, is that we think about *all* library and information services operations in terms of specialized librarianship, simply because the goal of an information delivery operation must be to provide the information the user needs, regardless of whether that user is in the public sector or the private sector, and regardless of the purpose for which it is to be used. This is not our concern.

In this regard, it is appropriate to also characterize the present as 'the age of the information customer', for at no time in the history of librarianship and information services has the authority of the customer been so recognized and so respected. Here again, special librarians are leading the way, for they have learned through experience that in the field of specialized librarianship the very survival of the library is dependent on its success in delivering what the customers require and expect. Both national and international trends indicate that information workers in the future will be more concerned than they have ever been with connecting their work to the specific needs of their customers.

Current trends

As we move towards the twenty-first century and into the much-vaunted 'information age' it has become clear that, in all societal endeavors, information is the key to success. In such an environment, information services practitioners have never been more valuable to the organizations in which they are employed, and never has so much been demanded of them as information providers. At the same time, it is becoming more and more obvious that certain influences are affecting how information is delivered today, and it matters not what kind of parent organization the information services unit is affiliated with, these influences are affecting the work we do and the way in which we deal with change and change management. Five which can be identified immediately are:

- A broader concept of information services

- Extending the librarian's domain

- The customer point of view

- What we're dealing with: the artifact? its content? or both?

- The integration of information.

All of these have been discussed in other books in this series, but from the point of view of organizing a quality management initiative for the information services unit a quick mention of them is useful to set the stage, so that the establishment of the quality program takes into account these driving and compelling influences.

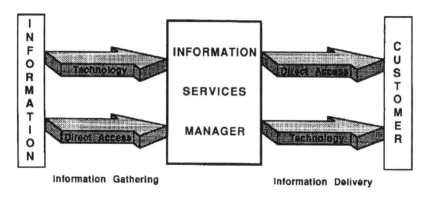

Information Gathering   Information Delivery

We find, for example, that as we think about how these influences are affecting the work we do as information services practitioners, the service connection is a strong and determining one. This connection is first noticed when we think about the terms and concepts we use to talk about what we do. When we speak of the discipline or subject of 'information', for example, nowadays we are obliged to look to a broader, more inclusive construct, what some are calling 'the splendid information services continuum', and a fuller discussion of this umbrella concept of information services appears in the 'Introduction to the series' at the beginning of this book. If we are willing to recognize the fact that in much of society today 'information services' is being used as a very inclusive term, we stand a better chance of providing our users with what they need, for we then begin to understand how they think about information.

This broader concept is itself connected to much else that is going on in information services management, such as Woody Horton's (1994) important admonition that those who have been trained to provide information services shift their primary focus from describing, organizing and cataloging objects to planning and managing the information requirements of the decision-makers in their organizations, and that they move out of the traditional information domain into the organizational domain, becoming part of the organizational team and not operating as standalone information provision units.

This movement and this change in direction are also connected with looking at information delivery from the customer's point of view, with rejecting the notion (for which we are often criticized by people outside the information services field) that our information units have become too institutionalized and too rule-bound to be of much value to our customers. When we and our staffs take a proactive quality perspective, moving the library from a collection-focused position to one that is customer focused, as Miriam Drake has characterized it ([Drake 1995], p. 1), we are ready to provide successful information delivery in this new information environment.

As is noted throughout this book, this authority of the customer is basic and important for information services practitioners, but it is unfortunately a subject from which colleagues often shy away. Some professionals are uncomfortable when they cannot play the role of intellectual arbiter, for many information services practitioners connect their work with education – which is right and in many cases appropriate – but they often take this role beyond what their customers need from them and put themselves in the position of making decisions about what the customer does or does not need, or should or should not have. This is not the way to do it, according to Karl Albrecht:

> Service management is a total organizational approach that makes quality of service, *as perceived by the customer*, the driving force for the operation of the business (Albrecht 1988, p. 20).

This is a concept that can and *must* be translated into the information services context, for it is the foundation on which the principles of successful information management and delivery are built. It expresses why we do what we do, and when we allow other influences to interfere with the successful achievement of that goal we are failing to live up to the terms of the service contract that has been established between ourselves and our information customers.

In fact, this commitment to the successful delivery of information is not such an unusual objective, for many organizations now recognize the value of information and are making special efforts to see that the content part of the information equation is given as much attention as the management of the materials that contain or transport the information. Thus we are finding, for example, that more and more organizations are hiring a Chief Knowledge Officer to be in charge of the information – that is, the content – and to work with the Chief Information Officer, who is usually in charge of the information technology part of the picture. That the two have often been commingled has frequently been a point of contention in organizations, simply because, as Thomas Davenport has pointed out, many senior executives mistakenly think of information *technology* when they hear the word 'information'. It is not hard to understand why, since because of the obvious costs involved in the acquisition and installation of information technology (to say nothing of its continued implementation), the very term 'information' for these people relates to what they pay for the machinery. The content, the thing being manipulated, and the value of that content to the successful achievement of the organizational mission are not considered until they are pointed out (Davenport 1993, p. 27). When information services professionals find themselves concentrating on the one component when they should be concentrating on the other, or vice versa, they must back off and determine which it is they should be concerned with. Is it the information, or is it the artifact in which the information has been captured? Or is it, as would seem to be the case for most information services professionals, a combination of both?

Connected to this, Davenport, who is a strong advocate of an advanced level of process re-engineering (he calls it process innovation), identifies information technology as an enabler in this important activity. Like Sylvia Piggott, he makes a strong case for the variety of ways in which information technology can support process innovation (Piggott 1995, p. 11), and he connects processes and information delivery. He also makes the point – and one which librarians will recognize – that in the ongoing confusion between information and information technology, 'information always seems to get the short shrift in the analysis' (Davenport 1993, p. 214).

Mary Park, too, is concerned about this confusion between information and information technology. For Park, information technology is the conduit not the content, but it's the content that leads to acquiring knowledge, and information services practitioners have to educate the decision-makers about this distinction. This is a critical new role for information services workers, as Park points out: 'I believe that it is critical', she says, 'for providers of information services to educate decision–makers about the "benefits" of their services that speak directly to the interest of the decision-makers. Providers must change the metaphor so that they are no longer perceived as just as the people who "point to the information", but as the people who can not only help define the problem, but can get the information that solves the problem' (Park 1996, p. 3).

Another look at our new information environment builds on this, and recognizes that our customers are looking for what is being characterized, perhaps superficially, as 'one-stop shopping'. These information seekers, we are told, want to come to one central information resource and find the information they need. Obviously in these situations the pleasures of serendipity and browsing as an information-gathering activity are lost, but certainly for some people this is a small price to pay to ensure that they are given the precise information they need. In any case, customers don't want to be told to go to this department or that section, where they *might* find the information they need. They want to ask the question once and then rely on the specialists to deliver the information to them. Of course, this is something of an ideal scenario, and those who work in the real world of information delivery recognize that it doesn't always happen, but it is nevertheless a scenario that information customers would like have in place, and as quality management programs are planned for information services units there is a need to recognize that this desire exists.

A logical and wise extension of this concept comes from Elizabeth Orna, providing another optimistic look at how information services as a discipline will be practiced in the future. In 1990, Orna wrote a very important book on managing information flow in organizations, in which she did not limit herself to traditional concepts about information. Instead, she pointed out, quite appropriately, that within the organization information will be found everywhere, 'not just in formal repositories like libraries or information systems, and not just in those functions where people spend a lot of time reading, writing, or interacting with com-. puters'. For Orna, the touchstone for identifying information is simply: 'Is this something that people need to know and apply in their work, to achieve their and the enterprise's objectives?' (Orna 1990, p. 46). The list of items that meet Orna's criteria is long. It includes such things as customer records, financial records, internal information, external information, technical information and information about the environment in which the enterprise operates, and, significantly, the form in which the information is held is irrelevant. As information workers face the new millennium and a period in history when information as a commodity with a tangible value will be organized, manipulated and disseminated in unheard-of ways, Orna's all-inclusive definition makes much practical sense.

Coming through all this is a healthy and ultimately rewarding final reason for optimism, identified by Sylvia Piggott, who points out that this is a very exciting time for information services because we are working in what she calls the 'second era' of the information age. We have passed through the childhood and adolescence of electronic delivery, and as a consequence of enabling technology, businesses and professions are re-engineering. Libraries and other information operations can benefit from applying the same concepts, leading to the realization of what Piggott – and many others of us – have for our organizations: a library or information center that exists as a seamless, borderless service, 'a place where information can be sought from wherever it exists and can be used immediately by local or remote customers' ([Piggott 1995], p. 3).

Others have come to the same conclusion. For example, Pat Molholt, with the CHIPS Project at Columbia University Health Sciences, writes that at her institution it is the technology that is the link enabling her to connect curriculum planning with information services planning. 'The tie is technology', Molholt says. 'With an automated, integrated information program, the library can become a true "service" operation, combining the faculty perspective with the librarians' perspective. It's an opportunity we've not had before' ([Molholt 1994], p. 3).

Finally, as we think about the information services environment at the end of the twentieth century and the beginning of a new millennium, a third era of information delivery can be identified, one that is likely to have enormous societal as well as organizational/community impact. This is what is being spoken of as 'knowledge management'. It is a concept that relates closely to the integration of information as described earlier, but it takes that concept much further, since it commits an organization or community to a major rethinking of the information services construct.

The move toward knowledge management is not an unnatural evolution, for as libraries and other services facilities have moved from warehouse and depository functions to the delivery of information through enabling technology, the integration and delivery of external and internal information as a unified transaction becomes an appropriate reaction to providing what the information customers are looking for. Doing this, of course, is the goal of total quality management, and provides the framework for incorporating the quality focus into information services management. It is only appropriate that it be done.

References

Abram, Stephen A. 'Adding value . . .' *InfoManage: The International Management Newsletter for the Information Services Executive* 3 (3), February, 1996.

Albrecht, Karl. *At America's Service: How Corporations Can Revolutionize the Way They Treat Their Customers*. Homewood, IL: Dow Jones-Irwin, 1988.

Ashworth, Wilfred. 1979. *Special Librarianship*. London: Clive Bingley.

Barker, Joel. *Paradigms: the Business of Discovering the Future*. New York: HarperBusiness, 1993.

Davenport, Thomas H. *Process Innovation: Reengineering Work Through Information Technology.* Boston, MA: Harvard Business School Press, 1993.

[Drake, Miriam A.] 'Mimi Drake at Georgia Tech: Ten Years Online and the Future is NOW!' *InfoManage: The International Management Newsletter for the Information Services Executive* 2 (6), May, 1995.

Ferriero, David S. and Wilding, Thomas L. 'Scanning the environment in strategic planning.' *Masterminding Tomorrow's Information – Creative Strategies for the '90s*. Washington, DC: Special Libraries Association, 1991.

Horton, Forrest Woody. *Extending the Librarian's Domain: A Survey of Emerging Occupation Opportunities for Librarians and Information Professionals*. Washington, DC: Special Libraries Association, 1994.

Levinson, Marc, 'Not everyone is downsizing.' *Newsweek* 127 (12), March 18, 1996, pp. 42–44.

[Megill, Kenneth] 'Relaxed at the revolution: Ken Megill takes us into information resources management.' *InfoManage: The International*

Management Newsletter for the Information Services Executive 1 (10), September, 1994, pp. 1–4.

[Molholt, Pat] 'Pat Molholt's bold CHIPS project.' *InfoManage: The International Management Newsletter for the Information Services Executive* 1 (2), November 1994, pp. 1–5.

Orna, Elizabeth. *Practical Information Policies: How to Manage Information Flow in Organizations.* London and Brookfield, VT: Gower, 1990.

[Park, Mary] 'Mary Park thinks "Partnering" is a good idea – if the partner is senior management.' *InfoManage: The International Management Newsletter for the Information Services Executive* 3 (2), January, 1996, pp. 1–5.

[Piggott, Sylvia] 'Sylvia Piggott at the Bank of Montréal: re-engineering information services for the 2nd era of the information age.' *InfoManage: The International Management Newsletter for the Information Services Executive* 2 (3), February, 1995, pp. 1–4.

Piggott, Sylvia E.A. 1995. Why corporate librarians must reengineer the library for the new information age. *Special Libraries* 86 (1), Winter, 1995, pp. 11–20.

Strable, Edward, G. 'Special libraries: how are they different?' Illinois *Libraries* 62, March, 1980.

Chapter Two

Managing information services

Much has been written about the theory of management, but in this context it is appropriate to give some attention to how general management practice as applied in an information services organization can be effectively and appropriately refocused into a total quality management effort. The concept of management has been quite thoroughly studied and analyzed, and the many professional workers who perform management roles will have no difficulty in describing what they do as managers. Whether management is a scientific discipline or not is a moot question; in the management of information services, certainly, the subjects studied in the sciences and the theories and experiences drawn from those studies influence the work that managers do. On the other hand, much of what constitutes management is almost personal in its make-up, and has as much to do with personal attributes and aptitude as with scientific study. So, the answer to the question is probably something along the lines of 'management is both an art and a science'.

There has long been controversy about whether the disciplines in which information services workers work can be 'managed' in a businesslike manner or whether they are, in fact, operating in a sort of management netherworld in which the hard-and-fast rules of management theory do not apply. The best response to this concern is to refer to what might be called the non-scientific aspects of management theory, and to suggest that the flexibility of management, especially quality management, provides wide latitude for the establishment of businesslike and objective practices in the management of the very subjective field of information services. In one of the most important studies in this area, Miriam Tees established that librarians can be trained as managers, but she noted that some studies (with respect to librarianship) had indicated that

> people entering the library profession rarely do so because they expect to follow a career in management. Rather, they enter because of an interest in information, a love of books, or a desire to serve people, and they learn

cataloging, bibliography, information retrieval, indexing, and a number of special skills which they want to practice (Tees 1984, p. 175).

Obviously Tees was writing in an earlier era (the paper, in fact, appeared in 1984), and certainly much has changed since she conducted the study. Graduate schools of library and information services, for example, now routinely offer management courses, and although these are usually electives and are not required for the awarding of the graduate degree, they are available for those students who seek a career in library and information services management. Nevertheless, despite the fact that some of the language has changed, the attributes which Tees identified in prospective librarians are still present in the candidates for admission to the graduate schools of study, and there continue to be plenty of graduates who want to get their degrees, go into the workplace, and then – as far as management is concerned – to 'be left alone to do her work', as Tees indicated that one student had made clear.

The crux of the matter is that there really is no choice. In today's information services environment the *management* of information is expected by the organizations and communities that hire information staff to work for them. However, it is not so much a question of whether one should or should not understand management theory if one is to be an information services practitioner: rather, it is more a reluctance on the part of some to be responsible and accountable for the services they and their staffs provide. There has been and continues to be a resistance to responsibility and accountability in the various fields that make up the information services disciplines. For example, resistance by some practitioners to such ideas as certification, required continuing education and professional development, effectiveness measures, the authority of the customer, the authority of senior management and similar 'managerial' issues, continues to cause much hard feeling between practitioners and their managers. As society takes a more hardline approach to the delivery of services, and as more and more organizations demand more accountability of their employees, information services workers, too, will be required to face up to the demands of responsibility and accountability.

A useful distinction between what happens in a service operation and a business was well made by Peter Drucker in his famous book on the management of non-profit organizations. He asked: 'What is the bottom line when there is no bottom line?', and of course he answers his own question in terms of responsibility and accountability:

> Non-profit institutions tend not to give priority to performance and results. Yet performance and results are far more important – and far more difficult to measure and control – in the non-profit institution than in a business.
>
> In a business, there is a financial bottom line. Profit and loss are not enough by themselves to judge performance, but at least they are something

concrete. Whether business executives like it or not, profit certainly *will* be used to measure their performance. When non-profit executives, however, face a risk-taking decision, they must first think through the desired results – *before* the means of measuring performance and results can be determined. For each non-profit institution, the executive who leads effectively must first answer the question, How is performance for this institution to be defined? (Drucker 1990, p. 107).

It is this reliance on measurement and performance that enables the information services manager to move beyond the mere providing of a service. Once accountability and responsibility become a part of the information services mission – as they do in an operation that is based on quality management principles – the functioning of that operation becomes serious and customer-focused, which should be the goal of any organization, regardless of whether it fits into the service economy or the production economy.

There are many definitions for the management concept, and one of the most reliable comes from the field of management education: 'the process of integrating resources and tasks toward the achievement of stated organizational goals' (Szilagyi 1988, p. 5). It is a definition that lends itself well to the information services arena and to the movement towards a total quality management environment. In managing information services, the head of the department must be prepared to reconcile the responsibility and accountability required in offering information products, services and consultations to a specifically identified customer group, and at the same time be prepared to seek opportunities for continually improving the delivery of those products and services. Thus the information services manager is required, before all else, to devise and implement a process that permits the integration of resources and tasks, so that organizational goals can be realized. It is this process that moves the information manager from being responsible merely for the *delivery* of information to *managing* the information services.

A first step in this process looks at the dichotomous organizational structure in which information services are to be provided: there are two entities to which the information services manager must be responsible, the parent organization or community and the unit itself. Both are organizations in the sense that both must be organized and managed in such a way that the ultimate mission of each is achieved. To be sure, the information services operation is only one part of the parent organization, but as a support function the information services unit is required to have a mission that supports the overall mission of the parent organization or community.

At the same time, however, the information services manager has management responsibility for the information services department itself, which exists in management terms as an organization of its own. So the information services manager must in effect be two managers, one who is

**LOYALTIES PULL THE INFORMATION SERVICES
MANAGER IN THREE DIRECTIONS AT ONCE**

part of the management team of the parent organization, and one who functions as senior management with responsibility for the information services unit. In recognizing this dichotomy, the information services manager positions himself or herself to practice management theory by using methodologies that are applicable and relevant to both entities, but each of which will have a different focus and different perspective in terms of how decisions are made.

A third allegiance (perhaps not so obvious in this context, but certainly a key concept once the total quality management process begins) looks at who the customers are: in many organizations the customer is seen as the person receiving the information. On the other hand, there is a management trend that looks at this customer as being simply an *intermediate* customer, whose query is technically part of a management process that looks to the ultimate customer of the organization's offerings. So, if the company is one which manufactures, say, garden hose, the scientist who approaches the technical library to find a history of a particular chemical compound that is being used by competitor firms is merely an intermediate customer, as the true customer in the transaction is the person who will ultimately purchase the newly designed garden hose that the company will develop and eventually bring to market. It is a useful concept, for it moves the information services operation and its employees beyond their support role to being participants in a corporate endeavor that makes each employee a part of the corporate team. Again, this is a basic TQM concept, and it works well in the management of information services.

A final allegiance, of course, is to one's profession: keeping up with what is going on in that profession, understanding the newest concepts and trends (and, whenever possible, acting on them), identifying who the 'movers and shakers' in the profession are and seeking to emulate them – these and similar activities all work together to position the information services manager as a leader, not only in the profession but in the organization or community in which he or she is employed.

Thus, as with determining the environment in which the information services operation will be managed (as discussed below), the information services manager must also be continually balancing the allegiances that affect the work he and his staff will perform. Ultimately, these various interactions are all part of the practice of information services management, leading to improved delivery of information services, products and consultations for the identified information customers.

The role of management: embracing opportunity

In thinking about information services in the TQM context, the first function of management is to recognize opportunity. The information services manager must understand that when the information function is matched to organizational or community goals it is imperative that he or she be able to recognize changes in society and in the workplace that can lead to better information delivery and then, whenever possible, act on the opportunity the changes provide, in order to create new and better information delivery systems. In the last decade, for example, the dramatic change in the availability of and access to information has been almost overwhelming for information workers. Each new workday, it seems, brings new tools and potential (and frequently easy) access to information that was previously difficult to find, if it was available at all or even known about by those who might have occasion to use it. Related to these 'technical' changes (although they are not all necessarily to do with information technology), the role of the information provider has changed as well, as indicated in the earlier reference to comments by the departmental manager about what librarians do (the quotation from *Newsweek* Levinson, chapter 1). In that changed role lies a splendid opportunity for better information delivery.

There are information practitioners who are looking at their changing role and matching it to the changes now taking place in the information delivery process. Gloria Dinerman, for example, looks at librarianship and challenges librarians to seek new opportunities for service:

> The prototype of yesterday's librarian is today's endangered species. As end

users become more proficient in researching their own answers, the librarian is transformed into an information technician who propels that user toward the discovery of information resources. The librarian must serve as the specialist, the promoter, the interpreter, the disseminator, and the trainer. Never before has the profession had such an explosive opportunity to lead other professionals into a dynamic world of search and discovery. Now a new persona is emerging that changes the behavior pattern from passive to active, and with that new leadership role, librarians have the opportunity to exert more influence on management decisions. Not only must we become proficient at information retrieval through automation, but we must also learn to interact with MIS departments, human resources, and communication services. Only then can we become a vital part of the corps of decision makers (Dinerman 1996, pp. 1, 11, 14).

In London's business and information community, Ann Lawes is considered something of an original thinker, and in the years that she has been managing training and consultation services marketed to the business and finance community in London's City, she has come in contact with a great number of practicing librarians and information services workers. This exposure has given her a unique vantage point for observing how the library and information services profession is being practiced, and at the same time has provided her with a unique perspective for thinking about what the profession needs.

'I'm not a pessimist by nature', Lawes said in an interview, '[Lawes 1995] and I am really uncomfortable commenting about some of our failures in the library and information services field, but I really think we don't seem to recognize what enormous change agents we are. There is so much change going on in society at large – and in the information field – that the words "change" and "change agent" have almost become devalued. We say them so much that we don't really think about what we're saying. But in fact we information managers have a tremendously important role. We are the very people who influence others in how they use information, who change the way they access information. And it is incumbent on us to recognize and manage how the changes we introduce affect our users.'

'That's a formidable responsibility', Lawes continued. 'We've got people coming into our organizations, coming out of university and other training programs, and they're going to have key roles in these organizations in the future. And look at how comfortable they are with information. They come to work with us, and they're so comfortable with information it's almost as if they've got computers hanging off the ends of their fingers. They are a far different breed than the people for whom we have previously provided information. These and other trends, factors, affect the way we are going to be managing information. We have to step back and think about them, about how they affect the way we do our work, and about how they affect users of information.'

'The first bit, for example, has to do with what I just said, the people who are going to be looking for information, the people who will be managing organizations in the future. Right now they're the end-users, and they want fast information. And we must give it to them, that is, we must give them the means for finding it, show them how to get it themselves. And that means we must persuade them to change their working practices, to change how they use information, to think about things that they weren't thinking about before. If they're going to be end-users – and if we are going to be working with them to help them find information – they must change how they think about information. And that's our job, to show them how to change and to convince them that the change is worthwhile.'

'We have to do it, because if we are going to be working in knowledge-based organizations – which we know we are – then the whole organization becomes information focused. And the information is not limited to external information or internal information or what the librarian finds or what the records manager finds. Those categories will become irrelevant, as information customers begin to demand one-stop shopping in an integrated information environment. There's just no way information staff will be able to deliver all that information by using traditional methods, so we've got to transform the information customers into information end-users and give them the help that they need to get the information they want. Look at what's happening: now we're talking about a massive consultation and training job, and it's the information professionals who will be called upon to do this work. And as they do this work, they do it while bearing in mind the huge changes they're asking people – the information customers – to undergo.'

'At the same time', Lawes continued, 'there's another thread to this, and that's the hodgepodge of delivery mechanisms that we're all frantically trying to keep up with all the time. They're changing so fast that even information services staff can't keep up, so how must the end-users feel? That's what we've got to know, and then we have to work with them so they can learn to use and exploit these changed delivery mechanisms.'

Even then it is not easy, for there are other factors Lawes has identified that influence the way we work with these 'new' information customers. For example, we all talk a great deal about the amount of information that is becoming available, about how information as a commodity is increasing globally ('by leaps and bounds' is the way Lawes puts it), and how it is not just the amount of information that is increasing but the access points, the amount of accessibility that is also increasing incrementally. So there are more challenges for librarians and information managers: how to keep up, just so they can advise the end-users, for if it's hard for the professionals to keep up, the end-users aren't going to have a clue, except in the specific areas of expertise in which they work. The information professionals are going to have to lead the way.

It will be a collaborative effort, and it will include both traditional information providers such as librarians and the 'newer' information workers.

'It's very much a cooperative arrangement', Lawes said, 'for in fact it's the librarians and the information technology people working together who become the change agent. The information workers who understand the content of the information – the librarians, the records managers, the archivists, and people like that – will need to join forces with the IT people, and together they take on the enormous responsibility of showing people how to manage and use information.'

Obviously what Ann Lawes is looking at is a new and very different role for librarians and information services managers, a role that moves them almost into the 'pop psychology' realm, where they are to take responsibility for the satisfaction of their customers in their quest for information, which is, of course, the first rule of total quality management. This is very different from what most librarians and information services professionals are trained to do. In fact, one can't help but wonder if librarians and information professionals, given the way they are currently being educated, are up to these tasks, to taking on this 'ownership', this almost psychological direction they are being asked to embrace.

As far as Ann Lawes is concerned, 'We don't have a choice. This is a different situation than we had as recently as two years ago. Then, we were just thinking about these change agents, and wondering what was going to happen. Now we know. They're all coming together, and it's nothing less than a revolution for the information services profession. And how we got there isn't important. Recognizing that we're there is what's important, and that means letting go of a lot of baggage. We've simply got to do it.'

As an example, Lawes described the excitement in the UK when Tony Blair, the Labour Party leader, obtained a commitment from British Telecom for getting libraries and schools wired into the Internet. The uproar was political, of course, about whether Labour could really do it and why the Conservatives didn't do it, and the verbal taunts were flying back and forth, but the point was not whether the action was going to take place or not. It is going to happen, and what will be needed will be changed mindsets, especially within the library and information services community. The implications, Ann Lawes was quick to point out, are tremendous, because when the change comes it will give focus to the Net. And when there is focus, there is a market. This is a pretty powerful paradigm for information workers.

So, according to Lawes, you end up with a picture of the current state of information services management that is almost visual: on the one hand you have got these change factors, the things that are influencing how information is delivered, the 'new' end-users, the disorganized and uncoordinated delivery mechanisms, the huge amount of information and the multiplicity of access points, the cooperation that will be needed between the IT people and the content people, and the integration of information. On the other hand you have the information customers, the people who need the information, and in a knowledge-based organization they are going to be required to find that information for themselves. In the middle, linking it all together and making it happen, are the change agents, the librarians, the archivists, the records managers, the information managers, the information specialists, the IT people, the information scientists.

The big issue for the people in the middle is taking on board how the end-users feel about change and how they react to it. It is not going to be easy, and this new thinking will require the leading players in the information services field to take on a vision of information delivery that makes the end-users the focal point, recognizes them as the key, and requires information managers to act proactively across the entire organization. This is a vision that requires an information services operation that is not static, not a standalone operation, and is organic to the organization as a whole. What it requires, in effect, is a quality management organization.

This is a vision of information services that asks a very important question, which is a tough one to answer. Nevertheless, Ann Lawes insists it be asked: 'Where do we find the people, the information workers? If we are going to meet the challenges that we are now able to identify, where does business, industry, the arts, government agencies, and all other organizations that rely on information find the people who will be the information managers of the twenty-first century?'

Obviously some information services workers will be educated and trained in graduate business schools or other professional educational programs, in continuing education and professional development courses and seminars, and even in vendor-sponsored programs. On the other hand, information services managers – the 'leading players' Lawes talked about – will continue to be educated in graduate programs of library and information science. Certainly the ones headed for careers in public, academic and school libraries will be educated in these institutions, and as long as some of these graduate schools continue to give attention to specialized librarianship many of the leading players in the business and organizational information community will be educated in the library schools as well.

So now the question becomes one of direction, accountability and responsibility, and it's a question Ann Lawes is very comfortable in asking: 'Are the library schools willing to provide the information workers the fiercely competitive information community is going to need?' She admits she doesn't have all the answers, but she demands that the question be asked for, as she puts it, 'If they don't, someone else will.'

These education and training issues are a major component in any quality initiative an organization might pursue, for part of the new role for information services workers is to be prepared to do this work. And opportunity continues to be part of it, especially for information services managers, who are continually confronted with the difficulty of determining whether the purchase of a new information service or tool is worthwhile when matched against the costs (staff training, marketing efforts etc.) involved in bringing it into the workplace. A few years ago, the classic cry of woe from information managers was that their managers wanted the organization to have access to the Internet. When asked why, these senior people often did not know how the Net would be used in gathering information for the organization: they had simply heard about it, knew that other organizations had access to it and thought that they should have access as well. As it happened of course, access to the Internet has indeed been a boon in the information-gathering process, but in 1992 this was not a foregone conclusion and much soul-searching was experienced by information services managers who were attempting to provide 'standard' information delivery and organize Internet training classes at the same time.

On the other hand, the smart information services managers recognized the opportunity that the Internet provided, recognized that for all its disorganization and difficulty, the Net would be a standard transmission medium in the future, and that training in and use of the Net would be a good use of staff time. For these managers the opportunity was there and it was simply another part of the managerial picture for them. Other examples seem to crop up with some frequency in the information management workplace, and information managers are frequently challenged to decide just how far they want to go in responding to the opportunity that has been presented to them.

Planning, the environmental scan, and the information services mission

Seeking opportunities is generally not considered a classic managerial function, but in terms of change management and the role of quality management in information services it is one that is now as basic to good management as the standard managerial functions which have been identified as central to effective organizational management: planning, organizing, leading and controlling. These are generally accepted within the management community as being the four basics of managerial work, and most of the work of the manager comes into these categories. The same elements are required in information services management, and because they lead to excellence in the end result – the delivery of information products, services and consultations – they can be the basis for a quality management initiative within the information services operation.

What we do as we manage is to ensure that the organization achieves its goals, that the people who have responsibility for contributing to that achievement participate as they have agreed to participate, and that the societal and organizational benefits of participating are realized. The goal of the information services operation is to support the organizational mission, and that support must be spelt out and codified so that each information stakeholder is aware of what these parallel goals are and how they are to be achieved. In a quality management environment the mission of the information services operation is matched to the organizational mission, and all participants in the information delivery process, however far removed from the actual information interaction itself, are expected to perform with this linkage in mind.

In an information services operation moving into a TQM framework, planning is built on the successful achievement of three managerial activities: the information services manager must identify the environmental influences that affect the information delivery process; departmental goals must be established and matched to organizational goals; and strategies and plans for realizing the information services operation's goals must be developed. The successful accomplishment of these endeavors enables the information services manager to set a 'tone', so to speak, for the level and quality of service that will be provided by the department.

In undertaking to study the environment in which the library or other information services unit will be operating, the quality-focused information manager looks at the environmental scan. Defined by Ferriero and Wilding as 'a systematic review and analysis of data about the universe in which the library operates', the environmental scanning process looks at 'a number of overlapping environments, each of which has an impact on and in turn feels the impact of the library' (Ferriero and Wilding 1991, p. 5). The five environments that Ferriero and Wilding identify are: the global; the industrial; the competition to which the customers might go for the same information they could find in the information unit itself; forces within the information services profession or discipline which affect how information is managed; and the internal environment within which the information services unit operates. The environmental scan is an essential component of strategic planning, and although there are some in the management community who might dismiss environmental scanning as a tired relic from the 1960s, it is in fact a management methodology that has not been replaced by anything nearly so successful.

That the environmental scan continues to be successful is demonstrated in the number of writings about the technique as a management subject. One of the most important books in this field was written by Chun Wei Choo and published as an ASIS monograph in 1995. In his work, Choo describes a process model for information management in the intelligent organization, and the environmental scan is a featured element in the achievement of organizational success, since the environment itself is recognized as a source of continually provided, critical strategic information. At the same time, the environment is recognized as a source of resources 'upon which the organization depends', and as a source of variation, 'an ecological milieu that differentially selects certain types of organizations for survival on the basis of the fit between organizational forms and environmental characteristics' (Choo 1995, pp. 3–5). It is, of course, the first two of these that significantly affect the workings of an information services organization, but the third cannot be ignored by information services managers.

For Choo, the definition of the environmental scan reflects these connections, and he uses the thinking of several different management scholars to flesh out his definition:

> Environmental scanning is the acquisition and use of information about events, trends, and relationships in an organization's external environment, the knowledge of which would assist management in planning the organization's future course of action. The external environment of an organization includes all outside factors that can affect the organization's performance, even its survival. Although many factors exist, it is helpful to divide the external environment into a small number of sectors. For business organizations, the environment may be analyzed as consisting of six sectors: customers, suppliers, competition, socioeconomic, technological, and governmental. Alternatively, one may distinguish between a macroenviron-ment comprising social, economic, political, and technological sectors, and a task/industry environment comprising mainly the customer and com-petitor sectors' (Aguilar; Choo and Auster; Jauch and Glueck; and Fahey and Narayanan; Lester and Waters; all quoted in Choo 1995, p. 72).

Choo goes on to quote another definition which puts the environ-mental scan in terms of its use in decision making, and notes that it comprises three activities:

1. the gathering of information concerning the organization's external environment;
2. the analysis and interpretation of this information;
3. the use of this analyzed intelligence in strategic decision making (Lester and Waters, quoted in Choo 1995, p. 73).

Karl Albrecht thinks about the environmental scan from a position that looks at management in general and is not restricted to the information services field, and he broadens the environmental scan to include additional 'environments', each of which, in one way or another, can be related to library and information services work. For Albrecht, the environmental scan is a management technique for getting beyond the immediate concerns of the organization:

Executive teams vary considerably in the discipline with which they study their environments. The more sophisticated of them devote continuous attention to what's happening outside their doors. Some organizations even have what amount to "environmental intelligence" units. They have people with no other job but to read the signals and alert the leaders to their implications.

Many organizations, however, are remarkably out of touch with the wider world. Their executives may be so preoccupied with near-field problems and issues that they feel they have no time to think about the far field. These organizations tend to be the sitting ducks that take the worst punishment when the shock wave hits. A major shock wave may come through a particular industry only once in a decade, and nine years of complacency can leave most of the players dangerously vulnerable.

But environmental intelligence has more value than just in averting disasters. It is the very raw material for creating new opportunities as well. Indeed, it is the starting point for the whole strategy development process. The environmental scan, the first component of the model, gets us grounded in reality and may enable us to see what our competitors may not see. It is the figurative crystal ball of strategic thinking ... (Albrecht 1994, pp. 72–73).

For Albrecht, the environments to consider are these (of course, there are some similarities with the Ferriero and Wilding list), and their identification in terms of the information services operation's customer base is critical, so that the operation avoids being 'remarkably out of touch with the wider world':

1. **Customer environment.** Not only must the information manager identify the users, he or she must also look at and understand the implications of the "demographic and psychographic truths" that influence the information needs of these customers.
2. **Competitor environment.** The information services unit provides its customers with information. Can they get it elsewhere? Then why do they come to this particular information unit? Can a competitive information provider lure them away? Why? Why not?
3. **Economic environment.** What economic factors influence how information is handled in the community or organization that supports the information services unit? How does the unit perform when money is tight? Are there economic factors that determine whether users come to the information services unit or not?
4. **Technological environment.** Of course the information services management and staff are aware of new technology products and processes, and how they help (or hinder) the work of the unit is usually clearly and very well recognized. But what about the old technologies? Do not information staffs spend time dealing with them as well?
5. **Social environment.** The corporate/institutional/community culture has enormous impact on how the information unit's products, services and consultations are received. Is the culture identified and examined as new products are planned?

6. **Political environment.** Who calls the shots in the organization or the community? Is there government intervention? Are power groups affecting information stability in the units the information services management is responsible for?
7. **Legal environment.** Intellectual property issues, employment law and litigation, and information liability are now firmly entrenched in information services management. Is the manager of the information services unit keeping up? What happens if he or she doesn't?
8. **Physical environment.** What is the physical arrangement of the information services unit? Does the location have any effect on whether customers (and potential customers) come to the unit or not? Is it easy to find? Or at least to be in touch with (e-mail, fax, voicemail etc.)?

It is important to recognize that in the above descriptions of the environmental scan, Choo's work is connected only with *external* environments, a distinction that compromises it somewhat as a management tool for the information services unit, since so much of that unit's work is directly related to dealing with *internal* customers, management and other information stakeholders. Nevertheless, all three approaches are valuable contributions to the study of the environmental scan, and certainly something can be gleaned from each as the information services manager seeks to incorporate environmental scanning into the quality management process.

The environmental scan is, however, only one step in moving towards quality management, and equal consideration must be given to the development of the departmental mission statement. It is when this action is taken that the information services manager begins his or her focused quest for a quality management environment.

In today's highly specialized information marketplace, professional librarians and others who are responsible for the management of information delivery units often find themselves at odds with patrons and/or senior management over the role of the unit in the organization. Whether the information services department is a standalone unit; a traditional book-oriented or reports collection which patrons access for themselves and for which the staff's responsibilities are primarily custodial; a research operation in which the information providers' role is essentially one of literature searching and document delivery; or a consultancy/advisory operation in which the staff are recognized as the organization's central information 'counselors', the fact that the unit is structured as an information services operation (and frequently characterized as a 'library') often leads to confusion among the various information stakeholders.

Adding further confusion is the fact that in many organizations information-oriented tasks are often connected to other functions, as, for example, in a small research and development firm where the one-person librarian has records management responsibility, or a legal practice in which the records manager is in charge of office operations. In these situations we often find librarians referring to themselves jokingly as the company's 'one-half' librarian, or the law firm's 'part-time' records manager. Whether or not it is really a joking matter depends on the employee's sense of humor.

Given these wide disparities it is not surprising that there is a certain amount of confusion about what these information workers do and how a library or information services unit is defined; especially as information services move toward the twenty-first century and an even more fluid approach to information management, there is also confusion as to how information practitioners should be trained and educated.

Many graduate schools of library and information studies now offer courses in the management of information services. Additionally, much continuing education and training is being offered through professional organizations (both within and outside information-specific fields), and commercial training organizations also address the needs of the information worker. All of this educational activity is of course very helpful from the point of view of the workers themselves.

On the other hand, the information workplace itself continues to seek employees for these different kinds of information operations, often without a clear idea of what the competencies and qualifications for success in these jobs should be, and in the workplace the confusion continues. How it can be abated is in the hands of the practitioners themselves.

The confusion is the result of a number of factors, nearly all of which can be linked to customer/management perceptions about what an information services operation is supposed to be doing. Therefore, to eliminate confusion the unit manager must ensure that everyone connected with the organization and who has any interaction (however remote) with the delivery of information within the organization understands the unit's function. In fact, it is not only within the organization that the information services manager must direct his or her efforts: suppliers, external clients (of internal staff), laypeople with an interest in the operations of the library, and anyone else who is in a position to comment on or relate to the work of the information services unit should be targeted to ensure that they understand what the unit is supposed to be doing.

It is this 'supposed to be doing', so similar in the English language to 'ought' and 'should' and their allusions to accountability, responsibility, 'right-and-wrong', and so forth, that the information manager must grapple with. In every interaction an effort must be made to educate, elucidate and raise awareness about what the library or information services unit does, and why it exists in this particular form at this particular time in the organization's history.

What this means, of course, is that the unit manager must have a clear understanding of what the information services operation does, and of what 'business' it is in. Two essential factors must be addressed:

1. **Library mission vis-à-vis organizational mission.** For every organization with a library or information services unit, the organizational information policy must clearly and succinctly define the mission of the library in terms of the organization or community at large, which means that the library's mission statement must directly correlate with the organizational mission statement. To attempt to operate outside this direct correlation is to invite disaster.

   A negative example best illustrates this situation. Although it is not a common occurrence, it does happen that a financial management firm might decide to close its library, often after an expensive study by an outside consultant (sometimes with the participation of the one-person librarian, sometimes not). Such actions take place in firms (usually older ones) where a 'library' has long been in place. The library, having been created in an earlier period in the company's history when senior executives required a handsome room full of books to provide them with business information (and offering them as well a 'prestigious' space to show off to impressionable clients), was no longer viable. As financial information delivery methodologies changed, the financial managers in the firm now made decisions based upon real-time information delivered to their personal workstations, delivered when they needed it, and exactly when they needed it. The library or information services unit, which had a mission that focused on acquiring materials to have available if they might be needed, no longer delivered materials that were required for the company's success, and thus fell victim to the changing information needs structure of the industry of which it was a part. The library's mission had not changed to match the different information needs of the company.

2. **Library mission vis-à-vis customer expectations.** In each library or information services unit, early and conscientious effort must be made by the information professional with management responsibility for the operation of the library to ensure that the library's mission is clearly spelled out for its constituent users, and for all other information stakeholders as well. Thus a succinctly worded mission statement – in terms that library patrons can understand, and not in library/information services jargon – will define the role of the library in the organization or community of which it is a part. Using the examples suggested above, the sample mission statements suggested in the sidebar might be considered.

If the library or information services unit is a standalone unit devoted exclusively to the procurement of external information for the organization, the mission statement will so state: The Osmosis Company exists to identify and develop companies which can profitably manufacture environmentally safe products. The Osmosis Company Library is a resource for the provision of external materials (that is, materials not generated within The Osmosis Company) to support the work of the company. All employees who require information that cannot be obtained internally are invited to use the resources of the Osmosis Company Library.

If the library or information services unit is a traditional book-oriented collection of materials which patrons access for themselves and for which the information staff's responsibilities are primarily custodial, the following mission statement, following a brief statement about why the company exists, might be appropriate: The Library of The Osmosis Company is a self-service facility where books, journals, technical reports, and other materials owned by the company are housed. All materials are listed in the general library index, which is available through the company's networked information system.

If the library is a research operation in which the librarian's role is primarily one of literature searching and document delivery, the mission statement might read: The Osmosis Company library exists to identify and acquire documents which the employees of the company require for their work. All employees requiring external information are invited to meet with a member of the library staff, who will conduct an information interview with the employee, develop an appropriate search strategy, and search appropriate databases and other sources for the documents required.

If the library is a consultancy/advisory operation in which the library staff are recognized and authorized as the organization's central information 'counselors', the mission statement might read something like the following: The Osmosis Company exists to identify and develop companies which can profitably manufacture environmentally safe products. The company librarian is an information adviser who will meet with all company employees seeking advice about their information needs, and the company librarian will direct employees to the best sources for finding the information they require.

If the library or other information services unit is one in which library-oriented tasks are connected with other information-related functions, such as records management etc., the mission statement will so state: At the Osmosis Company, the records and library services (RLS) unit exists to provide upon request any information which is needed for the successful achievement of the corporate mission. External information is collected and stored in the RLS unit or obtained from external sources when required. Internal records are stored in and accessed through the RLS unit according to procedures established by the RLS unit and available with each departmental manager.

In this last example, the addition of other, non-library information delivery requires the addition of a statement of procedures, in order to prevent the library from becoming a dumping ground for materials that are indiscriminately discarded by other departments. In the other situations described such specific cautions are not necessary, as they are covered through the ordinary development of policies and procedures for the management of the library or other information services operation.

A final point should be made in that mission statements are developed in consultation with others in the organization, including representatives of the users, other staff in the organization or community, and senior management. In particular, the mission statement is developed with the specific participation of the manager to whom the library manager reports.

Nevertheless, although consultation is part of the process, it is the library manager who must finally agree to the terms of the library's mission, as it is he or she who will be administering the provision of information products, services and consultations referred to in the statement. Thus a certain amount of negotiation is required, because if the statement is to work, and be taken seriously by other information stake-holders in the organization or community, management must sign off on the statement and agree to its implementation in its agreed-upon form. Following the successful development of a mission statement for the library or information services unit, procedures and policies will be developed and strategies built. With a solidly crafted mission statement, the information services manager is in a position to provide the information delivery expected by the organization and, in doing so, to eliminate much of the confusion that has hindered that delivery in the past.

The other management functions: organizing, leading and controlling

In quality management terms, the first two functions of management in information services are the seeking of opportunities for the improved delivery of information and the planning of information services. It is through the application of the organizing, leading and controlling functions that information products, services and consultations are brought to the customers. As has already been stated, our job as managers is to ensure that the organization or community achieves its goals, and it is in the seeking of opportunity and planning that these goals are realized. As organizers, leaders and controllers, information services managers ensure that the information workers who have responsibility for contributing to that organizational or community goal participate as they have agreed to participate, and that the organization (and the organization's stakeholders, however they are identified) benefits from that participation.

In fulfilling the organizing function, the information unit manager creates and develops a framework for delivering the information the customers require. In most cases, of course, there will already be a structure in place, but whether the task is to create a new information entity or to reorganize an existing one, the process is the same. The information services manager must determine, by a needs analysis and, when necessary, an information audit, how information is managed in the parent organization or community, how it is captured and stored, how it is disseminated and how it is used.

An example from a trade association illustrates the role the organizing function plays in the delivery of information. In this relatively new organization – only five years old – the management of 'information' appears to be well under control. Since the association is so new, it has been able to begin its operations in a completely electronic environment and all membership records, billing records, publications sales, conference arrangements and the like are organized in a state-of-the-art system that lends itself to a high level of efficiency in the distribution of information throughout the association. In the last year or so, however, the association's leadership has decided that a 'library' should be established, so that members and others interested in knowing about the organization will have access to externally produced materials about the industry it represents, and the association will become known for its 'academic-level' library.

The job of organizing the library was given to the manager of the association's very sophisticated information technology unit, and although this man and his staff are very well versed in the delivery mechanisms that move information around, they are not specialists in the industry represented by the association, nor are they librarians or information specialists. Their role, as they see it, is to deliver the information, to control the conduits the information travels through, and it is up to subject and information specialists to determine a policy for how information is managed. They recognize this difference in approach and, to their credit, recommend that the association bring in specialist librarians and consultants to organize and create the operational

A "COMMON-SENSE" APPROACH TO
PROVIDING QUALITY INFORMATION DELIVERY

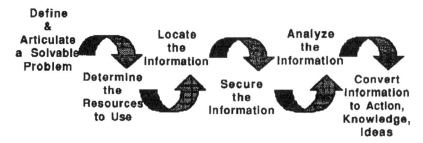

framework.

The IT manager agrees to participate in the effort as a member of the planning team, but it will be the expertise of the librarians and the consultants that will determine how the unit is organized and what its organizational framework will be. They will do this by determining, with the association's management and leadership, what the enterprise-wide information policy is (and help them to establish one if there is no such policy in place), and they will conduct an information audit to determine the information-gathering behavior of the current members, the organization's management and leadership, and any potential information customers who might be interested in using the new 'library.' Part of their effort, of course, will be to create the various plans that make up the operational structure of the library: a library mission statement, a strategic plan, an operational plan, a customer service plan, a marketing plan, and any other plans or schemes that will affect how the library will be used by its identified constituent base. As a fundamental theme, the tenets of quality management and the delivery of quality information services is built into all planning.

However, in an information services operation the organizing function includes more, for the development and implementation of appropriate communication arrangements is essential to the success of the operation. Patterns and networks that enable the information services employees to communicate with one another, with customers and with all other information stakeholders, both internal and external, are a critical part of the quality delivery process, and whether the operation is being organized by internal staff or external consultants, the communication function is the backbone of the operation and determines whether or not the unit will be successful.

The purpose of communication is to influence and direct the work that is being done, to permit all information stakeholders to express how they feel about the information delivery process, and to provide the information that is required to accomplish the information unit's specific mission. Obviously much communication with respect to information services is face to face (customers with information staff, information staff with management and so forth), but since the information services unit is also dealing with artifacts, things that contain information that have to be delivered back and forth (books, technical reports etc.), written communication is part of the picture as well. And in today's workplace, the presence of organization-wide network systems drastically changes traditional communication patterns. All of these elements must be considered as the information services manager attempts to put in place a communication structure for the information unit, regardless of its focus or the content of its collections.

Another element in the organizing function is the staffing of the unit, that is, hiring, training and managing the professional development of the people who will support the actual delivery of information to the customers. In seeking to organize a quality-centered information delivery operation, the manager must give much consideration to information expertise, competencies, skills and the like. In looking at the competencies required for the successful performance of an information transaction there are many different lists and standards, but one of the most useful, which Mary Park identified for the information worker in the business community, requires only a commonsense approach in order to provide quality information delivery:

1. Defining and articulating a problem that can be solved by information resources, determining information strategies
2. Determining what resource to use (i.e. print, electronic, people etc.)
3. Locating the information
4. Getting the information
5. Analyzing the information as it applies to the original problem
6. Converting the information to action, knowledge, ideas (Park, p. 4).

Staff concerns do not end with a list of competencies, however. At the same time, the staff must be trained to keep up with the seemingly unlimited changes going on in the delivery of information, and staff training has become one of the essentials of staff management; organizational training budgets reflect this.

Discussing staff and management–staff relationships forms an introduction to the leadership function, for much of what is done in the name of leadership relates to staff. Motivating and influencing employees and establishing trust in the workplace is an essential element in the leadership process, and certainly the creation of effective teams becomes a primary focus to the leader/manager's work. At the same time, the creation of advocacy and support groups for the information unit results from a manager's leadership function.

When we speak about the controlling function of management, we are not delving into the realm of lost personal freedom nearly as much as the term might imply. Control is, in western society, a frightening concept, and certainly the history of industry and business has demonstrated that controlling workers – in the absolute sense of the term – leads to unhappy and dangerous workplace situations. On the other hand, a lack of control leads to a lack of success, for the purpose of control is simply to see that what *is* accomplished matches what was *planned* to be accomplished. The control function usually includes input controls, process controls and output controls, and it is in the establishment of a basic control process that the information services manager ensures that the other functions he or she has put in place are all successful. The control process is usually based on the following formula: performance standards are agreed upon, performance is measured, and the measurements are compared to the standards. If performance meets the established and agreed-upon standards, the information services operation is succeeding; if it does not, corrective action is required.

So the manager's first task is to devise and implement a control structure that permits the establishment of standards, and it is at this point that the information services discipline tends to break down, because the delivery of information is most generally perceived to be intangible and thus not measurable.

The quality management objectives

The future of information delivery continues to be a major concern for information managers, regardless of the information environment in which they are employed, and establishing a framework for excellence in information delivery might very well be suggested as a primary objective in the development and implementation of a quality management initiative.

Picking up on this, and remarking that his 30 years in the information industry have made him, 'if nothing else', a qualified observer, Ira Siegel offered an ancient sailors' superstition to frame his subject when he discussed these matters in a presentation in early 1996 (LEXIS–NEXIS Executive . . . , 1996 p. 5). The sailors' belief, Siegel said, 'was that, inevitably, one wave will come along that is far greater than any other that has ever preceded it. It's called the ninth wave – the most powerful result of the cumulative efforts of sea, wind, and temperature. To ride – and not be swamped by – the ninth wave as it approaches requires special skills, first in the ability to anticipate it, and second, in timing your movements to mount it cleanly at its peak.'

Siegel suggests that those working in information delivery are witnessing an equivalent wave, 'bringing with it significant changes from the waves of the recent past'. And, not surprisingly for an executive whose operation provides a product widely used in the information services community, Siegel has very firm opinions about how information professionals should be thinking about the ninth wave.

'Clearly', he said in his presentation, 'when the ninth information wave arrives, the most exciting place to be will be the crest . . . On the other hand, the worst place to be is underneath it – knowing you've been overtaken – and the fear of falling even further behind.'

There are, of course, strategies for avoiding being overtaken, and Siegel listed quite a few that can be of benefit to information services managers. For example, he notes that successful librarians no longer wait for information requests to come to them. 'They seek them out', Siegel said, and take a proactive approach to incorporating information technology into the organization's regular activities.

The positioning of the information delivery unit is key, too, and Siegel noted that, in successful organizations, 'the corporate library is managed like any other technical group within the company'.

Similarly, quality control is critical in the successful library operation, and in one example Siegel used he described how each information request is reviewed by two librarians and the data edited so it can be presented 'in a valuable form' that the customer understands.

Finding a virtue in being noticed, Siegel urged librarians and other information workers to be visible outside their units and to develop relationships with their customers, in order to 'better understand their needs and to market the library's services more effectively'.

Finally, though, the goal that we should all be looking for as we seek to incorporate the quality perspective into an information delivery operation is one that was well expressed by Lucy Lettis, who manages Arthur Andersen's Metro New York Business Information Center ([Lettis 1996], p. 4). When asked about what it takes to organize a successful information services operation, Lettis's answer revealed an honesty and a new way of thinking: 'Let's not be too self-effacing about this', Lettis said in an interview. 'Of course there are rewards, and it would be slightly disingenuous for me to pretend that I'm not pleased. In the kind of work we information services managers do, especially at this level, there is a certain amount of ego satisfaction involved. Of course we do it for the customers, and of course we do it so our organizations can succeed, but we also do it because we're good at what we do, and there is satisfaction in that.'

This is the way the world works, and when there are information practitioners (especially at the management level) who can recognize that three-way success, there are benefits all around. That level of service and satisfaction is the result when the information organization is managed from a total quality management perspective. The information customers get what they need, the information services operation is contributing to the corporate success, and the information services manager is happy. This combination is what a lot of people are looking for, and it is what TQM provides in an information services environment.

References

Aguilar, Francis J. *Scanning the Business Environment.* New York: Macmillan, 1967.

Albrecht, Karl *The Northbound Train: Finding the Purpose, Setting the Direction, Shaping the Destiny of Your Organization.* New York: American Management Association, 1994.

Auster, Ethel and Choo, Chun Wei. 'Environmental Scanning: Preliminary Findings of Interviews with CEOs in Two Canadian Industries.' In *Proceedings of the 56th Annual Meeting of the American Society for Information Science held in Pittsburgh, PA, October 26–29, 1992,* edited by Debora Shaw. Medford, NJ: Learned Information Inc., 1993.

Choo, Chun Wei. *Information Management for the Intelligent Organization: the Art of Scanning the Environment.* ASIS (American Society for Information Science) Monograph Series. Medford, New Jersey: Information Today Inc., 1995.

Curzon, Susan C. *Managing Change.* New York: Neal-Schuman, 1989.

Dinerman, Gloria. 'The information professional: a portrait of progress.' *The SpeciaList* 19 (5), May, 1996, pp. 1, 11, 14.

Drucker, Peter F. *Managing the Non-Profit Organization: Practices and Principles.* New York: HarperCollins, 1990.

Fahey, Liam and Narayanan, Vadake K. *Macroenvironmental Analysis for Strategic Management.* St. Paul, MN: West Publishing, 1986.

Ferriero, David S. and Wilding, Thomas L. 'Scanning the environment in strategic planning.' *Masterminding Tomorrow's Information – Creative Strategies for the '90s.* Washington DC: Special Libraries Association, 1991.

Jauch, Lawrence R. and Glueck, William F. *Business Policy and Strategic Management.* New York: McGraw-Hill, 1988.

[Lawes, Ann] 'Ann Lawes: thinking about the information manager as change agent.' *InfoManage: The International Management Newsletter for the Information Services Executive* 3 (1), December, 1995.

Lester, Ray and Waters, Judith. *Environmental Scanning and Business Strategy.* London: British Library Research and Development Department, 1989.

[Lettis, Lucy] ' 'Determined?' 'Driven?' Perhaps even 'Relentless?' At Arthur Andersen in New York, success in the company's business information center connects of Lucy Lettis's own career path.' *InfoManage: The International Management Newsletter for the*

Information Services Executive 3 (5), April, 1996.

'LEXIS-NEXIS executive focuses in on the 'ninth wave' for information services.' *InfoManage: The International Management Newsletter for the Information Services Executive* 3 (5), April, 1996.

[Park, Mary] 'Mary Park thinks "Partnering" is a good idea - if the partner is senior management.' *InfoManage: The International Management Newsletter for the Information Services Executive* 3(2), January, 1996, pp. 1-5.

Szilagyi, Andrew D. *Management and Performance*. Glenview, IL: Scott, Foresman, 1988.

Tees, Miriam. 'Is it possible to educate librarians as managers?' *Special Libraries* 75 (6), July 1994, (pp. 173-182).

Chapter Three

Defining quality management in information services

Total quality management and its various permutations offer splendid opportunities for service workers to excel at what they do, but for a quality 'foothold' to exist all workers and their customers must understand what quality service means, and the people who will be affected by the implementation of a quality service effort must be identified. Establishing a quality structure is a complex task, and there will be many nay-sayers in the organization who will challenge the efforts of those who are attempting to create a quality framework, especially if the effort is mandated by senior management. The most popular arguments against the move towards a formalized quality initiative will be that quality management is not a realistic goal for the organization, that seeking to attain perfection in the workplace is an impossible quest for the various subunits of the organization, and that the effort involved in moving toward a quality workplace simply gets in the way of other work that must be done.

To these arguments, the manager who is supporting the development of a quality program has ready answers. Quality management is a realistic goal simply because it has been shown to work in those organizations and communities that will take the time to make a commitment to the process. Just the act of organizing a quality management effort makes workers immediately aware of their obligations to the organizational mission, and provides them with a stimulus they had not had before. Even in organizations where the commitment to an ongoing quality program is weak and the effort is discontinued, employees and management become aware of the role of quality in their working lives and recognize that without a formal quality program they have no way of determining whether they are providing quality outputs or not.

As for the quest for 'perfection' in the workplace, it is silly to expect total quality to lead to perfect quality. In any management activity one must be wary of setting unrealistic goals, and of course mistakes will be made along the way, but recognizing this fact does not mean that a quality perspective is out of place. What the information services manager must do is look toward the organizational mission and the departmental mission, to look beyond the immediate needs of the workplace and to focus on the overall organizational purpose. Taken from this point of view, the effort to introduce a quality framework becomes simply a matter of recognizing what business the organization is in, what its employees have agreed to provide, and then to move toward providing it as well as possible.

Whether quality management gets in the way of other work is not an arguable point. It does not. The perception that working with a quality program inhibits productivity in the department arises because many workers (and managers) fail to see their work from this broader perspective, and as they give their attention to the day-to-day work that must be done, it naturally assumes a larger and larger role in their planning. What is needed is for them to be persuaded to recognize that the tasks involved in implementing a quality management program are as essential as the other work they are doing. When this change in thinking is established, when a quality culture is accepted and built in to the management process, management and staff alike soon come to learn that the return on that investment is a healthy one. The excellence of the services provided, the building of teams and trusting relationships in the workplace, and the empowerment that comes to every employee are indeed well worth the effort.

The information stakeholders

In an information services environment quality management is linked to the delivery of information through the interactions of the information stakeholders in the organization or community. These individuals and groups can be variously defined, and each organizational entity will have different individuals and groups who can be so characterized. The most prominent, of course, must be the information customers, the constituent user groups and individuals who have been identified as the people who will seek the services the information unit provides. If the concept of 'the authority of the customer' means anything, it is that the work of the information unit must unequivocally be structured around the needs, interests and expectations of these people.

Equally obvious as information stakeholders are the information workers, that is, the unit manager and his or her staff. Various suppliers (both internal and external) who furnish the goods, services, support materials (including information) and other tangible resources required for the successful operation of the department can be classified as stakeholders, simply because information staff are required to interact with them in the course of their work and their participation or lack of it can seriously affect whether a quality program is successful or not.

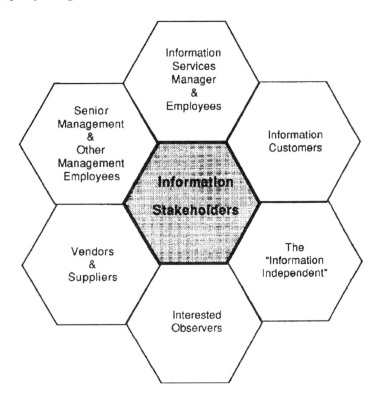

External vendors especially are often thought of as appendages to the operation of the information unit, but in fact without clear-cut and specifically coordinated routines and safety mechanisms for working with vendors, the information services manager can find himself or herself in a serious bind with respect to quality service. In fairness, however, it should be noted that many external vendors see themselves as part of the information services team, and are happy to work with the department because it is in their own organizations' best interest to ensure that their work with the information unit matches the quality standards that are established for internal operations.

Other information stakeholders include senior managers, each of whom has an organizational responsibility to see that the organization or community as a whole is managed in such a way that success is ensured. Managers on the same level as the head of the information services department are invited and encouraged to work with him or her to ensure that their respective units move the organization forward, and if the quality initiative is enterprise wide the likelihood of success is increased as the various managers come to depend on one another in realizing the benefits of the effort.

Depending on the nature of the enterprise, other information stakeholders might be interested leaders, observers and/or political (for lack of a better word) players in the organization or community. Many of these people will also be members of the constituent user groups. There will also be others who, despite expressing great enthusiasm and support for the information unit, for various reasons never need to use it. A typical example might be found in an professional association, in which the elected members of the board of directors might be very supportive of, say, the association's membership records department, but who have no reason to avail themselves of its services. Similarly, in a research institution a senior scientist might have all the subscriptions to the journals he needs sent to his office through his own efforts, or because he is a member of various scientific groups for which the journals are provided as a benefit of membership. With a collection of books, technical reports and similar materials of his own he has no need for the services of the library, but he is nevertheless interested in its wellbeing and continued success. In both of these cases, the people concerned are information stakeholders.

A final group of information stakeholders do not know that they have this role, and in fact many of them will assiduously deny any connection with an information services facility, for they do not see themselves as using information (particularly any information that is not generated or acquired at their own workstations). These people are often information literate, and the amount of information they use might be prodigious, but because they are end-users they see themselves as 'information independent' ([Ginsburg 1993], p. 1). They do not require the services that might be provided by a formal information delivery operation and because they function very well (by their own information standards) without those services they do not think of themselves as having any affiliation with the information services unit.

In fact they do have an affiliation, and so do those who might be called the 'information indifferent', the people whose work and personal lives simply do not require them to use libraries, computers, records, or any of the standard paraphernalia associated with the information-gathering process. Their lives move along quite reasonably without the benefit of any specific attention to information matters, and their information needs, being minimal, are met through ways they have devised and been satisfied with long ago.

Both these groups can be considered information stakeholders or, more specifically, *potential* information stakeholders, because as society changes and their interests change, they very well may come to require the services of the information unit in question. It is to the benefit of all that these 'non-users' be considered as the quality initiative evolves.

In moving toward a quality-centered information operation it is important to recognize that all of these groups and individuals will be working together to identify the barriers and enablers that inhibit or permit effective and successful information delivery. That is their role as information stakeholders, and although in most cases their involvement is simply advisory (since it is the information services manager and his or her superiors who have actual decision-making authority), their advice and good will is important in the successful achievement of the information unit's mission. Certainly in any quality initiative the leadership will come from the information services unit and its own constituent members (even if it was not especially sought by the unit in question). Nevertheless, the involvement of all information stakeholders is critical to the success of the process.

It is not difficult to understand why. It is in all their interests and that of the parent organization that information delivery be as good as it can be. What the information stakeholders require and what they are seeking is nothing less than excellence in information delivery, and the only way this can be achieved is through a structured, formalized quality management program. In participating in such a program, all information stakeholders come to an agreement on standards of performance, on mutually sanctioned objectives and goals, and on the elements of delivery and the methodologies that will lead to the attainment of these information-focused goals and objectives.

Defining TQM

Having developed a mission statement for the information services department that connects directly to the mission statement of the parent organization, the information stakeholders put their energies into defining quality management and determining how it will affect the delivery of information in their immediate situation. Led, more than likely, by the manager of the information services unit, they will begin to think about quality in the workplace, and one of their first tasks will be to define quality as it applies in an information services environment. Almost from the beginning they will recognize that quality management is not a passing fad or management buzzword. There are plenty of popular management techniques and trends that come and go, but quality management is not one of them, primarily because it is built on the fundamentals of all good business practice, which in the information services environment might be stated thus:

> Know what the *customers* want and provide it in a manner that meets their perceptions and their expectations. At the same time, do it in such a way that in providing it, you are positioned to do it for them *better* the next time they need it.

What quality management does, in effect, is to set the standards of service delivery so that the customer is given what he or she is seeking and the service provider is positioned to provide the service as well as it can be provided. Since this concept is the basis of all transactions (or should be), it should come as no surprise that quality management, built on this essential framework, is here to stay.

It is a little harder to define exactly what quality management is, but much has been written about the subject and many organizations, large and small, have achieved phenomenal success by putting their managerial structure on a quality footing. In information services terms, quality management is not simply a process, a management tool or a management style, and it is certainly not simply a management technique or procedure. Notably, despite the fact that it was developed for the production of goods, quality management has been demonstrated to be an effective methodology for achieving positive results in the services field. In fact, despite some well-known failures in some service disciplines, there have been remarkable successes in health services, in community and government agencies, in merchandising, and in numerous other fields as well. In information services, where there is already a tradition of attention to the needs of the customer and a long-established desire to provide excellence in information delivery, the potential for success in the development and implementation of a quality management initiative is great.

That this is so should be no mystery, considering the fact that quality management is a combination of process, technique, management tool and management style put together with a commitment to an ongoing effort that establishes quality management as the basis for all process decisions in the organization (which can be the parent organization or community of which the information services department is but a part, or it can be the information services unit itself). These elements then come together to form an information services culture, built on an unwavering commitment to customer satisfaction that utilizes a wide spectrum of quality-focused management procedures and policies leading to con-tinuous improvement and the provision of the highest levels of excellence in information products, services and consultations.

One point that must be made without hesitation is that quality management is not a quick-fix, fast-turnaround management technique. The concept of *culture* cannot be overemphasized, for what happens in a quality-focused information environment is that the quality effort is woven into the very fabric of the unit. Some information services managers like to assert that theirs is a department in which quality is emphasized. Emphasis is not enough, for an emphasis is often temporary and related to a specific event or set of conditions. Quality management must be ongoing, permanent and long term. It is not a commitment to be made without serious thought, and it is not in the best interests of the information services unit for it to be attempted without full commitment. Quality management is a philosophy of service that obliges its participants to take seriously their roles in the information delivery process, and to entrust to themselves and to those with whom they interact an assurance that their participation will move the information services unit forward toward the achievement of its mutually agreed-upon mission. As is often noted when the subject is discussed, particularly by managers who have successfully developed and implemented a quality initiative in their organizations, quality management is characterized as 'a journey, not a destination'.

Another important characteristic of quality management is that it is not a formula or template that can be dropped into a specific management environment and expected to work simply because it has been developed and codified in other environments. One of the ongoing difficulties with TQM is that internal staff with quality implementation responsibilities, or external consultants hired for the purpose, will seek to employ a TQM formulation that has been created to work in a variety of settings, and often across several different service disciplines. Such an approach cannot be expected to succeed, because each management entity (particularly in information services) is operated differently and is frequently organized differently. In fact, when working with information services operations, the one element that must be carefully factored in to the management of the operation is the human relations part of the picture: the success of any information-related transaction is going to be based very heavily on the relationship between the information customer and the provider, the information staff and organizational or community management, indeed, between the various and many information stakeholders that have already been referred to. Certainly the quantitative and measurable aspects of TQM must be studied and considered, but for the methodology to work in an information services environment the role of subjectivity (with particular reference to the people) is equally important, and not to be dismissed lightly.

Quality management and quality assurance

The quality management approach goes under many names and TQM is but one of them, although it certainly is the term that appears to be the most popular. Initially originated by the Naval Air Systems Command to describe its Japanese-style management approach to quality improvement, the term has come to take on many meanings, as has been noted by many writers, including William Duncan. His own definition is fairly straightforward:

> TQM is a system by which continuous improvement of all value-adding processes performed by the organization may be achieved. The customer determines if value has been added based on his or her own satisfaction.

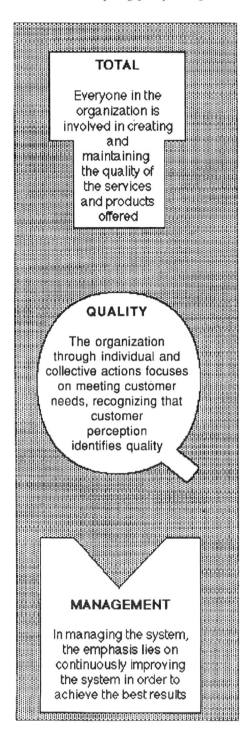

TOTAL

Everyone in the organization is involved in creating and maintaining the quality of the services and products offered

QUALITY

The organization through individual and collective actions focuses on meeting customer needs, recognizing that customer perception identifies quality

MANAGEMENT

In managing the system, the emphasis lies on continuously improving the system in order to achieve the best results

TQM is predicated on the participation of each organization member in improving products, processes, services and the company culture (Duncan et al. 1995, p. 174).

In a related definition, and one which lends itself well to being adapted for an information services operation, Peter Capezio and Debra Morehouse also emphasize the importance of having all stakeholders involved, and they specifically call for the participation of senior management:

> Total quality management refers to a management process and set of disciplines that are coordinated to ensure that the organization consistently meets and exceeds customer requirements. TQM engages all divisions, departments, and levels of the organization. Top management organizes all of its strategy and operations around customer needs and develops a culture with high employee participation. TQM companies are focused on the systematic management of data in all processes and practices to eliminate waste and pursue continuous improvement (Capezio and Morehouse 1995, p.1).

In the library/information services discipline, there have been attempts to define quality management in information-specific terms, and one of the most useful was formulated by Jennifer Younger, who returns to a basic description of quality management to provide a framework for applying the methodology in information delivery:

> To the untutored ear, phrases like "total quality management" have the sound of jargon. Yet once these phrases are dissected and understood, they can be seen for what they are – shorthand methods for representing three ideas central to addressing quality:
> **Total** Everyone in the organization is involved in creating and maintaining the quality of the services and products offered by the organization.
> **Quality** The organization through individual and collective actions focuses on meeting customer needs, recognizing that it is the customer's perception that identifies quality.
> **Management** In managing the system, defined as the steps taken to produce the services and products, the emphasis lies on continuously improving the system in order to achieve the best results. Together, these ideas form the foundation on which to build an organizational commitment to quality (Younger 1992, p. 3).

In the United Kingdom John R. Brockman has become well known for his work in quality management, and he offers a continuum that moves the development of quality management in the library and information services discipline from quality control through quality assurance to total quality management (Brockman 1992, p. 283). He uses BSI/ISO definitions for the terminology and they can be repeated here to help set the framework for establishing a quality program in a library or information services operation:

Quality control: The operational techniques and activities that are used to fulfil requirements for quality. Quality control . . . aims at eliminating causes of unsatisfactory performance at relevant stages of the quality loop in order to result in economic effectiveness.

Quality assurance (QA): All those planned and systematic actions necessary to provide adequate confidence that a product or service will satisfy given requirements for quality.

Total quality management (TQM): A management philosophy embracing all activities through which the needs of the customer and the community, and the objectives of the organization, are satisfied in the most efficient and cost-effective way by maximizing the potential of all employees in a continuing drive for improvement (BSI 1992).

Younger is quick to acknowledge that although the emphasis is on customer satisfaction, the information services unit itself has to be acknowledged for the role it will play in the quality process:

While customers can and do make choices based on their perception of quality, the usefulness to them of the services produced, the obligations to improve quality and to invent new services rest with the producing organization. The whys of improvement are obvious and shared by many outside the formal quality improvement circle. The quality management approach focuses, however, on finding and reducing the causes of variation that occur in the systems used to produce the results. The desired level of quality is defined at the outset and the process is then designed to produce services or products of uniform and high quality. Determining when and how to adjust the system depends on systematic data collection and analysis to indicate when the system is reliably producing the predicted quality (Younger 1992, p. 2).

In moving toward the establishing of a quality program, employees in an information services operation will quickly discover that there is other terminology that describes what is very much the same philosophy of service. It is this wide variety of terms (having sprung from the work of many different quality 'gurus') that causes the most confusion and builds the first barrier to the acceptance of a quality program. The information services manager will be confronted with many different names for this initiative, and phrases like quality improvement (QI), company-wide quality control (CWQC), total quality assurance, quality assurance and service reliability, marketing quality assurance, quality service, service quality, quality circles, quality function deployment (QFD) and quality improvement strategy (QIS) will be thrown about with considerable ease, and although at some point a decision will be made about what to call the program the basic tenets of the various approaches will vary little. In employing quality improvement strategy, for example, the application of statistical tools is emphasized, but the primary goal – to ensure that customers are obtaining the services they expect – remains the same.

Similarly, as Brockman points out, as quality assurance evolves toward total quality management, 'the most important changes involve the roles of management and measurement'.

> In the case of the former, the responsibility for quality ceases to be delegated to QA staff and becomes the concern of all employees, but especially top management. The emphasis on measurement systems also changes from being internally to externally orientated and more customer-focused (Brockman 1992, p. 283).

Nevertheless, quality assurance is an approach that has been successfully established in the library and information services field, and Anne M. Fredenburg has written about the subject. Fredenburg defines quality assurance as:

> a systematic method of establishing standards, identifying and monitoring problems, and looking for ways to improve where improvement is possible. Continuing education does not ensure quality, though education is part of it; nor is QA crisis intervention, characterized by a rally to respond to a crucial situation (Fredenburg 1988, p. 278).

Given the success of quality assurance programs in library and information services units, it is important to recognize how such programs can be initiated. Fredenburg reports that a primary benefit in her experience was the high level of 'both *inter*departmental and *intra*departmental cooperation', and suggests that for some information services facilities a quality assurance program might be the key to strengthening the relationship between the information unit and senior management. It is, she writes, 'the vital link in acting on, rather than reacting to, an administrative mandate to produce results, justify the library's worth, and relate what the library is and does to the organization's strategies and goals' (Fredenburg 1988, pp. 277, 283). The ten suggestions that Fredenburg offers for beginning a quality assurance program (see sidebar) ensure that a proactive, creative perspective is established.

Establishing a quality assurance program

1. Put yourself on the same wavelength as decision makers, using their process, record-keeping system, and recommended methods. Adopt their vocabulary and jargon . . .

2. Talk with the quality assurance administrator in your organization to keep current on developments in QA adaptable to the library and to coordinate the library's activities with the institution-wide program.

3. Be flexible, keeping an open mind to changes in the method.

4. Realize that QA is an idea with many approaches. Adapt what works for you and omit the ideas that don't apply.

5. Also realize that QA is as individual as each library . . . hence no instant QA guide and no "canned" programs with answers for all libraries' questions. Because of this individuality, any prepackaged program for purchase should be avoided.

6. Be attuned to the library's relationship with its clientele. Educate and get to know your users, asking for their opinions and following up on work done for them. Be an effective, focused listener.

7. Use informal evaluation methods, such as "corridor conferences" or 15-minute meetings with administrators or department managers to gauge the library's effectiveness.

8. Don't get bogged down with statistics, studies, questionnaires etc. Be selective in what to study and analyze, avoiding studies for the sake of studies or because, historically, that's the way a task has always been done. Planning to do a study means focusing on a specific library issue or service which can be especially useful as a baseline to evaluate future performance in that area.

9. Since some statistics are necessary, decide which ones are important and what is an appropriate amount of information to gather.

10. Keep a folder or notebook on QA to make note of ideas to put in practice.

Source: Fredenburg, Anne M. 'Quality assurance: establishing a program for special libraries.' *Special Libraries* 79 (4), Fall, 1988. Reprinted with permission of the Special Libraries Association.

In an information services operation it needs to be recognized that much of what is done in a quality context is not necessarily according to a specific and ironclad formula. In fact, attempting to put the management of a company's archives department, say, into a quality program that has been developed for the MIS/information technology staff might very well lead to disaster. At the very least much confusion would ensue, and much time would be lost as staff attempted to deal with the exceptions that did not match between departments. So, flexibility is a primary requirement in the establishment of a quality program for an information services unit, and different components of different methodologies will be incorporated into the work.

ISO 9000, for example, published by the International Standards Organization, is a set of five international standards having to do with quality assurance and quality management. The standards are necessarily generic, but they are nevertheless an important move in the direction of establishing quality standards worldwide. Because the certification (called 'registration' in America) of an organization's performance in accordance with these standards is acknowledged through third-party examination, the ISO 9000 program is useful, providing objective measurement standards.

With respect to ISO 9000 and information services, however, there is still work to be done before the value of the application of the standards in information services is established. For one thing, according to Helge Clausen, 'the process which may lead to the sought-after ISO 9000 certificate is a long and labor-intensive exercise', and smaller and less well-financed libraries and information services units may find the costs (especially in staff time required) to be impractical. A second finding which Clausen reports, which may be connected to the first, is that for those libraries and information services units connected with a larger parent organization, if the parent organization is seeking certification 'this will also be the case for the library in about 40% of the cases (19 out of 48). If the parent company is not involved with certification, the library was in only two cases out of 67' (Clausen 1995, p. 39).

Benchmarking, re-engineering, and the learning organization

There are three management concepts which relate closely to the success of any quality initiative, and they are now recognized as significant auxiliary tools in the management of a quality focused information services operation.* During the past decade, the attention paid to benchmarking, re-engineering, and the learning organization as useful methods for approaching effective information delivery has been remarkable, proving once again that managers in the library and information services fields are not as resistant to the management techniques of the business community as some would have us believe. All three concepts grew from efforts in the business community to do better what business managers were expected to do, that is, to provide the management expertise so that their organizations could provide the products and services that their customers were expecting them to provide. With benchmarking, re-engineering, and the development of the learning organization as management techniques, so to speak, the

---

*Benchmarking and the Learning Organization as "new management paradigms" in connection with Total Quality Management were the subject of a special issue of *Special Libraries* 84(3), Summer, 1993.

connection with quality management becomes a natural progression, and each of these is now frequently used – at varying degrees of involvement – with quality management efforts.

Benchmarking, for example, has become one of the basic tools of the quality improvement process, and a standard definition can demonstrate why:

> Benchmarking is a process by which an organization continuously compares its processes, products, and services to those of the world's best organizations with the same or similar functions. It is a comparative investigation that analyzes the gap between an organization's present level of performance and the best that exists. Finally, benchmarking is a way to study the methods of "best" organizations, to adapt their ideas, and to become, quickly and efficiently, the best in the world (Balm 1992, p. vii).

At a level that relates more closely to the concerns of information services managers seeking to organize a quality initiative, Annette Gohlke has created a definition for libraries which can be altered to fit any information-delivery function:

> Benchmarking is a total quality tool used to measure and compare your library's work processes with those in other libraries. The goal of benchmarking is to increase your library's performance by adopting the best practices of your library benchmarking partners. Since best library practices are always evolving, benchmarking should be applied at least annually. (Gohlke 1996, p. [1]).

Obviously, then, benchmarking is a process of comparing and measuring which can be integrated into a quality management program. In fact, it would be difficult to undertake a quality program without some attention to benchmarking, since the objective of benchmarking, as noted in the benchmarking 'bible', is 'to provide goals for realistic process improvement and an understanding of the changes necessary to facilitate that improvement' (APQC 1996, p. 5).

Benchmarking as an effective management tool is described in an article about a US federal government agency's response to Vice-President Al Gore's call for 'reinventing government'. The agency used the benchmarking process 'to take a hard look at every job located in a senior level function with middle management "oversight" responsibilities' and among the work studied was the library function. A five-step process was applied, and the questions used can be asked in any information services benchmarking exercise:

1. What causes this job to be done [that is, in very specific terms, why does this job exist?]

2. Work and output:
   (a) List the steps involved and output resulting from performing this job.
   (b) Identify non-critical output.

3. Benefit analysis:
   (a) Explain the benefit of the critical outputs to the corporate mission.
   (b) Explain any mission degradation that would occur if the task were eliminated.

4. Job assessment: Should the job continue to be done?

5. Job enrichment:
   (a) List the steps, output and associated manhours that could be reduced by revising this job.
   (b) Could the job be done another way to save manhours if it is still required to be accomplished? (Gohlke 1996, pp. 1–2).

In these benchmarking efforts, the relationship with quality management, specifically in library and information services management, can be most clearly demonstrated in the comments contained in a pamphlet distributed by the Australian Council of Libraries and Information Services. It is difficult to address quality issues in an information services environment because, as the authors put it, 'one problem for libraries [and other information services operations] is the paucity of indicators that relate to value, as against indicators of level of activity encompassed in the traditional library statistics'. Recognizing that many information delivery units are being questioned as to their value, and connecting this situation with the difficulties traditionally inherent in determining the effectiveness of information delivery, it is helpful to look at how some of the relevant concepts are defined:

> **Best practice:** simply the best way of doing things. It is working for outcomes and empowering the workforce. It relies on problem solving, objective setting, planning, and measuring at the operational level. It fosters the concept of continuous improvement as part of the organizational culture. Most importantly, it focuses on meeting the needs of the customer.
> **Benchmarking:** a process of measuring performance across the organization, or within a particular function, and then comparing it with the performance in another section or organization which is regarded as "best in class".
> **Performance indicators/measures:** The purpose of the performance indicator is to measure performance or progress against a set target within a time period. The measures are locally based, i.e. they are internally derived according to strategic goals and operational objectives. Performance indicators should accord with the SMART principle: they should be specific, measurable, achievable, realistic, and sit within a timeframe (ACLIS 1996, pp. [1–2]).

Another management process closely linked to quality management but which requires a radical approach to the effort (and 'radical' is the operative word in this context) is re-engineering. Now firmly established as an accepted methodology for achieving organizational vision, re-engineering calls for the establishment of new management procedures and discarding old ones, to the extent that what is left is only what is germane to the objectives being sought. Re-engineering, in the definition of its best-known authority and teacher, 'is the fundamental rethinking and radical redesign of business processes to achieve dramatic improvements in critical, contemporary measures of performance, such as cost, quality, service, and speed' (Hammer and Champy 1993, p. 32).

The re-engineering process is totally visionary, which is why it is so appropriate for an information services operation whose management is seeking to organize a quality initiative. Recognizing that much that has been developed in the library and information services discipline over the centuries is not specifically customer-focused, the information services manager who embarks on a re-engineering effort goes back to the proverbial 'blank page', to asking very basic questions about why the information operation exists, what it was created to be doing and what it *should* be doing. In the process, every step, every action is questioned as to its relevance to the attainment of that goal, that information services mission. When necessary, radical redesign is instigated to ensure that each step in the information process is relevant.

In the Hammer and Champy model the 'new world of work' that they envision is singularly appropriate to the library/information services community, if management is willing to commit to a new philosophy of coaching instead of supervising. Here are the changes that Hammer and Champy project; they can work in an information services environment:

- Work units change – from functional departments to process teams.

- Jobs change – from simple tasks to multidimensional work.

- People's roles change – from controlled to empowered.

- Job preparation changes – from training to education.

- Focus of performance measures and compensation shifts – from activity to results.

- Advancement criteria change – from performance to ability.

- Values change – from protective to productive.

- Managers change – from supervisors to coaches.

- Organizational structures change – from hierarchical to flat.

- Executives change – from scorekeepers to leaders (Hammer and Champy 1993, pp. 65-82).

A third management direction that should be given attention is the learning organization. This concept relates to quality management because, in the words of Peter M. Senge, the man who is generally credited with bringing the idea of the learning organization to the business community, 'Human beings are designed for learning'. Senge defines learning organizations as 'organizations where people continually expand their capacity to create the results they truly desire, where new and expansive patterns of thinking are nurtured, where collective aspiration is set free, and where people are continually learning how to learn together' (Senge 1994, p.3). Surely there is no organization more poised to become a learning organization than an information delivery facility, and the recognition of the learning organization as an organizational construct that can be linked to quality management is an approach that has special resonance for information services. By moving the information services department in the direction of becoming a learning organization, the manager positions the role of the information provider as the information 'leader' in the organization or community of which the department is a part. At the same time, looking at information delivery in this light positions the information provider to think about his work in an intellectual framework that builds on systems thinking, as opposed to an individualistic and, as Senge puts it, 'snapshot' view of the organizational history and environment.

In describing how new leadership models are required for organizational success, Senge provides a useful device for information services, if the information provider (or at least the manager of the information services unit) is willing to see himself or herself in the role of a new leader in a learning organization:

> Our traditional view of leaders – as special people who set direction, make the key decision, and energize the troops – is deeply rooted in an individualistic and nonsystemic worldview. Especially in the West, leaders are *heroes* – great men (and occasionally women) who rise to the fore in times of crisis. So long as such myths prevail, they reinforce a focus on short-term events and charismatic heroes rather than on systemic forces and collective learning.
>
> Leadership in learning organizations centers on subtler and ultimately more important work. In a learning organization, leaders' roles differ dramatically from that of the charismatic decision maker. Leaders are designers, teachers, and stewards. These roles require new skills: the ability to build shared vision, to bring to the surface and challenge prevailing mental models, and to foster more systemic patterns of thinking. In short, leaders in learning organizations are responsible for *building organizations* where people are continually expanding their capabilities to shape their future – that is, leaders are responsible for learning (Senge 1990, pp. 8–9).

In the new skills that Senge's leader will seek to develop, building vision becomes almost a blueprint for moving quality management practices into the information environment, for they include the following skills which Senge has identified and which information services managers can use as a basis for thinking in quality terms:

1. Encouraging personal vision;

2. Communicating and asking for support;

3. Visioning as an ongoing process;

4. Blending extrinsic and intrinsic vision;

5. Distinguishing positive from negative vision (Senge 1990 pp. 13-14).

For Senge, the route to building learning organizations then leads through a second critical skill, the 'surfacing and testing of mental models', to the third set of skills, engaging in systems thinking.

It is in the area of systems thinking that the information manager seeking to bring a quality perspective to the information services unit will realize the new leadership role, for it is the integration of systems thinking into the information service management process that will enable him to construct a 'historical' infrastructure that will lead him to a quality-focused approach. Systems thinking, which Senge defines as 'a conceptual framework, a body of knowledge and tools that has been developed over the past fifty years, to make the full patterns clearer, and to help us see how to change them effectively', is the 'fifth discipline' that he identifies. The characteristics of which have been listed as follows:

1. Seeing interrelationships, not things, and processes, not snapshots;

2. Moving beyond blame;

3. Distinguishing detail complexity from dynamic complexity;

4. Focusing on areas of high leverage;

5. Avoiding symptomatic solutions (Senge 1990, pp. 14-15).

For the information services manager, the inclusion of new leadership models and systems thinking can provide a workable and practical framework for the organization of a total quality management initiative in the information services unit, but the success of the effort will be determined by the seriousness with which these ideas and concepts are organized. Once again, it is imperative that information services managers recognize that no one formula or process is going to work for every organization, and even linking such logical and reasonable methodologies as benchmarking, re-engineering and the learning organization will require approaching each from a point of view that asks 'What is the best attribute of this technique?' and 'Which parts of it will work in my organization?' At the same time it is important to understand that each of these methodologies, as connected to a quality management endeavour, requires a certain ability to step back from the process and determine where it is doing good and where it is not. With these conditions in mind, the information services manager can confidently move into using the techniques of benchmarking, re-engineering and the learning organization in managing the information services operation from a quality perspective.

References

ACLIS (Australian Council of Libraries and Information Services). *Bench-marking, Best Practice, and Quality Management: What's it All About?* Canberra, ACT, Australia: Australian Council of Libraries and Information Services, 1996.

APQC (American Productivity & Quality Center). *The Benchmarking Management Guide*. Portland, OR: Productivity Press, 1992.

Balm, Gerald J. *Benchmarking: A practitioner's Guide for Becoming and Staying Best of the Best*. Schaumburg, IL: Quality & Productivity Management Association, 1992.

British Standards Institution. *Quality Vocabulary: Part 2. Concepts and Related Definitions.* (BS 4778: Part 2: 1991). Quoted in Brockman, John R. 'Just another management fad? The implications of TQM for library and information services.' *Aslib Proceedings* 44 (7/8), July/August, 1992.

Brockman, John R. 'Just another management fad? The implications of TQM for library and information services.' *Aslib Proceedings* 44 (7/8), July/August, 1992.

Capezio, Peter and Morehouse, Debra. *Taking the Mystery Out of TQM: A Practical Guide to Total Quality Management,* 2nd edn. Franklin Lakes, NJ: Career Press, 1995.

Clausen, Helge. 'ISO 9000 and all that: is the information sector ready for the big quantum leap?' *Online Information 94 Proceedings,* London: Learned Information, 1995.

Duncan, William L. and Luftig & Warren International. *Total Quality: Key Terms & Concepts*. New York: American Management Association, 1995.

Fredenburg, Anne M. 'Quality assurance: establishing a program for special libraries.' *Special Libraries* 79 (4), Fall, 1988.

[Ginsburg, Carol]. 'The information independent organization: Carol Ginsburg's bold approach.' *InfoManage: The International Management Newsletter for the Information Services Executive* 1 (1) December, 1993.

Gohlke, Annette. 'Reinvention effort provides model for libraries.' *Library Benchmarking Newsletter* 3 (1), January/February, 1996.

Hammer, Michael and Champy, James. *Reengineering the Corporation: A Manifesto for Business Revolution.* New York: HarperBusiness, 1993.

Senge, Peter M. 'The leader's new work: building learning organizations.' *Sloan Management Review* 32 (1) Fall, 1990.

Senge, Peter M. *The Fifth Discipline: The Art & Practice of The Learning Organization.* New York: Currency Doubleday, 1994.

Younger, Jennifer. 'Total quality management: can we move beyond the jargon?' *Central Ohio Bulletin Special Libraries Association* 27 (2), February, 1992.

Chapter Four

Relating information quality to organizational quality

Miriam A. Drake

For the manager of an information services unit, relating the quality management program of the unit with those of the organization is essential to the success of that quality program. No matter how conscientious and forward-thinking the information services manager might be, the value of a quality management effort is going to directly connect to the organizational attitude towards quality, and a successful quality initiative must be in concert with the culture of the organization or community in which the unit resides. If that culture permits, the information services unit can create its own quality program even if one does not exist for the whole organization, and certainly such a lack should not be an excuse for not undertaking a quality information services program. In either case, the scope of the quality effort will reflect the organizational climate with respect to quality management.

As discussed in an earlier chapter, the framework for the mission of information services units is the organization's mission. Any unit involved with information storage, retrieval, transfer or systems needs to thoroughly understand and internalize the organization's mission and the nature of its business before formulating its own mission or purpose. To understand quality information services and their relationships to organizational quality, we need to explore the attributes of quality organizations, the nature of services, why people seek information, knowledge of the organization, quality information and learning, and quality organizations and the information services quality team.

Quality organizations

In an ideal world all organizations would have continuous quality improvement programs. They would strive to improve the quality of their products, services, marketing, selling, customer support, employee relations and other functions. They would have systems to make it easy for employees to gather information and to learn about the company's business activities, customers and trends affecting the business. In addition, the ideal organization would create an environment that encourages employees to do their best work.

Quality is often an elusive concept. It is difficult (but not impossible) to define and measure, especially when the service is intangible and abstract. And while many articles and books have been written about quality organizations, producing gurus, rich consulting practices, and corporate heroes and heroines, no single concept of quality and quality management has yet been developed which crosses all disciplines and can be implemented in all environments, so naturally whatever quality focus is being considered for an information services operation must fit into whatever quality program is appropriate for the larger organization or community. The task for the information services manager is to seek those elements of quality management that will work in his or her specific information workplace, and to match them to the elements that work in the organizational entity.

The quality of an organization can be measured in many ways: financial results, good employer, zero defects in goods produced, customer satisfaction, successful marketing or innovation. For the information services manager seeking to match his or her quality program to those in place in the organization, Oren Harari's three definitions of quality make sense. First, he writes, 'Quality is the total experience that a customer has with the vendor organization' (Harari 1993, p. 58). This experience involves every aspect of the customer–vendor relationship and includes expectations, product performance, sales, technical support and follow-up.

Secondly, 'Quality is the ease, convenience, excitement, interest, and/or fun that the organization provides the customer with' (Harari 1993, p. 59). Information managers need to ask: Do we make our services accessible, convenient and easy-to-use? Do we maintain interest by following up? Do we create a sense of excitement with new services? Do we tailor our services to the needs of our customers?

Thirdly, 'Quality is the ability to provide customers with high value solutions' (Harari 1993, p. 60). Do our information products and services solve problems or create them? Do our information services deliver value to our customers? Are we constantly striving and looking for ways to enhance value and solve problems for customers?

There are no paragons in the corporate world, and no organization achieves quality in every aspect of its operations. Some organizations have genuine quality programs; some pay lip service to quality. Many organizations proclaim their commitment to quality and, for a variety of reasons, continue with business as usual. Many executives spend millions of dollars and hundreds of staff hours on 'cookie-cutter' approaches to the management technique of the year, the craze that is in fashion at any particular time. These managers' desire for instant gratification and the need to belong to the 'instant-answers club' often doom their experiments to failure. Eileen Shapiro observes:

> The hard truth is that there are no panaceas. What is new is the sheer number of techniques, some new and some newly repackaged versions of older models, that are now positioned as panaceas. What is not new is the need for the courage to manage: to assess situations, set an overall course or focus, think through the options, develop plans, take actions, modify plans, learn and go forward (Shapiro 1995, p. xvii).

Managers in the information services environment can avoid the traps of the instant-answers club by adopting a plan, modifying it as needed and maintaining flexibility. Patience, resilience, courage and commitment can overcome the imposition of new techniques. Often, the new cure is the old cure in a new package which imposes new names and new labels on old diseases and techniques.

Information managers need to internalize the notion that quality is in the eye and mind of the customer. Improvements in the quality of information products and services can be pursued without an organization-wide effort. A commitment to excellent service, which is both responsive to and anticipates customers' questions and problems, is the first step in a quality program.

Some products and services may exhibit a range of qualities dependent on raw materials, skill in manufacturing or skill in creating and delivering a service. In manufacturing, quality may relate to the number of defects or the percentage of output meeting specifications. Through statistical quality control techniques manufacturers can measure the number of defects and the percentage of output not meeting specifications. However, even in the case of manufactured goods quality is often subjective: a quality item for one person, for example, may not be a quality product for another because each person is looking for different characteristics.

Quality in personal services is more difficult to define and measure than quality in manufactured goods, and all personal services are not equally measurable. Air transportation, package delivery, postal services and utilities such as telephone service and electricity are more tangible and have more measurable attributes than information services. We judge the quality of air transportation by on-time performance, price, comfort, baggage handling and how well we are treated. If an airline has flights at convenient times, arrives on time and without incident, provides reasonable comfort, produces baggage quickly and in good condition, and charges a reasonable price, we are satisfied. The attributes of the airline's service can be easily and immediately measured.

In the information services environment the realization of value may not be so immediate, and the connection to an organizational focus on quality will reflect the expectations of information customers within the organization. Information is abstract and unique, and the quality of information delivery depends on the need and the context in which it will be used. In this respect information is both static and dynamic, for an information item does not change even if it is used many times. Data and facts may change with time and when combined with other information. If the information consumer wants a quick answer to a relatively straightforward question, the payoff may be immediate. If the question involves research, proposal preparation, a patent filing or another relatively long-term outcome, the customer will not judge the quality or value until the research has been completed, the proposal accepted or rejected, or the patent filed.

An impersonal category of information services are online carriers, such as AOL, CompuServe, Knight-Ridder (DIALOG) and the various Internet providers. These services operate through computers and networks, and judgment of their services will depend on easy connections, availability, reliability and price; their personal service operations are customer technical support. Convenience, availability and informed technical support personnel are essential; however, there are daily reports of people getting repeated busy signals, being kept on hold for hours and dealing with support personnel who could not solve their problems. If databases are involved the judgment will depend on the value consumers place on having the information, the cost of not having the information, and whether the databases deliver the information in a timely, reliable, complete way at a price related to the value.

In the case of personal services, the category into which information services delivery belongs, at least two people are required to create the service: the service provider and the customer. The service provider is usually a professional, an expert offering selling knowledge and experience. Such services are intangible: they do not exist until the consumer engages the provider in an interaction, and they cannot be taken from a shelf and distributed. They have fewer measurable performance characteristics than airlines or databases, and the determination of quality in personal services is made by customers subjectively.

Some people will judge the quality of personal services on the perceived competence of the professional, on how they deal with the consumer, and on the outcomes. The role of pricing and who pays for the service depends on how services are funded. For example, in medical care price may be a small factor because the providers are being paid on a transaction basis by a third party, an insurance company or a government, and consumers may pay a portion of the price or nothing at all. If people had to pay directly for medical care, price would be more important than standards and treatment.

In the case of a public library, most or all services are provided at no direct cost to the consumer. The costs are paid indirectly through city, state and/or country taxes, and are based on a budgetary appropriation rather than on transactions. In such cases the lack of direct payment may lead to a different way of judging quality. On the other hand, in many corporate libraries and information centers customers are charged for services. This helps determine the true cost of a product, project, case or serving a customer, and before agreeing to purchase an information service the customer will have the opportunity to make a decision based on price and the perceived value of the information. After the information is delivered and used, the customer will judge the quality and value of the information itself and the quality of the service. In companies and academe, where information services are added to overheads, customers' assessment of quality and value may be different from when customers make direct payments.

In some professional service situations all elements may be of a high quality except the outcome. If the outcome does not fit with the consumer's expectation, the service may be judged to be poor quality. In other instances the outcome may be disappointing or grim, and the consumer will still feel that the service was of good quality. For example, a person may go to a physician and find out that he or she has a serious disease and yet, because the patient was treated on time and in a caring way he or she will feel positive about the experience. Thus the view of quality depends on expectations, process and outcomes. An outcome of good health may result in a judgment of poor quality because the consumer was treated badly, subjected to long waiting periods for tests, or treated as a 'number' instead of being given the respect that should be accorded a person. If physicians treated people who buy their services as valued customers instead of as patients who are ill, health care might improve.

Information managers and all professionals selling their services need to keep in mind that:

> ... in quality service settings each person is treated as a respected individual. There is a diversity of response between the consumer and the organization. Quality service is an art, not a science. It is subjective, emotional, and abstract. In quality service, process is as important as results (Drake 1993, p. 45).

In information services customer satisfaction depends on expectations, mindset, knowledge, experience and the goals of the transaction. Customer experience and knowledge are as important as professional experience and expertise, for information customers do not want standardized services. They want service that will work for them and improve them in some way. Unfortunately, it often is easier for an organization to standardize service, since then no one has to think, analyze or make decisions or adjustments. In information services standardization does not work because each information request or

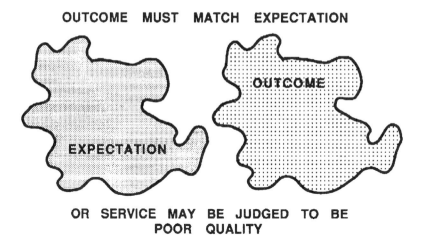

question is unique. People consult experts or professionals because they have problems they cannot solve for themselves, which are individual and unique (at least in their own eyes) to their specific situation. They consult accountants for assistance with keeping the company's financial records, performing audits and filing tax returns. They consult attorneys for legal assistance. They consult information professionals and librarians because they need to know or learn.

Quality personal services thrive on enthusiasm for problem solving, knowledge, experience and the love of working with people, and consumers quickly know if they are dealing with someone who likes to work with people and cares about them. The professional or service provider who is detached and distant may be very competent and knowledgeable and still not be able to provide services that meet or exceed the expectations of customers. Successful personal services (including the delivery of information products, services and consultations through an information services operation) rely on the active involvement of the client or customer. Personal service is not one-way: it is an interaction. The knowledge and experience of the customer must be respected in information interactions, and a service encounter will be judged to be of poor quality if the service provider fails to listen actively to the customer.

Quality service is not a single event, it is a process. Whereas a transaction may have a beginning and an end, service providers usually want to build long-term relationships with clients, and long-term relationships are especially important in information services. As information managers gain knowledge about their clients, their information needs, how they use information and how they want services delivered, the great long-term relationship develops.

Why people seek information

Knowing why people seek information and how they will use it can make a critical difference in the success of information transfer. It also is important to know the difference between data, information and knowledge. Data are raw facts and essential ingredients of information. Data become information when they are processed, organized and made available in a useful form. When we acquire data we need to filter, combine, organize and transform it into information. The next step is to integrate it into our mental knowledge base and synthesize it with existing information to produce knowledge. The creation of knowledge takes place in the minds of individuals.

Why do people spend time, energy and money to seek information? Sara Fine tells us, '... people come to libraries to reduce ambiguity, to increase their ability to cope with a situation, to make a decision, or to find something that will lessen their anxiety ... In other words, people come to libraries to solve problems ...' (Fine, p. 445). People seek information for the same reasons they come to libraries: to find answers, to find ways of doing things, and to learn about processes, devices and ideas.

When people seek information they have made an implicit decision that answering their question was worth spending the time and money. In making this decision people make implicit assumptions about the cost of finding the information, its value and the cost of not having it. Naturally, in life and death matters people often are willing to spend great amounts of money, and they will also spend time and money when large investments are involved. The amount of time people are willing to spend depends on the nature of the information needed and the value they place on their time. People often are willing to spend hours seeking information because they are not willing or able to hire an expert to do the job, they do not trust anyone else to do it, or they are vague about what they need to know or learn.

Many people enjoy spending hours browsing in libraries and bookstores. The benefit they derive from this is not immediate or clear; however, they see a benefit from exploring, scanning and being with printed material. People browsing outside their fields or disciplines may find useful personal information or learn about methods and techniques used in other fields.

Knowledge of the organization

It is impossible to establish a quality information services program without a working knowledge of the parent organization. If the organization has a quality program, the information services unit must be an active participant and contributor. A quality information program will have a higher likelihood of success if it is based on the knowledge and culture of the organization. This knowledge begins with understanding the organization's mission, business and goals.

Whether the organization is a company, firm, academic institution, government, hospital, not-for-profit enterprise or a community, the library or information center is an integral part. To acquire knowledge about the organization, key questions must be asked, among which are the following:

- What is the business of the parent organization, enterprise or community?

- Who are the customers?

- Who are the stakeholders?

- What is its purpose?

Knowing the answers to these questions and having an understanding of the mission and goals of the organization are basic to building an understanding of how the organization does its work. Information services that make a difference to the knowledge base of an organization rely on knowledge of that organization, its functions, goals, activities and desired results.

The organization's mission or purpose, business, strategic plans, marketing, finances, research and other operational elements are essential inputs into planning and implementing information services and quality programs for information units. In any organization, information professionals need to understand the language of the business, its industry, its culture and its economic, regulatory and political contexts. Effective communication depends on using the language of the business and speaking and writing within the context of business issues. Library and information professionals need to discard the language of libraries and information services when dealing with customers, since people outside the library world do not understand the more specific specialized terms, such as 'monographs' and 'serials'.

Practitioners in management information systems, the professionals who work in information technology, have been successful in using technological language to confuse and create a mystique, but the outcome has not necessarily been successful for their customers and their managers. For example, when managers question concepts, planning and likely outcomes of technology investments, these people often have problems translating their ideas into the language of the business and its issues. In the days when computing was done on mainframes, information technology appeared to be more complex than it is now and managers often gave up trying to understand and assumed the technical people knew what they were doing. Now managers realize that the mystique has been expensive and has not solved critical problems. The technology is no less complex, but it appears more comfortable when the unit on the desk makes things easy.

For the manager of the information services unit and his or her staff success in a corporate or organizational setting requires knowledge of the industry, the company, economics, planning, marketing and finance. This understanding is essential to relating information to business issues, and critical questions in understanding the enterprise include:

- What business is the company in?

- What are its main products and services?

- Who are its customers?

- Who are its competitors?

- How does the company earn its revenue?

- How does it spend this revenue?

- What is its profit? Cash flow? Marketing expenses? R & D expenses?

If a company is publicly held its published financial statements will reveal the answers to these questions, and annual and quarterly reports are essential sources. The company's strategic plan, which is likely to be proprietary and private, is equally important, as it will reveal where the company wants to be some time in the future and how it proposes to get there. Lou Parris, a corporate librarian with many years of experience, suggests that reading reports from earlier years is important to gain a perspective on the company's progress and how it arrived at its present position (Parris 1994, p. 53). The company's values and culture also should be studied, as it is these that reveal the politics of the company and how things are done.

Also, as the information services staff attempt to learn more about the company or the enterprise, its organization chart will indicate the structure and who reports to whom. If the company is a conglomerate, the chart will reveal how subsidiaries report to the parent company. Many companies have policy manuals documenting formal policies and procedures. Although this is useful it may not be an accurate picture of the way things are really done. Information managers need to know how policies and procedures are implemented and how to get things done efficiently.

Information technology may be handled by a chief information officer, an information systems department, or an MIS or other department with information technology responsibility. The technology people are valuable partners for other information services practitioners in the organization, as in all likelihood it will be necessary to work with or through the information technology department to establish networking arrangements, to organize the distribution of electronic materials, or to arrange access to external electronic information resources. In most organizations, these people provide logistics support for information specialists, who deal with content and substance, and are usually responsible for computing and networking, including hardware, software, maintenance etc. They may be involved with substance of the internal management information system but they are not usually involved with external information or with dealing with internal customers' information needs. Partnership with this group can be productive and useful for all.

Working in an academic environment requires the same sort of reading, observation and knowledge of the institution as working in a company. Colleges and universities aim to offer quality programs of instruction, quality research and public service. As a first step on this road of learning about the organization, the information professional needs to know how the college or university is financed. Other questions which must be reflected on include:

- What are its academic programs?

- How many students are enrolled in each major and at each level?

- How much and what is the source of sponsored research? How large is the endowment and how is it managed?

- How much emphasis is placed on sponsored research?

- Who are the key faculty members and administrators?

In academe politics plays an important role, and understanding the nature of politics in the specific institution is especially important for the information services manager seeking to organize and implement a quality management program. For example, the role of the faculty in decision making is not the same in all institutions. Some universities have elaborate faculty governance structures where decisions are made slowly, and in other universities faculty governance may be weak and create fewer obstacles to decision making. The quality-focused information services manager will determine what the faculty's role is in the decision-making process, and the level of interest and expertise that these faculty members exhibit, so that those findings can be put to use in organizing and implementing the quality initiative.

Librarians and information professionals interested in quality management need to thoroughly understand how things are done in small as well as large and complex institutions. In academe and other not-for-profit enterprises there are many constituent and stakeholder groups. The primary customers of an academic library are students, faculty and staff, alumni, local business, government, research sponsors, donors and foundations, all groups that have significant influence on policy, direction, funding and budgeting for the institution. Knowing the people in these groups and the roles they play in policy formation can be valuable for the information manager.

Government also has its complexities, many of which can affect the success of a quality initiative in information services. Information professionals need to know the mission of the agency, its relationship with the taxpayers, its relationship with other branches of government, and its legislative mandates. Many government agencies are charged by legislation to disseminate information to the public. Although the library may serve a relatively small group of government workers, its impact can be far-reaching.

In a public library it is essential that staff and other information workers understand the community, its income levels, education levels, number of children, older citizens and the political structure. The politics of funding are critical because the library is usually funded by an annual appropriation from tax revenues, funds which may be supplemented by endowments and private contributions. Knowing who holds the real power can make funding and policy making easier. The Board of Trustees of a public library can range from a relatively uninterested group of volunteers to a collection of anxious and determined officials, each of whom has his or her own agenda. Sometimes, a board may want to micro-manage the library and does not understand the difference between governance and management. It is necessary for the quality-focused library director to recognize that trustees are often elected or appointed for political reasons, and to be prepared for the barriers to quality that such trustees might present. They might, for example, be major contributors, volunteers, or (in the case of appointed trustees) friends of the official making the appointment; other people like to be on boards because it conveys recognition or prestige. In still other situations a person may be appointed to a board because of a single issue that is, at the time, of overriding importance in the community. In each of these situations the process of educating the board members to the value of quality services in the public library and bringing them to the point where they can make a positive contribution may be long and arduous.

Quality information and learning

Much has been written about the obsolescence of knowledge, the need for lifelong learning, and the need for everyone in an organization to acquire new knowledge and share it. As discussed in the previous chapter, Peter Senge brought the idea of the learning organization to the public with his book *The Fifth Discipline: the Art and Practice of the Learning*

Organization. It is important, in the quest for quality library and information services management, that the role of the information unit as a learning organization be recognized.

Learning is essential to continuous quality improvement. Through continuous learning people are made aware of changes in the internal and external environments of the organization, and important economic, social and technological trends that affect the organization and its business. New information helps to create new products, processes, services and visions. The employee who stops learning becomes a 'couch potato', a mindless consumer of goods, with obsolete skills. In today's world each person must assume responsibility for his or her own continuing education and learning. There is less and less opportunity for people who are unskilled or are not willing to acquire the necessary skills to enable them to earn the income they desire.

Peter Drucker observes that 'Goods, no matter how greedily desired, change consumption; information changes the imagination. Goods change how we live; information how we dream. Goods change how we see the world; information changes how we see ourselves' (Drucker 1995, p. 335). It is this opportunity to change how people see themselves that the information services manager takes advantage of in creating and implementing a quality initiative in information services management, and it is combining the concepts of quality management and the learning organization that enables him or her to succeed. For Oren Harari it is not a difficult connection to make, and he offers practical ideas on learning in organizations: 'I propose that the best predictor of a company's future earnings is its capacity to generate, consolidate, and use ideas from every possible source: employees, customers, suppliers, partners, outside experts, and myriad databases' (Harari 1996, p. 47). For the information services manager and his or her staff, the notion of using other sources is not a new idea and they are quite comfortable in going wherever they need to go to add to their resource base.

Harari offers other ideas for creating an organization where ideas and information flow: 'Challenge sacred cows in pursuit of bold goals, cultivate a culture of curiosity, and spread information everywhere' (Harari 1996, pp. 47-49). Challenging sacred cows means questioning assumptions and not taking anything for granted. As the external world changes and new technologies emerge, it may not be possible to keep doing business in the same old way. New information changes our thinking, our goals and the way we do things. It encourages us to get rid of practices that no longer work and find ones that do. It means internalizing new assumptions about the relationship of information to the work of the company, and using new knowledge to create, invent and innovate.

The creation of a culture of curiosity means that people are encouraged to ask questions and question the answers they receive. It means hiring people who are curious and like to learn and apply new knowledge. And, from the point of view of the information services manager who is moving the information unit into a quality framework, curiosity is an essential characteristic of successful information professionals.

Spreading information everywhere means giving everyone access to both internal and external information. In this day and age, no one can hoard or control information: financial statements, strategic plans, marketing plans, customer information, quality data and other information about the business needs to be readily available. External information also needs to be available, so that employees have the means to understand the external context of the business and competitor activities.

Collaboration with the information technology staff

In a recent book Peter Drucker cautions us as a society about becoming too enamored with technology: 'Too much talk focuses on the technology . . . Now that knowledge is taking the place of capital as the driving force in organizations worldwide, it is all too easy to confuse data with knowledge and information technology with information' (Drucker 1995, p. 13). The people who promote technology as a panacea for all business problems rarely think about content, meaning or understanding, but from the point of view of the information services manager who is seeking to bring quality information delivery to the workplace, it is necessary that he or she remember that it is the information services professionals who understand content and meaning. Arno Penzias, a Nobel Prize winner in physics, states the essence of the issue: 'Machines only manipulate numbers; people connect them to meaning' (Penzias 1989, p. 11). In business, academe and government, people believe that if they have computers and networks their problems will be solved. They have not thought about training issues and how to present information so that it can be understood and used effectively. Successful learning and business decisions are dependent on the context and a knowledge of business issues.

Although the role of information is critical to learning and creativity, not all information is useful. Control of information by information technology people may not be in the best interests of the company or its employees. Senge observes:

> While increased access to information may be a step in the direction of enhanced learning, more information is not always better. It can overwhelm and paralyze decision making, it can direct attention to highly visible but highly misleading facts, and it can place greater control in the hands of information systems designers who might not necessarily have the best understanding of business issues (Senge 1994, p. 529).

Senge's comments relate to the unique skills of information specialists who know how to find, filter and synthesize information. Practitioners in information technology do not generally have these skills. For example, individuals with little or no experience, searching databases or surfing the Internet, may retrieve far more data than they can handle. Experienced reference librarians, searchers and knowledge analysts know the structure and content of databases and can produce concise and useful packages of information from the chaos of data. By knowing the customer's need and context, a professional can use his or her expertise to find the right information, filter out irrelevant material, refine the information, make it useful and prevent overload.

Information systems analysts and designers are not trained to deal with information overload, filtering or packaging. Their training is technical: they think in terms of bits, bytes and bauds, not in sources and meaning. It is their role to provide the technical infrastructure necessary to disseminate information throughout the organization as well as the hardware and software that stores, transmits, receives and manipulates data. Librarians and other information services managers need the technical infrastructure and the expertise of technical people, and they need to work with information systems staff as partners with common goals. The integration of internal and external information is an excellent example of a project that will benefit from collaboration, and while this process is challenging both technically and politically, intranets, group software and the World Wide Web are making the job easier.

The more difficult task is to convince people to share information they create or acquire. People often feel threatened by communicating knowledge because it removes a sense of power: knowing what others do not know or cannot access gives power to the person possessing or controlling the information. As people gain more experience in sharing information the situation becomes less threatening and results in group synergy, creativity and productivity.

Collaboration between information managers and the information technology group can do much to overcome the obstacles associated with the integration of information. Librarians and information managers interacting with information seekers on a daily basis learn about how people access and find information and how they interact with computer systems. Librarians in academe, public libraries and corporate libraries design Web pages and screens based on their observations of human–computer interactions. These daily interactions give librarians a special understanding of how information is found and used.

Training is another area where collaboration can result in significantly better implementation of a variety of systems. Most librarians have extensive experience in teaching people how to use information systems, the Internet and databases. By relating instruction to the individual's problems and specialities, librarians ensure that training and learning are relevant. Technology people can train on the technical aspects of a system but they cannot relate these aspects to the substantive needs of individuals or business issues.

Collaboration in combining internal and external information is especially important in planning, marketing and competitive intelligence. Trends and developments in the economy, government, industry, demography, technology and a variety of other factors are essential inputs into the planning process. If company sales or contributions to a charity are declining, the reasons may be internal or external. Integration and easy access to both kinds of information is more likely to yield useful answers than just looking at internal information.

In competitive intelligence it is important to relate internal performance data to external data gathered about competitors. Barbara Ettorre defines competitive intelligence (CI) as '... the process by which organizations gather actionable information about competitors and, ideally, apply it to their short- and long-term strategic planning' (Ettorre 1995, p. 16). She also points out that intelligence gathering makes people uncomfortable because they think about it in terms of spying or illegal activity. CI relies primarily on published material, such as newspaper or trade publication articles, annual reports, technical reports and trade association publications. Ettorre speculates that 'Probably less than ten percent of American corporations know their way around the CI process and effectively integrate the information into their strategic plans' (Ettorre 1995, p. 15).

Effective CI relies heavily on knowledge of the business and industry and sources of information about industry trends and competitor activities. When materials are gathered and processed from external sources, they need to be packaged and integrated with internal information. Reliance on internal information alone is like living in a vacuum and not paying attention to the outside world. The resulting surprises can be very costly in terms of lost sales and lack of knowledge about new technological applications, competitor initiatives, or marketing techniques.

Information services quality program

Establishing a quality program in information services is one of the best ways to ensure that the organization has the information needed to move forward. If an organization has a quality improvement program, information services can meld its improvement efforts with this. In the absence of an organization-wide program, the information services staff can collaborate and lead the quality effort, contributing know-how, talent, experience and leadership to quality improvement.

Collaboration will facilitate the formation of ad hoc teams to deal with technical, training and information content issues. Using teams helps to ensure that the desktop computer or workstation will not be subject to malfunction because several people who work in different departments and who do not talk to each other change the system in the same way. Teams are not new. They have been functioning in organizations for years as people from different areas come together to solve problems. Teams should not be viewed as ends in themselves, but as the means to bring diverse talents together to work on projects, problems and planning.

When the staff of the information services department, whatever its form, and those with information technology responsibility get together as partners and approach customers as a team, they set an example for the whole organization. Everyone benefits, and they demonstrate that commonality of purpose and commitment can produce value for the company and its customers, and fulfilment of its mission.

Technology has changed and will continue to change the ways we find, analyze and use information, but the substance of that information is the same regardless of where it is stored and how it is retrieved. Internal and external information is essential to creative and productive work, and it is the customers for whom the information services unit exists. For the information services manager moving to organize a quality focus in information delivery, remembering the role of the information customer positions the department for success in the quality initiative.

References

Drake, Miriam A. *Libraries, Technology, and Quality. Advances in Library Administration and Organization*. JAI Press, 1993.

Drucker, Peter F.*Managing in a Time of Great Change*. New York: Truman Talley Books, 1995.

Ettorre, Barbara. 'Managing competitive intelligence.' *Management Review* October, 1995.

Fine, Sara. 'Research and the psychology of information use.' *Library Trends* (32) (4), Spring, 1984.

Harari, Oren. 'Think strategy when you think quality.' *Management Review* March, 1993.

Harari, Oren. 'Mind Matters.' *Management Review* January, 1996.

Parris, Lou B. *Know Your Company and Its Business. Information for Management: A Handbook*. Edited by James M. Matarazzo and Miriam A. Drake. Washington DC: Special Libraries Association, 1994.

Penzias, Arno. *Ideas and Information*. New York: Touchstone, 1989.

Senge, Peter M. *The Fifth Discipline: The Art and Practice of the Learning Organization*. New York: Currency Doubleday, 1990.

Senge, Peter M. *Microworlds and learning laboratories. The Fifth Discipline Field Book*. Peter Senge, et al. New York: Currency Doubleday, 1993.

Shapiro, Eileen. *Fad Surfing in the Board Room: Reclaiming the Courage to Manage in the Age of Instant Answers*. Reading, MA: Addison-Wesley, 1995.

Part 2

TQM – the Critical Components for Information Services

Chapter Five

Customer care in the information environment

The authority of the customer as a management concept is now beginning to make inroads into the information services environment, partly as a result of changing attitudes about the role of an information services operation in an organization or community, and partly in reaction to societal changes. There is no longer an easy acceptance of the existence of a library or similar information delivery facility simply because it is there. As has historically been the case in the private sector, funding authorities in all spheres in the public sector, as well as in the not-for-profit and non-profit sectors, are now demanding value in return for investment in information services, and that value is defined by the information customers.

This attention to the customer is taken seriously in all lines of work, and even in disciplines in which the authority of the customer was traditionally not addressed (especially if what was being delivered were services the customers needed, and about which they had no choice), serious attempts are being made to establish a rapport between the service provider and the customer. There is a good deal of cynicism and gallows humor when citizens begin discussing 'the role of the customer', but the fact of the matter is that attention to customers does make a difference to the perceptions and expectations of those customers. It is well documented that patients and visitors have a much less stressful experience in today's NHS facilities compared to what they would have experienced 15 years ago. Certainly the hospital environment is one in which the concepts of caring and empathy should be incorporated into the general fabric of management but, as everyone knows, those concepts were in the past frequently more honored in the breach than in the observance. This is not the case today, where NHS hospital administrators are attempting to instill a climate of customer care that matches the expectations of their customers with the actual services provided. In doing so, the NHS presumably expects to change perceptions about hospital care so that at some point in the future perceptions match expectations, and both will reflect the authority and wellbeing of the customers.

The same management approach is moving into the law enforcement field. In places like New York City, where the perceptions of the public about the manners of the police force have for years been based on incidents in which officers on the beat were described as being rude or offensive (to say nothing of perceptions about how they dealt with alleged perpetrators of crimes), serious attempts by police department administrators are being made to build a culture of care and empathy into the interactions between the police force and the citizens. Again, it is not an inappropriate response because the real role of police officers in society has in most societies been one of helpfulness and interest in caring for the people who come to them for help.

What is happening is simply that society, which provides support for public services through taxes, and those in the private sector who have resource allocation authority, are demanding a return on their investment. Since the mission of any service operation is to understand the needs of the identified customers and to structure the service so that those requirements are met, the customers must be the primary arbitrators in the transaction.

It is a subject that has been dealt with before:

> The definition of quality in quality management circles explains the emphasis put on customers. Quality is defined as the goodness of results, whether products or services, as judged by the customer. They [the customers] will decide what characteristics, e.g. timeliness, accuracy and detail of information, are important in creating their satisfaction or dissatisfaction with the results. Frequently, more than one category of customer exists, e.g. when the library's own staff are customers due to their extensive mediation of certain library services to the general public. In these cases, the definition of the characteristics that that lead to quality is correspondingly a more complex task but one that still must take place (Younger 1992, p. 2).

The quality service mission

In seeking quality in information services management, the mission of the information unit will link directly to the organizational or community mission, as has already been established. Beyond that, however, specific efforts within the information unit will be required to establish relevance, appropriateness to the particular environment in which the unit is positioned, and customer requirements. What is actually happening is that the quality-directed information services manager is seeking to balance customer perceptions and expectations with the role of the information unit in the organization or community. Thus considerable attention is

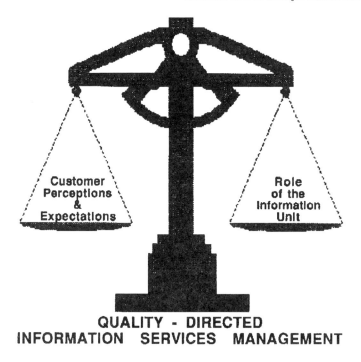

QUALITY - DIRECTED
INFORMATION   SERVICES   MANAGEMENT

given to the process that establishes the mission of the information services unit and its relationship to the organizational mission, and, at the same time, the mission statement of the information services unit is developed in a format that incorporates customer requirements.

We know what information customers are seeking, and for those who have not encountered the many studies about customer service in society at large and attempted to relate them to the information services discipline, the five 'dimensions of service quality' identified in the work of Zeithaml, Parasuraman and Berry provides a handy framework for information delivery with a quality focus. What customers want, they have determined, is a service delivery that has the following attributes (using their terms): tangibles, reliability, responsiveness, assurance and empathy (Zeithaml, Parasuraman and Berry 1990, p. 25). It is not difficult to translate these requirements into the information services marketplace, as was done in an earlier book in this series (St. Clair 1993, pp. 69–71).

In the current information services milieu the framework that Zeithaml and his colleagues have established is being reinterpreted, but the new way of looking at these attributes does not change their initial value to managers as guidelines for establishing quality service. New technologies are necessarily having an impact not only on the way people use libraries and other information services operations, but on the service dynamic between information providers and their customers. Customer service differs dramatically in an electronic environment from that in a paper-based environment, and while most information services operations use a combination of both formats, an awareness of how technology changes customers' thinking about information and their ideas about customer service is valuable in a quality-focused environment. Although the traditional service components of reliability, assurance, tangibles, empathy and responsiveness are equally important in either environment, adding technology to the equation puts an additional strain on both the information services provider and the customer.

Reliability in customer service is the ability to provide what was promised, dependably and accurately. For this to happen in the new information environment, however, new hardware and software must work effectively, every time, whenever needed, 24 hours a day, seven days a week. In addition, staff must keep up to date with new technologies in order to provide quality service and to have confidence in the equipment. When the information services worker does not understand the technology it is difficult to determine whether system failure is due to the equipment or to insufficient knowledge, but for the customer it doesn't matter. A customer waiting for an answer soon gets impatient with technology, especially as an excuse for poor service, and the reliability of the information services operation is soon called into question.

As for assurance, in the past a good firm handshake was sufficient to convey trust and confidence. Today the information services practitioner must not only behave in a confident manner, he or she must be able to direct the customer to the best possible answer, whether it is found on paper, in microform, online, on tape, in a CD-ROM product or through an e-mail source. Increasingly, the visitor to the information services department is more sophisticated, both in information technology and in information content, and the information provider is not always going to have the answer. Yet that person cannot compromise customer trust or the department's commitment to its established level of service with technical ignorance or misinformation. Previous generations of librarians, say, could suggest that the user peruse the stacks to find the answer he or she was seeking, but today, as Beth Duston has stated, 'looking for answers in the electronic ocean without adequate training is comparable to sailing the Atlantic without a rudder' (Duston 1994, p. 3). If there is any doubt about the quality of the information source, it is best that the information services worker say, at that point, 'I don't know how to help you with this particular problem, but I can find someone who can'. It is the second part of the comment that changes the information interaction from one of disappointment to one of encouragement (and which, of course, recognizes the authority of the customer in the transaction). Obviously, of course, the information worker must then go forward with the search for further information. The customer's expectations have not been realized, but his or her perceptions of the service have been changed and now it is up to the information services worker to see that the customer's new understanding is not a misreading of the situation.

For many library users in the past, coming into an area where staff members are working at neat desks, in a generally tidy library, have been tangible indicators of a well-managed and well-run facility. For today's information seeker, a cluttered assortment of electronic equipment for providing access to new information is often more comforting and reassuring than a well-organized room of hardcopy resources. For these customers, computer interfaces that are easy and intuitive to use permit them to query the system without assistance (which is a good thing, as customers usually cannot, and more to the point, will not, read documentation manuals). Since the customer is probably already acquainted with some form of automated information delivery, there is a level of intolerance when the information services systems are not user friendly, and his or her reaction to these limitations is necessarily going to affect the relationship between the information services worker and himself or herself.

Empathy has long been a characteristic of good librarianship, and it is expected in other information delivery operations as well. Librarians, of course, are known for having strong 'people skills', and their reputation for empathy and caring for each user and his or her needs is a long and admirable one. When this understanding of the customer's needs is also practiced by other types of information workers, the departments of which they are a part are moving toward quality information delivery. In fact, the information worker's sensitivity to deal directly with the customer's information requirements is a key element in the quality management of information services. In order to improve service the information services manager should seek to build on the staff's empathetic strengths, inviting them, for example, to encourage feedback from users as they begin to work with the new information technology. Doing so enables them to be able to provide user-friendly systems and to determine what the customers' realistic expectations might be, with respect to the new technology.

In this new age of technology the concepts of responsiveness and prompt service have been totally redefined. Although speed and accuracy have always been measures of quality service, today's information customers not only expect immediate answers but expect them to be in the format that is most useful to them. Thus it is that an information services practitioner will discuss frankly with a customer how long a requested search might take, or contacts the customer to advise that using this or that resource will mean extending the deadline, and seeking her advice, as the requester of the information, as to how to proceed. Similarly, today's 'high-tech' information services professional will learn to recognize the delivery expectations of the customers, thus determining whether they need materials quickly or if less immediate delivery will suffice, and whether the format and presentation package for the information will affect their judgment of the value of the service.

Information technology presents many new opportunities for interaction and service between the information services provider and the customer, and among these is the opportunity for a partnership. With more attention being paid than ever before to how resources are used, and with the expectation of a decent return on resources invested, librarians and other information services workers are now required to be better informed about their customers' specific needs, and it is through teamwork and partnering that the two can determine how best to work together and how best to construct the information activity they will share.

Relevance of the information

Probably the most important key to the delivery of quality information services is the relevance of that information to the customer's needs. There are few more unsettling scenarios than the one in which an information manager runs into a colleague and mentions that he saw her in the information services department earlier in the day. 'I hope you got what you were looking for', he comments cheerfully.

'Well, I didn't', the colleague replies. 'I was looking for the project reports on the Westover deal. Remember that job we did for them back about 1991? Susan gave me a batch of contracts and personnel folders, but the reports weren't in the material she sent to my office.'

'I'm sorry', the records manager says as he starts to move away. 'I'll go track them down those reports right now.'

'Don't bother', the colleague says. 'We've already done our review, and we don't need the reports now. We just went ahead and did the best we could from what we had in our own files.'

The moral of this tale is obvious. If the information provided doesn't match what the customer is seeking, the information transaction has been useless and a waste of time for all parties. Adding to the difficulty is the established and well-documented fact that most disappointed customers will make no further reference to the transaction, but will simply 'file it away' as another disappointment with the information services unit. In the example here, of course, the manager learned about the failed transaction because he happened to meet the colleague informally. In an information services department with a quality focus, there would be a procedure to ensure that the person providing the information followed up with the customer to determine whether the information provided was what was needed.

Appropriate information services for the organization

It is also important, in a quality-focused information unit, that the work of the unit be appropriate to the environment of which it is a part. While the assumption for many decades has been that all organizations and communities have a need for specifically structured information services operations, each serving different organizational or community markets, the trend within the last decade or so has been to look at these operations and attempt to determine whether or not they are actually necessary for the attainment of organizational or community success, or if the same (or a better) level of information provision cannot be achieved in a different way.

Outsourcing

There is much concern within the library community these days, especially in the specialist library field, about the closure of libraries within organizations and firms that have determined that they either do not need a library to obtain external information or that they can obtain the required information from a third-party vendor more cost-effectively. There are plenty of arguments on both sides of this issue, but for the discussion to have any real meaning it has to focus on the organization's core business and whether an internal library is required for the successful achievement of its business mission. In some organizations it becomes necessary to close the library and to outsource the gathering of the limited amount of external information that staff require.

In very real terms, however, the outsourcing controversy is not a controversy at all, but it has taken on all the characteristics of one as the fine line between vendor and librarian has finally been crossed. The long-simmering resentment from librarians about vendors providing services that they as librarians have been hired to provide is being addressed, but it will probably be some years before the discussions die down. The people who are most offended in this situation are, by and large, specialized librarians, information providers who work in the profit sector and who, naturally enough, dislike the idea of vendors doing their job.

On the other side of the table are the vendors, the people providing services they say are cost-effective and superior. These people are in the business of providing information, and the fact that they are doing it as an outsourcing assignment for a client makes no difference. They are in business, and they have found a client who is willing to pay for their products.

Hovering around the sidelines, sometimes feeling awkward and sometimes feeling arrogant, we have senior management, desperately trying to cut back on expenses and at the same time produce enough of whatever the company produces to make the profits the stockholders demand. This manager, believing – sometimes correctly, sometimes not – that the specialized library costs more than it returns to the company, targets the unit for savings. Why he or she targets the library is anybody's guess: maybe the company has done studies that have determined that the return on investment in having a library is too small to bother with, or maybe no one has told senior management what the library really provides for the company. Or perhaps the vendor came in and proved to management that he or she could provide information at a much lower cost than it costs to maintain the library.

In the middle of all this confusion are the information customers, nervous because they're beginning to wonder what's wrong with the services they've been getting from the library all along, and unsure about whether this outsourced information delivery will match their needs as well as the library does. So it is a complicated picture, and the most uncomfortable person is the customer, who is caught in the middle.

In attempting to deal with the situation, specialized information services professionals are finding themselves in the position of having to respond to a threatening situation. First, let us not forget where the power lies: management makes this decision, not the special librarian and not the customer or the vendor. And by the time management has made the decision, it is probably too late to do anything about it. If the management decision is ill-informed and consequently turns out to be wrong, the question then becomes: why did they make this decision without bringing the specialized librarian and his or her management into the discussion. How is it that decisions about information matters are made without the advice and counsel of the librarians and those who work with them?

Next, it is necessary to recognize that the tactics of many of those who succeed in the business world (and that includes senior managers and some of the vendors who approach them) are not necessarily the tactics we would use to gain the advantage. Does that mean that special librarians should sit back and get whipped? Absolutely not. If there are any indications that the organization might be considering a move to one of the vendors known for using aggressive marketing tactics, the librarian goes to work, building up his or her own campaign and putting just the right spin on it so that the librarian's 'presentation' is as impressive as the vendor's. Is it Machiavellian? Yes. Is it unethical? No. Does it work? Yes.

The next step is to think about how to put that presentation together, and this is where the librarian and his or her staff can really dazzle the competition: no one knows the information needs of the organization better than the people who work in the library, no one specializes in information content better than the librarians, no one else knows as well as the library staff who uses what information and how they use it, no one understands the information delivery process better, and, best of all, no one understands better how the library contributes to organizational success. This is valuable information and it is exploitable. What the librarian must do is use it to his or her department's own advantage. Those who work in specialized librarianship must never forget that they are part of the competitive capitalist society, and they must always, using every opportunity and every device they can muster, bring to management their own and their (satisfied) customers' success stories about the library's contribution to the achievement of organizational goals.

This, in a nutshell, is what this controversy is all about. We have not yet devised effectiveness measures for information services, and no-one has yet come up with a formula that works for all situations. Yet there are other measures (library statistics, for example) librarians use which, when passed on to management, are pretty meaningless. Perhaps what the librarians need is some combination that matches the statistics with quotations from information customers about what they have done with the information they acquired. If this can then be related to mission-critical issues attached to the organization at large, the librarian has a report that ties the special library back to the company, where it belongs. The library will not then be perceived as a standalone operation outside the organizational mainstream, but as a critical component in the organizational effort.

So who's the villain here? Is it the special librarian, the information expert, the employee who understands the content side of the information equation, who is merely trying to provide the best information that can be provided? Of course not. Is it the vendor? The vendor is merely doing what entrepreneurs are supposed to do: looking for opportunities to market his or her products, targeting the most likely prospects for those products and offering them a sales pitch and a promise of success. No, the vendor is not the villain. Is it senior management then? No, because management is only doing what it is supposed to do, i.e. organizing, planning, directing, controlling. So if there's no villain and no drama, what's the quarrel? Perhaps that's the point. Perhaps, when librarians are all doing what they are supposed to be doing, and doing it openly and honestly, there isn't any controversy at all.

Reinventing information services

Some organizations, in order to provide the information products, services and consultations that the identified customers need, have chosen to literally reinvent the information services they provide. This is probably best exemplified by the firm of Cooper & Lybrand, where the term reinventing is used to describe the changes that are taking place in the company in making the information services match the information needs of the customers.

Those needs are changing, and have been changing for a couple of decades. And they will continue to change. Change is the name of the game, and information services must go along with whatever changes are taking place in the environment itself. Patricia S. Foy, who is Director of

Libraries and Technology Research at Cooper & Lybrand, is clearly on to something, and reinventing the corporate information model is not just a trendy management fad. The requirements for change in corporate information services are very real, and Foy is determined to see that the products and services that are her responsibility measure up to the needs of the employees of Cooper & Lybrand. It's not change for change sake, certainly, and it's not simply managerial posturing. It's leading the way in the very real world of corporate information delivery, and nothing less than reinvention is called for.

It begins, Foy said when she was interviewed about her work, with a recognition that the traditional library model, even the traditional corporate library model, does not work in business any more. This is not to say that libraries are no longer appropriate, nor that traditional librarianship is bad and that business information provision is good: it simply recognizes that they are different, and proceeds to build on that recognition.

'The perspective is different', Foy said. 'In the public library community, which is what most librarians are trained for, the perspective is not geared to supporting a business clientele. I serve on the Board of Trustees of my public library, and I understand very well what that library is supposed to be doing. I support it and I am happy to be a part of it. But it is not what we do in a business environment. The concerns are not the same, and we have to think about those differences.

'The concept of traditional librarianship, with its broader-based constituency and its wide range of services, just doesn't fit in the business environment. In corporate information work, we're dealing with a variety of users, the majority of whom do not necessarily know where to go for their information. They might come asking for one thing, for example, and we have to work with them, guide them along, to find out what it is that they are really looking for. It's our job to let them know that many different "pieces" of information are available that might be applicable for what they need, and if they are focusing on just one of those pieces, they might not be getting the quality of content that they need.'

The reinvention of information services came to C&L because it was time. It's a big operation, this partnership, and is one of the famous 'Big Six' public accounting firms, with some 16,000 employees working in 119 offices in the US. And although it is known as an accounting firm, C&L identifies itself as a 'professional services' firm. In the fiscal year ending 30 September, 1994, its global revenue increased to $5.5 billion. So we're not talking about an information services operation that is 'nice to have': in this company, every function and every service must be justified and this is what led to the innovative initiative that Foy now directs.

'In any company this size, ongoing financial review is part of the picture, and as library and information services were looked at here, it became clear that some change in direction was called for. But in fact that was not a bad thing, for by looking at the information services role in the organization, the company is giving attention to information, and to the value of information. It sets the stage, so to speak, for moving beyond what isn't working.'

What wasn't working, they found, was an information services operation based on traditional library concepts, resulting in wide variations in the levels of services that were provided. There had even grown up an awkward mixture of 'have' and 'have not' offices with regard to information delivery. It was not a system that worked very well, and Foy and her working partner, Mik Chwalek, responsible for market research and analysis, saw that their work was cut out for them. It would be their job to design a process that established a responsibility for information throughout the company.

Fortunately, C&L is the kind of company where there isn't a great deal of holding back, and Foy did not have to be too concerned about her authority to move ahead with her innovative planning.

'At Cooper & Lybrand', she said, 'There is an expectation that if you step up to the responsibility of the job, you get to do it', and that's what has been happening over the past few years with the information services operation.

'Of course we work hard at justifying ourselves. There is always financial pressure, but what we've done is to establish an information services program that works for the C&L information customers, and as long as we are providing them with the services they need at reasonable cost, we can innovate. And besides, we're firm believers in the "it's-better-to-ask-forgiveness-than-to-ask-permission" school of management, and if we've come up with something particularly good, it can be "sold".'

The reinvented information services operation at Cooper & Lybrand has a number of specific features that characterize it, and among these is a remarkable attention to the role of communication in the information services effort. Not only are the information staff required to understand the value of communication, public relations and customer service, the marketing and promotion of information services is built into the success of the operation.

'Communication is the key', Foy said, a point she emphasized several times during the conversation. As she talked about how she gets the word out to customers ('If we need to, we put a marketing piece in the envelope with their paychecks. Then we know they'll see it.') about what she expects from new staff, about how the operation is identified ('Not "libraries". We are restructuring library operations into something else and we'll call them something else. We are changing expectation levels, and we can't call them libraries if we're going to do that.'), it becomes clear that communication is essential to the success of what she is doing.

'This is a different kind of operation, and any kind of change of this magnitude must rely on a successful communications effort. It is something we concentrate on all the time, and it pays off.'

Just how different is this information services operation? There are several defining characteristics, and each of them provides particular insight into how Foy and her colleagues are reinventing the corporate information model. In the first place, apart from the emphasis on communication, the role of information services is different.

'We are charged to take information responsibility', Foy said, 'to evaluate content and quality and to restructure library operations. We have recognized that in the last 25 years, as the structure of the corporation has changed, the enabling role of technology is having a tremendous effect on how information can be accessed and delivered. And on what customer expectations can be.'

Foy herself comes to this work with an information technology background, and although she has an MLS degree she has spent much of her career in information technology implementation and information analysis. For the past two years she has directed strategy planning for the C&L libraries, and for five years prior to that she headed C&L's Technology Intelligence group. So the place of information technology in this reinvented information agenda is critical, for which she must take much of the credit. And it is this IT connection that leads to the second major characteristic of this reinvented model, the structure of the service.

The work at C&L builds on three information 'layers'. A desktop layer helps, as Foy put it, 'to build the information-independent user', for the information the customer needs is retrieved from desktop tools or from a specialized information kiosk, and both external and internal information is identifiable and accessible in this format. The kiosk piece of this concept, now being tested in parts of the company, will meet the demands of what Foy called 'high-voltage' and vertical industry-specific groups, and is self-contained and interactive.

The information fulfilment center is used for simple factual reference, for directing users to specific product/service providers, gathering and transmitting research materials, controlling the C&L catalog, and basically eliminates the duplicative sources and expenditures that now occur throughout the firm. Its backbone is a company-wide internal information hotline, inaugurated in 1993, that operates from 8:00 am to 8:00 pm daily, staffed by knowledgeable professionals. They do no administrative or secretarial work, and their brief is information analysis, pure and simple. When staff at C&L ring up 1-800-KNOWHOW, they are confident that they will get 'true' information delivery. Linked to the information fulfilment center is a new fax-on-demand service for frequently requested internal and external reports. Now operating far in excess of original expectations, this service just might turn out to be the most successful of all of these new information products.

The third layer is a network of C&L information specialists, planned to include internal industry group experts, information center and library professionals, market analysts and C&L line-of-business experts, all interfacing closely with the information fulfilment center and there to synthesize and evaluate information. As many of the information specialists will have a thorough knowledge of a specific subject, they will also have quick access to other subject experts, thus compounding and dramatically increasing the potential for success in the information quest.

Of course the entire operation is based on the people who are part of it, and it is this people component that moves Foy's work into the winner's circle. It has not always been easy, of course, and there has been turnover, because what is taking place here is a sea-change in the information delivery system.

'It's not just different careers that these people are moving into', she said. 'It's a different operation, and what we require are information professionals who can sell "specialist" skills. As one of my colleagues says, we're not providing "baby" information any more, and so we're working very hard with our information staff to help them. With librarians, we need to show them how to see themselves in different, other roles. And when it's necessary, we look elsewhere in the organization, beyond the usual "library"-type activities, and we bring over people who are skilled at gathering particular types of information.'

Is it difficult to find the people to do this work?

'You must understand', Foy said with some emphasis, 'that this is a totally different operation. We are asking people to work in an entirely different way, to interpret, to consult, to add value, and the new job descriptions – with the new salary structures – that we have in place require a way of thinking that fits into this "different" picture. Of course communication is basic, as I've been saying, but we also have to have people who are comfortable with technology, who are creative, who are team players, and, as much as anything else, who are willing to take risks. These are the people who will make this new model of information services work.'

So, reinventing information pulls a lot of things together, and what is being done at Cooper & Lybrand makes a lot of sense. The characteristics described here – the enabling role of technology, the structure and the staffing – are all critical to the success of the new model. But riding above all else, from a management point of view, is the understanding that information delivery today is not the information delivery of the past (even of the very recent past) and that information delivery as practiced in traditional librarianship is not the same as information delivery in the corporate environment. Of course they are all part of the same information spectrum but in very different places along that spectrum. By reinventing the corporate information model for Cooper & Lybrand, Foy and her team are positioning information services where they belong: at the very heart of the company.

Insourcing

As senior managers begin to realize and recognize the critical role that information plays in organizational success, it is not surprising that they are coming up with innovative methodologies for information delivery. In addition to outsourcing and the total reinvention of information services, another approach being given serious attention is insourcing. This new management tool elevates the information management function to the same level as that of other management efforts in the unit.

In many respects the evolution of insourcing as a practical management methodology has sprung from the one-person library, which has long been predicted to be the 'wave of the future'. In fact, in the very first book on one-person librarianship the point was made that 'it is probably safe to assume that the number of one-person library operations will grow, as management comes to realize that one excellent, efficient and enthusiastic librarian or information specialist is preferable to two or more who do not provide the same level of service for users. It is these committed, enthusiastic librarians who will bring to the profession a level of service that their employers cannot help but appreciate, because they will bring to the parent organization, the employing corporation, hospital, society, or teaching facility, good library service, which is all they wanted in the first place' (St. Clair and Williamson 1986, p. 171).

In the ten years since that book was written the information services discipline has changed drastically, but if there is any one attribute of the information delivery function that has stayed the same, it is the one referred to in that last statement: management wants 'good library service' (now generally referred to as 'good information delivery'). More to the point, the information services workplace has changed to such an extent that it is now a commonly accepted practice in many organizations to have a single person to provide the information products, services and consultations that were previously delivered by a multistaffed operational unit.

There are very real reasons why these changes have taken place, and among these are several which should be given special attention:

- Advances in enabling technology that permit one person to provide the information that is required for an identified customer group;

- The now-established adherence to solid management practices in information services that avoids processes and deliverables that are not mission-critical;

- Participation in high-visibility enterprise-wide projects and activities that position the information function as customer focused and enterprise focused rather than library focused;

- Training and education that prepares practitioners sufficiently for single-staff information delivery;

- Among the practitioners themselves, a sense of professional self-worth and organizational allegiance that establishes a framework for the highest quality standards in information delivery.

These changes, combined with changes that have occurred simultaneously in society, in the general management community at large, and in the expectations and perceptions of information customers, have led to the insourcing of information services. Much attention has been paid in recent years to the outsourcing of those functions within an organization that are not part of the organization's core competency. Such activities as the hiring of a short-term research team, for example, to determine the validity of pursuing a particular course of action before resources are committed to the action, or the hiring of an external project management team to implement the activity, so that internal resources are not used, are commonly pursued, and commented upon. Little has been said about situations where organizational managers hire and add to staff employees for permanent research- or project-related work. Certainly in the information services field the trend towards outsourcing has elicited much comment (despite the fact that those same units have been themselves outsourcing tasks and projects that are not their or their staffs' core competencies, or that are not appropriate for information staff to perform – the use of subscription agencies, for example, or the contracting out of information technology projects). Now the pendulum seems to be swinging the other way, as managers and department heads realize that they need information, and while the organization at large might not require the services of a permanent library or information center, an individual unit of the organization might very well need an information specialist who can perform all functions connected with the management and delivery of information. When that unit's manager decides to hire a person to do that work, and whose tasks are limited only to that work, the unit is insourcing.

This new management methodology establishes the information services practitioner as the single-staff information 'point person' and requires of him or her not only a high level of quality in the information management function, but a parallel level of accountability and responsibility. The role of the information practitioner is not negotiable and is not subsumed beneath labels referring to 'professionalism', 'qualified', and similar external influences which are not part of the basic function of the job. That function is to provide the information that is required for the successful achievement of the unit's mission, to enable the unit to do its work, and while expertise and professional judgment are required, the end product – the information that meets the specifically defined needs of the unit and its employees – cannot be compromised.

Given these conditions, insourcing can be defined as 'the establishment of a departmental or other limited-sphere information management function in which the employee or employees who perform the function not only acquire the information that is required for the department to achieve its stated mission, but serve the department as information counselors, mediators, analysts and interpreters. In the department, an agreed-upon information policy defines the scope of the information management function, and all information specifically identified as falling within the agreed-upon range of services is requested through the information management employee, who is generally referred to as an "information specialist".'

Insourcing changes the focus of the work by emphasizing the relationship between the information specialist and the specifically defined customer base. Because the specialist is a member of the departmental team, he or she is in a position to know intimately the requirements of the people who are going to be using the information that he or she is providing; at the same time, the information specialist is responsible for determining how the searches will be constructed, what the best search strategies will be, the appropriate formats for searching, and, once the information has been received, for analyzing and interpreting the information before it is delivered to the customer.

Certainly insourcing represents an almost idealized version of the quality perspective in information delivery, for it provides the best opportunity yet for personal and immediate interaction between the parties involved in the information transaction. Significantly, in the insourcing arrangement the information function is no longer characterized as a 'support' function (that is, it is no more a support function than the work of the other members of the departmental team), and the role of information in the unit's operation is acknowledged as being critical to the unit's success.

As insourcing moves into quality information management as a recognized management tool, examples can be found in a number of environments. An early example goes back to the late 1980s. Working as a single-staff librarian in the pediatrics department of a major hospital, Laurel Blewett was effectively operating an insourcing service for the department. Here is how she described her work, in an article published in 1990:

> One of my more important responsibilities is daily attendance at a conference entitled 'morning report', [which] functions as an instructive as well as informative conference on the last 24 hours of patient admission to the Children's Center. During the conference, the various senior residents who have been on call discuss their patients with the Chairman of Pediatrics and the Chief Resident. I act as a resource person for the group. For example, if an in-depth discussion arises on the treatment of pertussis (whooping cough), I might be asked to search for specific articles on pertussis that the Chairman has read, or I might be asked to find several

articles on the different treatments of pertussis, or maybe a review article. . . .

Another aspect of the job is attending a weekly meeting called the 'case management conference', [which] discusses patients admitted to the Children's Center with a list of symptoms, but sometimes without a diagnosis. Faculty, residents, interns, nurses, ambulatory personnel and medical students attend this meeting. My specific job is to help the Chief Resident find pertinent information (Blewett 1996, p. 282).

Eventually Blewett's job changed to include accompanying doctors on their daily rounds, in order to better understand their information needs and to be positioned to provide the best information that could be made available for their work. By this time, the job had evolved into what would now be considered a classic insourcing position.

Other insourcing arrangements have been put in place in large manufacturing enterprises, where the engineering and design staff, for example, will have an information 'point person' assigned to specific projects, so that the information function can be focused on the needs of that project team. Historically, of course, marketing departments in many businesses have often operated their own information gathering and analysis units, as have multinational businesses, government agencies or research organizations with information needs involving security and privacy issues. The new attention to insourcing, however, is notable in that it looks at the information management function in terms of its critical role and accepts that critical role as a normal operational function, not as a separate standalone function to be turned to when necessary. As such, of course, it relates directly to the quality customer service model, for the very concept of insourcing establishes the critical link between the value of the information provided by the information specialist and use of that information by the customer.

Finally, though, it is up to the information services manager to set the tone when it comes to customer service, and it does not go unnoticed that when information managers get together, there is much talk about customer service, about how this plan or that policy has been put in place to satisfy customer needs and/or to measure customer satisfaction. When members of their staffs get together, on the other hand, there is much talk about lip service, about how there is supposedly much concern about customer service but that no one is really doing anything about it. Here are a few questions the manager of an information services unit might ask himself or herself before the next departmental staff meeting. After taking the test, the information manager seeking to initiate a quality management focus to his or her department might rethink some of the department's customer service initiatives.

1. In the information services unit for which you have managerial responsibility, does your professional staff have regular (not

occasional) customer service training?
Yes.
No, but they should.
No.

2. Do your non-professional staff have regular (not occasional) customer service training?
    Yes.
    No, but they should.
    No.

3. Can your staff members personally 'bend the rules' if the rules interfere with good customer service?
    Yes.
    No, but they should.
    No.

4. When you learn of bureaucratic interference in the customer service process, do you take corrective action?
    Yes.
    No, but I should.
    No.

5. Do you use personal visits to customers (in their offices, not yours) to measure customer satisfaction?
    Yes.
    No, but I should.
    No.

6. Do you regularly meet with customer group, and/or senior management to identify customer needs?
    Yes.
    No, but I should.
    No.

References

Blewett, Laurel A. 'Part of the team: profile of a pediatric librarian.' *The Best of OPL II: Selected Readings from The One-Person Library: A Newsletter for Librarians and Management, 1989-1994. Washington* DC: Special Libraries Association, 1996.

Duston, Beth. 'Technology changes customer focus and customer service.' *The One-Person Library: A Newsletter for Librarians and Management* 10 (11), March, 1994.

St. Clair, Guy. *Customer Service in the Information Environment.* London and New Providence, NJ: Bowker-Saur, 1993.

St. Clair, Guy, and Berner, Andrew. 'Thinking about . . . how insourcing changes the role of the one-person library.' *The One-Person Library: A Newsletter for Librarians and Management* 13 (4), August, 1996.

St. Clair, Guy, and Williamson, Joan. *Managing the One-Person Library.* London: Butterworths, 1986.

Younger, Jennifer. 'Total quality management: can we move beyond the jargon?' *Central Ohio Bulletin Special Libraries Association* 27 (2), February, 1992.

Zeithaml, Valarie A., Parasuraman, A. and Berry, Leonard L. *Delivery Quality Service: Balancing Customer Perceptions and Expectations.* New York: Free Press, 1990.

Chapter Six

The route to continuous improvement in information services

The phrase 'continuous improvement' is so closely linked with total quality management that it is hard to imagine the one without the other. Any organization seeking to establish a continuous improvement focus, regardless of the origin of the idea, is going to be moving in a TQM direction, and certainly any TQM initiative is going to focus on continuous improvement, one of those essentials of TQM that is referred to so often by managers and other organizational leaders seeking to ensure the successful achievement of organizational goals.

In information services terms continuous improvement is an enabling process, permitting those responsible for information delivery to concentrate their efforts on the needs of their customers, and at the same time to cultivate a departmental (if not enterprise-wide) awareness of the role of the information services unit.* In any operation that is responsible for delivering information products, services and consultations to an identified customer base, ongoing attention to the continuous improvement of the processes that provide for the delivery of that information assures a level of satisfaction that naturally reflects well on the unit. When continuous improvement is a fundamental component of the workplace environment, the information customers are satisfied, the information staff are contributing their best efforts for the successful delivery of information, and management is provided with specific and documented evidence that the work the department is charged to perform is being done successfully.

---

*The reference is to continuous improvement and the continuous seeking after new and better ways of doing what has to be done, not necessarily seeking to do better what is already being done. For more about this approach, see another book in this series, *Entrepreneurial Librarianship*.

Deciding what continuous improvement is

Continuous improvement has been defined as a process in which the many pieces of the operational picture are identified, examined and judged on their value to the overall organizational and departmental mission. To engage in continuous improvement is to agree to establishing ongoing evaluations regarding the validity of processes, about whether or not those processes contribute to the achievement of overall success, and to use those evaluations to structure a workflow that eliminates duplication, avoids unnecessary work and reduces costs.

In the management literature, continuous improvement has been part of the TQM methodology from the beginning, as the fifth of Deming's 14 points:

> Improve constantly and forever the system of production and service, to improve quality and productivity, and thus continually decrease cost (Duncan et al. 1995, p. 77).
>
> Constantly improve the system of production and service. Quality requires ongoing commitment to continuous improvement, elimination of waste, and reductions in cycle times. Management achieves this by rewarding the creativity and initiative of employees who try new things and who accomplish benefits for customers and gains for the company (Capezio and Morehouse 1995, p. 78).

For those who practice TQM and the many management scholars and practitioners who write or speak about it, continuous improvement is critical to the ongoing implementation of any quality initiative. It is not easy to get a TQM initiative in place, but to keep it in place and implemented on a continuing and perpetual basis is far more difficult, and it is the continuous improvement of the processes and procedures that brings in demonstrable results. Certainly this is the point that Richard Williams is making in his authoritative guidebook to total quality management:

> Continuous improvement is a philosophy that must permeate the very fabric of an organization. It isn't something you can fix overnight, but you can begin the process by doing everything possible to influence product and service standards to reflect the need for always improving standards. You can always expect more, something better, something stronger, and/or something that better meets customers' needs . . .
>
> One of the most important TQM principles for managers and supervisors is the nature and critical importance of continuous improvement. Too often, managers believe that quality is a fixed goal set by specifications, and once it is achieved it need not be improved. Managers must believe that no specification or goal is fixed: everything is subject to improvement. No goal is forever, and no specification is good enough to meet the demands or expectations of tomorrow's customers (Williams 1994, pp. 14, 86).

If any explanation is needed, surely this attention to the role of continuous improvement in the success of TQM in providing a framework for change management can justify a quality initiative in a library or other information services facility. There are few disciplines where the delivery media – information technology and its related tools – are changing so rapidly as in information services management. And certainly there are few disciplines where the changes taking place within the field are providing so much opportunity for the successful achievement of the discipline's service goals. Getting the information to the customer, in all its various guises, has been and continues to be the primary goal of the information services field, and the tools available for reaching this goal have never been so applicable and so available as they are now. Yet there are also few disciplines where there is so much resistance to the changing of processes to adapt to new standards in order to meet new customer demands and expectations. Certainly attempts are being made, and there are notable successes, but in many information services operations staff resistance even to the very idea of process review and the achievement of quality management objectives is so entrenched that it becomes almost impossible – without mandated compliance dictated by senior management – to ensure staff cooperation for embarking on such programs. The beauty of continuous improvement is that the activity becomes part of the work process and is 'written in' to the departmental work patterns. As such, improved information delivery becomes far less vulnerable to resistance.

However, continuous improvement is much more than a management tool for encouraging staff to participate in the achievement of quality service. In fact, as part of the teamwork infrastructure upon which total quality management is built, continuous improvement is but one more opportunity for information stakeholders to work together to achieve departmental goals. Continuous improvement becomes part of the organizational culture, a point that William Duncan includes in his definition of the process. For Duncan, continuous improvement is:

> . . . the improvement of products, processes, and/or services on an ongoing basis. The gains made through continuous improvement activities are generally incremental, small-step improvements, as contrasted with more dramatic and sweeping improvements typically associated with initiatives such as policy deployment. In Japan, the continuous improvement process is often called *kaizen* (Duncan 1995, p. 35).

For those organizations which choose to build the continuous improvement process into a formalized and codified continuous improvement plan (CIP), which is the usual pattern for the successful implementation of a total quality management initiative, the CIP is defined by Duncan as:

A plan designed to incorporate the philosophy of continuously improving every process and product into the culture of a company. The plan should outline specific training and improvement guidelines. The training included in this plan should prepare participants to seek out root causes in problem solving and stress prevention as opposed to detection of defects. The plans typically include initial awareness training; more detailed problem solving and TQM tool training; initiation of improvement activities; and the monitoring of regular, ongoing improvement activities, including reward and recognition systems to reinforce the application of continuous improvement throughout the company (Duncan 1995, p. 36).

This is all well and good for the theorist, but the information services manager in most organizations is seeking practical, 'down-to-earth' guidance on how to put continuous improvement to work. Barbara Spiegelman has created a remarkably user-friendly approach to TQM in an information setting, and the friendly tone is set up as she describes her own philosophy about quality management in a technical library, such as the one she manages at the Westinghouse Electric Company's Energy Systems Business Unit in Pittsburgh, PA:

There are those who try to make TQM complex. Do not let them do this. TQM is nothing more than an organized approach to improvement (Spiegelman 1992, p. 106).

In Spiegelman is successful effort to take the complexity out of total quality management, she provides a framework that sets up the effort with a five-step process. It begins with identifying the value of products and services offered by the library or other information services unit from the customers' point of view (thus beginning the process with attention to the first essential of TQM, the customer focus). Spiegelman then moves to the second step, which is to map the processes used to deliver those products and services and then to establish how improvements in those processes can be made. The fourth step is to measure the effectiveness of those improvements, and finally, the fifth step is to communicate improved measures to staff, customers and management. For those information services managers who want to move to a more advanced stage of TQM, a sixth step can be the incorporation of a benchmarking effort, which Spiegelman defines as 'finding out how others accomplish the same tasks, and choosing the best practices to reach your own goals' (Spiegelman 1992, p. 106).

In the context of continuous improvement it's the *mapping* that is of interest, for Spiegelman's *task mapping* relates quite importantly to work that Forrest Woody Horton in his work in *information resource mapping* (Burk and Horton 1983, p. 67). Although the contexts are not the same, the ultimate goal is: to determine what procedures and processes are used in establishing an information delivery pattern, and how they can be mapped or tracked so that their validity can be established. For example, in distinguishing between information cost and information value, Horton offers useful definitions that can come in handy for the information services manager seeking to institute continuous improvement and to relate the costs of information delivery to the processes being tracked:

> It's axiomatic that in order to manage any resource intelligently we must know both its cost and value. . . . Information cost [is defined as] the costs incurred in acquiring and/or producing information, as well as storing and maintaining it, using it, communicating it, and disposing of it. Included are the costs of the input resources used to produce information and other related expenses incurred in production, storage, and dissemination. From an accounting standpoint, this production is similar to the production (manufacture) of a physical commodity. Both involve converting something "raw" (unfinished) to a finished product by applying resources such as direct labor, equipment, overhead, and information in order to add value to it. . . .
>
> Information value [is] the value attributed to information produced or acquired by organizations, entities, and persons, and delivered in the form of an information product or service. The values may be realized immediately or at some later time. For example, the values attached to information created by scientific research are often realized long after it is created. The risk of realizing future values must be weighed against present and continuing costs of creating, storing, and accessing it (Burk and Horton 1983, pp. 78-79).

The conjoining of information cost and information value takes the information services manager back again to the processes: what are the steps involved in providing the information that the customer requires, and how can those steps be reviewed and their cost-effectiveness established? A prior effort must precede Spiegelman's first step of identifying a value for the products and services provided by the information unit, and that is the simple inventory of the products and services themselves and the less simple itemization of steps in each process required for their production and delivery. So in fact the 'mapping' will begin much sooner than would seem to be the case, for the information services manager and his or her staff must list the products and services and then list the activities that go into the production of each.

Difficulties in establishing continuous improvement in information services.

One barrier that is to be acknowledged and prepared for is the environment in which continuous improvement is to be implemented. It has been indicated (*cf.* Introduction) that information services practitioners,

BARRIERS TO CONTINUOUS IMPROVEMENT

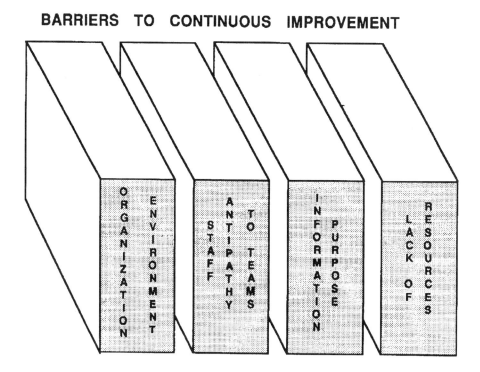

accustomed as they are to 'quick-turnaround' work, might not be the most receptive audience for a total quality management initiative, and the same holds true when we are looking at the continuous improvement element of TQM. Just thinking about the size of the effort, which must begin with an exercise that identifies everything a library or other information services unit does, and then taking each of those things and breaking it down into distinct and measurable parts, is an overwhelming idea for many. To move beyond the idea stage to a commitment to actually embark on such an effort is beyond the comprehension of many information workers, and the staffs of information departments must be sold on the concept.

Another point of resistance in organizing a continuous improvement program in information services is the natural antipathy of many information workers to participating in teams and groups in order to accomplish information-related tasks. Many of these people get far along with their preparation for these careers without participating in teamwork at any level. Thus, as many who teach at the graduate schools educating future library and information services workers will attest, there is much difficulty in assigning team projects, and the idea of participating in a group case study project is resisted. Much of this attitude carries over into the careers of these workers, and as the entire strength of TQM and the continuous improvement effort is built on the team approach to problem solving, there will be many who do not want to be part of the continuous improvement activity.

Within the organization or community a lack of understanding about the role of information, and of information delivery as a management function dealing with a commodity or a tangible entity, puts the information services manager in an awkward position. One of the manager's first tasks is to establish the information unit's place in the organizational culture. It is often commented that the success of an information services operation is directly related to the organizational or community attitude to information, and the information services manager who wishes to improve the workflow and the delivery of information in his or her unit is required to confront the organizational culture. If the organization is one in which information is critical to the successful achievement of organizational goals – the news library at a television station, for example – the culture is built around the value of information and the news librarian is in a position to require the highest standards of excellence in the delivery of information to support the news effort. In fact, in such a situation those standards are demanded by the organizational culture, for without them the organization's mission could not be realized.

On the other hand, if the organization is one in which the gathering and dissemination of information does not necessarily relate to organizational success, the value of the information services departments and their functions is going to be minimized, and the managers of these departments will have difficulty finding support for any quality effort. In a small manufacturing company, for example, the management library may serve primarily as a place for the collection and display of current management journals and popular magazines which are not routed to management staff in their offices. The books in the collection are few, and will be primarily those basic reference materials which provide information not available through electronic sources at staff workstations. In fact, for most of the management staff the library serves as a place to go to read a newspaper or magazine when they want to get away from their offices for a while, or to use as a study facility, a quiet place to escape to when they need to get away from ringing telephones and other interruptions. Thus the facility is hardly on the cutting edge as far as the company's information delivery procedures are concerned, and the librarian is going to be hard pressed to find support for engaging in a quality-focused activity. In fact, for people working in such units the situation becomes doubly disconcerting when there is a management emphasis on quality, when all other staff are given specific quality programs to initiate, and the information unit is particularly unsuited for such an activity. In these cases, by incorporating their work with that of others in the organization or community, a quality program can be initiated but the activity is pursued from a different and broader perspective.

Thus, in those organizations or communities where there is a noticeable lack of commitment to the information delivery process, and to the relationship between information delivery and organizational or community success, it is going to be difficult to organize continuous improvement awareness. Information staff (even those who are not interested in TQM or its results in better information delivery) are well aware of this limitation, simply because other signs are given off that support this assessment, and it is not difficult to ascertain where the information function is positioned in the organization. Many information workers can attest to these situations, and one of the most telling examples occurred in a large multinational company that was seeking to expand into a new area of business. To do so meant bringing into the parent company a number of new companies that would support the new line of work, and acquiring and merging these companies required much competitive intelligence and general business research. Because the project was so important, a specially designated member of the corporate library staff was assigned to the executive charged with putting together the various deals, and over a two-year period much high-level negotiating took place. Naturally, much information was requested and delivered, and the library staff member, a professionally trained and qualified librarian, became almost a personal librarian for the executive managing the operation. It was, of course, a highly secretive affair, and even within the corporate library no one knew what the librarian was working on. The end of the story is that the deal went through successfully, and after a two-year gestation the executive and his senior staff were understandably overjoyed and quite proud of themselves. To celebrate their success a grand dinner was planned, at which all senior executive staff were in attendance, as well as all members of the successful manager's mergers and acquisitions team, with one exception. The personal librarian was not invited, and when the manager of the corporate library enquired as to why this exceptional staff member had been excluded he was informed that she was 'just a librarian'.

It is difficult to understand how such a mean-spirited response could occur in today's information-ruled business environment, but in this case the situation says more about the company and its attitudes to information than about the personalities involved. The company is simply not an organization in which the information function is valued very highly, and the connection between organizational success – even in a situation as demonstrably clear-cut as the one described here – and the successful delivery of information has not been established. Perhaps if the librarian had not been very good at his or her work, or if the executive in charge of the new operation had been required to go to private information brokers for the information he or she needed, the role of the information transfer process would have been more highly valued, but probably not. The circumstances, it seems, are simply that this is a company in which information is taken for granted.

Such a situation highlights another barrier to the establishment of a continuous improvement initiative which must be recognized, and in a company or community such as the one described above this barrier is almost inevitable and almost impossible to overcome. It is, of course, the lack of resources that will be committed to a project of the sort being described here. One of the information services manager's most difficult tasks in the organization and implementation of a TQM initiative will be to find the funds, staff, time and other resources that will be required, and unless senior management has mandated the quality program, or has bought in to the concept, the effort is doomed to failure. Even if some initial start-up resources are made available, senior managers often don't expect the commitment of resources to be a long-term need. 'Let's just get it started' is a typical response from many managers when they are trying to bring quality management into an organization but are not willing to commit the resources that are required. 'Once we have TQM up and running, we'll be able to use those resources for other things.'

It is not going to happen unless a serious commitment is made, and that commitment must be permanent.

Selling continuous improvement to the information stakeholders

Certainly the commitment that is required is a major stumbling block to the initiation of a continuous improvement program. This is a point that has been well made in reference to quality management in the general management community, and it certainly applies in information services. 'TQM as process improvement requires commitment', write Capezio and Morehouse. 'Commitment means being the best you can be in your job, as well as continuously looking for opportunities to improve the work' (Capezio and Morehouse 1995, p. 31). Yet even before we get to the commitment stage we must convince information stakeholders that it is to their benefit that continuous improvement and total quality management be insinuated into the organizational culture. It is at this point that information services managers fall back on their persuasive skills, using them to establish a cultural framework in which the power of information and the influence that it brings are used to manipulate organizational culture so that it becomes more information focused, and thus more in tune with the efforts being made to bring quality information delivery to the organization.

Even in a situation as negative as the example presented above, if the library manager is willing to build on the distinctive role his staff member played in the company's new success, this work can be used to the library's advantage. In most situations, of course, the information services unit is not so precariously positioned, or even if it is with respect to one particular department or function there are others in which its services are held in high esteem. The smart information services manager will recognize where this esteem is to be found and exploit it to his or her unit's advantage. No one knows more about information delivery than the staff of the various information services departments in an organization, and those people can come together to organize a TQM management picture if there is in that group the necessary leadership, vision and information knowledge. Obviously such an effort has a far greater chance of success if the various units are managed by one person, but even if this is not the case, the effort still has the potential for success if some of the different department heads are committed to an integrated information services quality picture.

Certainly the support and enthusiasm of senior management are required. According to Capezio and Morehouse, companies that embark on the road of continuous improvement through TQM make the following commitments:

1. The CEO and senior management lead the process through visionary leadership and provide enough resources for TQM to succeed.
2. A steering committee, composed of senior management and key players from throughout and outside of the company, receives ongoing TQM training in problem-solving and conflict resolution – as well as direction in leading a change process within an organization.
3. Preparation for implementing TQM or any change process must be finely tuned and integrated before it is launched. Time to assign roles, develop strategy, assemble resources, and ready the environment to accept change are key tasks to accomplish at this point.
4. The principles of TQM – elimination of waste, error-free work, and continuous improvement – are captured by focusing on
   • customer requirements
   • measurement (baselines and benchmarks)
   • existing programs aimed at quality
   • customer service and satisfaction.
5. Training guides the entire process and never stops for the company's employees or suppliers if continuous improvement is the goal.
6. Evaluation provides an ongoing process for assessing the value and impact of quality on the performance of the company (Capezio and Morehouse 1995, p. 28).

A final point should be made: although it is a charge that is almost routinely made against continuous improvement, it is not 'change for change sake'. The benefits of continuous improvement must continually be talked about and included in the organizational culture. Creating customer satisfaction, raising the level of employee participation, training to provide the framework for a better workplace (and better jobs), teamwork and process improvements are all concepts that cannot be argued with. In the information services environment they lead to better information delivery, which is what a service-oriented department expects to do anyway. Information services, staff *want* to provide the highest levels of information delivery they can, but they are prevented from doing so by procedures and processes that impede or prevent the quality they want to provide and which their customers expect. By initiating a total quality management focus for information delivery, one emphasizing continuous improvement, the information unit is positioned to assume its critical role in organizational success.

Continuous improvement in the information services context

For the information services manager who is ready to begin a continuous improvement plan, Capezio and Morehouse offer what they call 'a few success factors' to consider:

1. Are you committed to continuous improvement? Is your leadership?
2. Do you know your internal and external customers' requirements?
3. Do you have opportunities for education and training to upgrade your skills?
4. Do you have a vision for the future?
5. Do you have clear direction for your job? (Capezio and Morehouse 1995, p. 33).

Each of these can provide a useful point of departure in the information services environment. For example, the first question raises important personal issues with respect to one's work, and the answer must be delivered before any attempts at TQM can be seriously undertaken. If the information services manager himself or herself is not committed to continuous improvement, there is hardly any purpose in going on with the attempt. On the other hand, if there are occasions when word gets back to the senior manager that the delivery of an information product, service or consultation could have been better than it was on one or another specific occasion, and the senior manager regrets that the department is not structured to permit such refinement, there is a good chance that a continuous improvement program would be appropriate and would succeed.

As for the commitment of organizational or community leadership to continuous improvement, information managers must interview them and determine what their attitudes to information are. Of course they are going to want to achieve the benefits of any continuous improvement activity, and the attractions of eliminating waste, error-free work and an ongoing effort to improve processes are going to be received with much enthusiasm. Nevertheless, when it is time to begin negotiations about the effects that some of the changed processes might have on some of the information customers, or for resources to bring the TQM effort to fruition, there might be some backtracking, and new persuasive efforts will be required from the information services manager. However, many senior management personnel are quite strongly drawn to quality programs, and are happy and supportive when the information services manager brings the matter up for discussion. So if there is commitment from senior management the information services manager can take advantage of this and move forward with his or her plans.

Although some of the information staff know the information requirements of some of the internal and external customers, it should be remembered that few trends or generalizations can be made from such knowledge. For a continuous improvement initiative to be truly effective in an organization, an information audit is required. This, with its emphasis on accountability and responsibility, combines with the basic pattern of the needs analysis to provide the information services unit with documented, factual information about the information-gathering behavior of identified information customers. The data gleaned from such an audit can provide surprising information about the perceived purposes of the information facility, and in most cases can provide the basis for establishing and implementing a continuous improvement initiative.

Regardless of the organization or the subject speciality of the discipline in which the information services operation is positioned, the manager of the unit and his or her quality planning team will need to find opportunities for education and training to upgrade their skills. Like other management skills, TQM and its component parts require expertise, and in this particular management task the information services manager cannot 'learn by doing'. It is critical that serious training be undertaken, either by bringing professional trainers in-house or by sending staff to seminars and workshops sponsored by professional associations, quality specialists etc. Attention must also be given to the training of non-managerial staff (particularly frontline staff), as they are the people who first come in contact with the customers and set the tone of the information transactions.

The information services manager's vision for the future of the unit is of course critical, and must not be underemphasized. Anyone in a management position should be visionary, but since so many people are promoted to managerial positions without appropriate training and education, there are often those in positions of considerable responsibility who do not understand that part of being a manager is to have an idealized or best-case-scenario vision of just how good the information services unit and its products could be. TQM and continuous improvement are simply one means of attaining that vision, but the manager must understand this before he or she embarks on the TQM initiative.

As far as the manager's clear direction for the job is concerned, we come again to the relationship between the information services manager and his or her supervisor, and the corporate culture. Before the move toward continuous improvement is undertaken, the manager must examine the relationship between the mission of the information unit and the organizational mission, and a clear understanding of the information unit's role must be established. In many cases there are information functions which continue to operate simply because they always have, and one of the first questions to be asked will be: 'Is this function necessary at all? Should this information services unit be in existence, or can the products, services and consultations it provides be provided through another means more efficiently and effectively?' If the answer is negative, the TQM/continuous improvement exercise will be futile.

However, if all the right questions have been asked and a decision is made to establish a framework for continuous improvement, some attention must be given to what the exercise will be doing. Will it be simply a regular process review, one of the general controlling functions of any management effort, or will it be a total commitment to change, to re-engineer the entire information services function?

Continuous improvement links closely to re-engineering (discussed earlier), but before the information services manager goes too far and commits himself or herself (or senior management and additional resources) to a re-engineering-focused TQM/continuous improvement effort, certain considerations must be made. There is a basic need to understand what re-engineering is and what it is not. Michael Hammer, the man who brought re-engineering to the management community, cautions that organizational leaders seeking to embrace the re-engineering mantle should be careful about what they mean to do. For example, only processes can be re-engineered – not organizations, not departments, and not the people who make up those organizations and departments. And processes, Hammer points out, are cross-functional and results oriented: they defy rather than respect organizational boundaries (Hammer and Stanton 1994, p. 18).

Here we run into one of the fuzzy areas of the TQM/continuous improvement effort that must be approached carefully. When do we use re-engineering, looking at processes that are cross-functional and enterprise-wide, and when do we look at intradepartmental activities that relate specifically to the work of the information services unit itself (and only to that unit and its products, services and consultations)? It is a question that has important connotations in the information services setting. Spiegelman has noted that process improvement at Westinghouse includes attention to four different elements: products; processes and procedures; information; and suppliers. Each of these must be considered in terms of whether it is organization-wide or specifically related to the information unit itself.

Like Spiegelman, Laurie McFadden has come up with a specific formula for process improvement which was developed as the information staff at AT&T Bell Laboratories sought to bring a continuous improvement framework to their technical documents management system. The seven steps for process improvement that McFadden identified are:

1. Establish process management responsibilities.

2. Define process and identify customer requirements.

3. Define and establish measures.

4. Assess conformance to customer requirements.

5. Investigate process to identify improvement opportunities.

6. Rank improvement opportunities and set objectives.

7. Improve process quality (McFadden 1994, pp. 10–14).

Richard Hodgetts believes that a well-formulated continuous improvement program is built on four steps 'of paramount importance', and it is in implementing these four steps that the information services manager is going to find direction for establishing the continuous improvement element of the total quality management initiative:

1. Develop quantitative measure, such as percentages, costs, revenues, time, or dollars, so that you know the status of your quality efforts and do not look at mere anecdotal data as truth.

2. Use benchmarking and similar approaches to help generate, creative unique situations and learn how to think "outside the box", by looking at problems in new ways.

3. Focus on achieving small, incremental improvements in quality, as opposed to trying for large advances that come as a result of occasional major breakthroughs, because it is more important to have continual improvement than the starts and stops that characterize these giant periodic increases.

4. Working within the three previous guidelines, develop a continuous improvement system that will work best in your own organization (Hodgetts 1996, pp. 179–198).

References

Burk, Cornelius F. Jr. and Horton, Forest W. Jr. *InfoMap: a Complete Guide to Discovering Corporate Information Resources*. New York: Prentice Hall, 1983.

Capezio, Peter and Morehouse, Debra. *Taking the Mystery Out of TQM: a Practical Guide to Total Quality Management*, 2nd edn. Franklin Lakes, NJ: Career Press, 1995.

Drake, Miriam A. and Stuart, Crit. 'TQM in research libraries.' *Special Libraries* 84 (3), Summer, 1993.

Duncan, William L. and Luftig & Warren International. *Total Quality: Key Terms and Concepts*. New York: American Management Association, 1995.

Hammer, Michael and Stanton, Steven A. *The Re-engineering Revolution: A Handbook*. New York: HarperBusiness, 1994.

Hodgetts, Richard M. *Implementing TQM in Small and Medium-Sized Organizations: a Step-by-Step Guide*. New York: American Management Association, 1996.

McFadden, Laurie. 'AT&T Bell Laboratories creates a quality team to study technical reports.' *Special Libraries* 85 (1), Winter, 1994.

St. Clair, Guy. *Entrepreneurial Librarianship: The Key to Effective Information Services Management*. London and New Brunswick, NJ: Bowker-Saur, 1995.

Spiegelman, Barbara M. 'Total quality management: how to improve your library without losing your mind,' in Matarazzo and Drake.

Williams, Richard L. *Essentials of Total Quality Management*. New York: American Management Association, 1994.

Chapter Seven

The measurement of quality in the provision of information

To measure the work we do is to give meaning to the claim that the products, services and consultations provided by our information services departments have some value. Everyone knows that libraries and the like are important. Ask anyone in the company if the archives department should be done away with, or outsourced to a private archives management firm, and you'll get a wide range of responses but they will all fall into the category of 'Don't touch it! We need to be able to get to those materials.' In fact, just moving the archives collection to an off-site storage facility, which of course is an action considered by practically all organizations at some point in their history, is a decision to be made with some difficulty, as the outcry by the people inconvenienced by the decision can be expected to be substantial. And if the subject under consideration is the outsourcing of the work of the archives unit, any suggestion of change will be met with considerable resistance. Archives are 'good'. The presence of a well-managed, easily accessed archives department is perceived by customers and non-customers alike as being worthwhile, as being something that is good for the company.

A more dramatic response comes when you ask the proverbial man in the street if the community should consider giving up its public library. Even people who never use the library, who have no intention of ever using the services that a library offers, cannot restrain themselves when the subject is raised: 'How dare you?' they ask, meaning that, as far as they are concerned, just raising the question is an attack on their quality of life, their own 'goodness'. For libraries, like churches, schools and similar institutions, are 'innately good'. Even when they are badly managed and perform badly, these institutions are part of the framework of society, and to not have a library means that a community does not have even the most rudimentary society in place.

These are, of course, values and perceptions about information services that have evolved over many generations, and although they are comforting and provide information services managers with a modicum of ease as they attempt to match service demands with resource allocation realities, for the most part these same perceptions lead to a great deal of confusion about how information services are or should be supported.

The fact of the matter is that claims that the information services operations we manage are of value are empty unless they are backed up by documentable, verifiable data. To assert that the products, services and consultations provided by our information services units are of value is to state the obvious, but in today's society the obvious is only of interest when it can be taken apart, dissected and analyzed. Of course no one is going to suggest closing an archives department or a library out of mean-spiritedness, but all of society's institutions are now being asked to justify why they should be supported. It doesn't matter whether the information services unit is in the private sector, the non-profit sector or the not-for-profit sector, questions about its value will be raised, and measurement determines value.

But measuring goes beyond simply determining value because it's the current societal trend. In today's information workplace there are five distinct influences that must be recognized and incorporated into the information services management plan: in addition to financial justification we are experiencing a new interest (for library and information services managers) in exploring management theory and its application in information services; there is competition for the services our departments and other information entities provide; and there is pressure for information workers to measure what they do because every other work unit is required to measure. Finally, and not to be overlooked, the very act of measuring, if done properly and if the results are properly disseminated, makes for very good public relations for the library or other information services unit whose value is being measured.

The resistance to measurement

Given these very reasonable – and not difficult to understand – motivations for measuring, many in information services still continue to resist. Why? Once we move beyond the very natural resistance to being asked to justify what we are doing and why we should be permitted to use resources that might very well be used elsewhere, there are three reasons why information services managers avoid measuring if they can. First, there is the intrinsic value that is built in to most information services operations, that 'innate' goodness that is automatically assumed about libraries, records management departments, computer services departments and so forth. They do 'good' things, they provide 'valuable' services for the organization or the community, they exist to 'be there', and any attempt to codify or measure them or the services they provide is perceived to be an attack on that intrinsic worth, compromising the organization or community at large for having established the entity in the first place.

Unfortunately, this natural sort of goodness is related to the role the information services unit is expected to perform within the organization or community and it often leads to a second, more insidious, problem. The perceived role of the unit affects how it is supported, of course, but equally important is the effect this perception has on how its products and services are utilized. Because most information use is based on specific need, and because most of the constituent user base is not thinking about an information services function on an ongoing basis (the way they would be thinking about the human resources department, say, or the payroll department), the unit itself in many organizations is simply not considered a 'real' activity. Its role is seen as one that is nice to have, but hardly essential to the successful achievement of the organizational mission. In these cases, any attempt to measure value is equally 'fringe'. In these cases the librarians, say, are told not to worry about whether the library is important to the organization: after all, it exists. Any concern about how good or bad it is is seen as rather pointless.

In these situations we have little power games going on, for there are always those people in organizations or communities who need to assert their own importance and who delight in having the opportunity to do so with respect to a function that is not considered critical. For these people measurement becomes a nasty little tool, and measurement techniques are used to put the information services manager and his or her staff in an awkward or subservient position, to 'catch them out' so that they appear to be foolish or innocent when compared to the 'serious' business that the organization deals with. In one research firm, for example, there is the story of the member of the library committee who refused to acknowledge the value of the library's success in providing information that the scientists and engineers used in their work. For him, the library (despite the fact that most of its work was project related, including literature searches, sophisticated research and analysis and similar tasks) was a place where people came to borrow books. At each meeting of the library committee this person labored the fact that book loans were 'down' by 20 volumes from the previous month, or that book loans for the current year were not 'keeping up' with the loans of the previous calendar year. It was futile to attempt to educate him about the other work that was performed in the library, and he went on his way, continually judging the library's success by his own limited measures. To be fair, this committee member in his ignorance probably did not do much harm, and he surely provided quite a bit of amusement to the other members of the committee and the information staff, for this was the same man who measured the value of a book using a page/price ratio (meaning that a 200-page book advertised for $19.95 was considered a good value, but a 200-page book that was offered for $39.95 was 'not worth the money'!). In such circumstances, as long as the information services unit is not considered a mission-critical function, there is little the information manager can do to change these perceptions. About all he or she is in a position to do is to convince someone that measurement might raise awareness of the information function, but even so, the advocate would need to be convinced first. In this example it might be the chairperson of the library committee, who might be influenced to see his role as one that could advance him in the organization, but unless he wants to be advanced the effort will lead to nothing.

There is, however, another more important phenomenon in information services management that prevents managers from attempting to measure the value of their unit's services. This would appear to be based on fear, on a certain concern that those in authority in the organization or community that supports the information operation lack respect for what it does. Related to this, of course, is an associated fear that those same authorities are determined to destroy or weaken the unit in some way, and if the unit itself is weakened, naturally its manager and its staff are weakened. When this is the situation the manager is going to avoid measurement, because to attempt to measure the value of the services the unit provides is to call attention to it, and that is the last thing these managers want. They have discovered that they and their staffs have found positions that demand little of them, and they are reluctant to provide more.

However, perhaps the best explanation of why measurement is resisted in the library/information services discipline probably has more to do with the view of the practitioners themselves that the discipline is a distinct service, unlike any other. There are probably as many reasons why this state of affairs has come about as there are practitioners, and some of these have been touched on earlier. In the final analysis, though, a move toward a more modest opinion might be in order. Certainly the work that is done by information services practitioners is important, and there are many fields in which the information provided is essential to the existence of the organization and to its success in achieving its mission. But information services practitioners have a tendency to see their work as *more* important than the work others in the organization or community are doing, and by not measuring that work and its value to the information customers they are able to keep alive the mystique of information services. Thus, those who don't have their understanding of information and information services aren't in a position to judge whether the information products are of real value or not.

Certainly this is the point that Marilyn White and Eileen Abels made in an article they wrote about the applying methodologies from the service marketing field to information services management: 'Libraries and information services can benefit significantly by stressing their commonalities rather than their differences with other segments of the service industry. . . . They often have a membership relationship with their clients and usually provide services in discrete transactions. The services themselves are highly customized, and staff exercise considerable judgment in meeting individual needs. The extent of demand probably fluctuates only narrowly over time, and, in most cases, peak demand can usually be met without major delay' (White and Abels 1995, p. 41).

Of course the information delivered to the customers is valuable: they wouldn't have come to the information services unit to seek it if it were not valuable to them and if they did not need it. On the other hand, there is, a requirement on the part of information services practitioners for a certain level of objectivity in this respect, for without measuring how good the service is, without recognizing that there are influences within the organization or community that can affect whether the unit is going to succeed or not, the information manager and his or her staff continue in a sort of organizational limbo, never secure in the knowledge that they are doing a good job, and never secure in the place of the unit in the organization or community it was created to serve.

Quantitative measures

When it comes to valuing the information services operation every information services manager is aware of the tension that exists between themselves and others in their organizations and communities. Despite a supposedly firm commitment to the place of the information service unit in the organization, there is an ongoing requirement for *verifying* value, and for most managerial units measurement is required.

Quantitative measures are typically employed in most information services operations, for it is these that permit managers to compare what they do and how they do it (and how much it costs and how long it takes). In fact, since control is one part of the management function it is through the use of quantitative measures that most managers exercise control. This is not to say that quantitative measures are used to replace observation and experiential evaluation, for these are just as much a part of the managerial control function, but the successful information services manager must carefully construct a management practice that gives equal authority to each, and which attributes to each the role for which it has been chosen. There is nothing worse than a library basing its request for resource allocation on statistics without any attention being given to the effectiveness of the library in the community or organization of which it is a part. On the other hand, if the director of that library went to the funding authorities and sought allocations based on the results of customer satisfaction surveys alone, questions would be raised about the specifics of the operation.

So there is a long history of using quantitative measures, and although these provide a less than complete picture the fact that they are so well established in the information services discipline means that they will continue to be used for evaluative purposes. No library, for example, is going to *not* count the number of books loaned to its patrons, even when the library is used less and less for book borrowing and more as a place to come to for up-to-date information delivered through electronic media. Libraries are expected to count the number of books borrowed, and will in all likelihood continue to do so.

The counting of books borrowed, the traditional 'circulation count' that libraries use to track how their services are being used, is a typical quantitative measure. The term 'to measure' can also be used to describe the *value* in terms of quality or 'goodness' that customers attach to particular services (effectiveness measures), but in most information services settings measurement generally refers to quantitative measures. These have been variously identified, but for information services the distinctions provided in a guidebook written by Don King and José-Marie Griffiths can offer useful direction:

> Evaluation of information centers involves four generic types of measures, including input cost measures, output measures, effective measures, and domain measures. The first two types of measures (input cost and output) involve information center operations and they, individually or together, help to establish the performance of resources, activities, services, functions, or the entire information center. Such measures include the amount and attributes of resources applied to services and output quantity and attributes of services. Effectiveness measures are those involving the effects of center services from the perspective of users, such as amount of use, purpose of use, consequences of use, etc. Domain measures involve descriptions of the environment or context of the information center. Such measures include the total number of persons in the service population, their information needs, etc. (Griffiths and King 1991, pp. 16-17).

The question that must be asked with respect to quantitative measures concerns the value of the measures themselves. For quantitative measures to have any meaning, attention must be given to what is being counted and how the statistics will be used. In most information services operations quantitative data are used for two purposes, to provide a picture of current services, practices and usage, and to be used in comparison with other quantitative data that have been or will be captured. The use of quantitative measures to provide a picture of current services has generally been motivated by a request from senior management, so that the return on investment for the support of the information services unit is seen to be worthwhile. Thus a records management unit which reports that 4,500 documents were received in the unit within an identified 30-day period, and that during the same time period 165 documents were prepared for retention and filed is sending a very clear message to management that there is a breakdown in the system and steps need to be taken to narrow the gap between documents received and documents filed.

Likewise, usage statistics are a valuable quantitative measure for senior management, giving them a picture of how much the facility is being used. In an engineering consulting firm, for example, by recording who comes to the corporate library for research, or who calls or e-mails requests to the library, the library staff has a profile of who the information customers are and, if proper statistics are being recorded, the kinds of services they expect from the library.

Of course one of the major disadvantages of relying on usage statistics, particularly as information delivery formats change, is that they provide only part of the picture, and while this limitation is generally recognized by management, there are occasional surprises. For example, Beth Duston has identified the 'phantom user', a concept that until a decade or so ago would not have been thought about. This is the person who accesses online databases from his or her workstation, uses CD-ROM products and other library materials after hours in the organization's library, and, although never counted among the library users in the statistical counts, considers the library an important and valuable part of his or her work. The librarian may never see this 'fugitive' user, since the information is usually accessed from another location, or in the library when the librarian is not there, but as the librarian plans for future needs and services for the library it is important that the fugitive user be considered (Duston 1993, p. 7).

Quantitative measures are also used for comparisons, the classic bench-marking exercise. Again, usage statistics and circulation counts can be of value if they are what management needs to know about how the information services department is used, but by comparing current figures against past data (or proposed objectives), the information services manager can answer the age-old management question: 'How are we doing?'

There are three ways we use quantitative data for comparisons, and they match the three types of benchmarking that are commonly accepted in management practice. Internal benchmarking refers to a comparison with other departments or operations within the organization or, in terms of historical or time-framed comparisons, within the same unit. For example, turnaround time for the delivery of documents may be 48 hours in a medical center's teaching hospital library, and 12 hours in the consumer information center. If this is the case, the manager who has responsibility for both operations will see the data and be able to compare them and raise questions with the respective departments as to why the situation is as it is.

On the other hand, for historical or time-framed comparisons, the quantitative data are simply compared to the same data that were collected at the time for which the comparison is to be made. In the example above, if the hospital's large library currently requires 48 hours for document delivery, but there are statistics that show that the turnaround time was as low as 16 hours five years ago, and began creeping up at that time, serious study and analysis of the inhibitors to faster turnaround time will be called for.

Quantitative data can also be used for competitive and functional benchmarking. In the former, data on the number of literature searches per month, say, are compared to matching data for similar information services operations, and while these data are not always easy to come by, they can be made available through various networking arrangements and cooperative activities. In functional comparisons the data collected are matched with similar data from other industries or disciplines which have some of the same goals as the information services unit. For example, if the manager of a records management operation is attempting to learn how to encourage customers to access records electronically (instead of their coming to the records unit, as is now the practice), he or she might look at how another industry persuaded its workers to move to electronic mail from hard-copy interoffice memoranda.

The kinds of data used for these quantitative measures are those which Griffiths and King have identified as input cost measures, output measures and domain measures, and all can be used for reviewing current operations or for comparison (obviously with varying results, depending on how the data will be used). Input cost measures, for example, which include such measures as collection cost, can be used to describe the current status of the collections budget, or to compare collection costs as spent, say, in the current month with the same month last year. Similarly, if the information is available (and it generally is, in the public and non-profit sectors), collection cost figures can be gathered for information operations of a similar size and function, and can be compared.

Output measures, too, can and will be used, in addition to usage data, measures such as number of items processed, number of transactions with customers (both total numbers and transactions broken down by type or service), timeliness, number of hours of service, and physical accessibility. As Griffiths and King have pointed out, 'the time taken by users to get to an information center and waiting for services is a portion of the "price" paid by users to use center services. The more users are required to "pay" in terms of their own time, the less likely they are to use the services' (Griffiths and King 1991, p. 17).

Domain measures are not generally used in quantitative measures, simply because the information services manager has no control over such demographic and already established conditions, but such quantitative data as the size of the service population, or within that group the size of the user population (including potential users), and attributes of those people can influence the kinds of services that are offered by the information services unit. Domain measures will also include such elusive data as how people use information, whether they are accustomed to and prefer hard copy as opposed to electronic media, and similar measures. Determined through the implementation of a well-constructed information audit, the data gathered about the information-seeking and –using behavior of identified customer groups will be helpful to the information services manager in deciding about what types and levels of information products, services and consultations will be offered.

Feedback about customer satisfaction and quality management

Although any attempt to find out how well the information services department is working will necessarily focus on formal and informal measurement methodologies, a basic measurement effort relates directly to customer care. One of the fundamental tenets of any successful customer service plan is that it include a mechanism for feedback, for determining customer satisfaction with the service, and a quality management initiative that focuses on the authority of the customer requires the same attention. In fact, in their essay on TQM in libraries Carson, Carson and Phillips assert that 'with the TQM approach, quality is determined not by conformance to professional library standards but by compliance with the expectations of the patrons' (Carson, Carson and Phillips 1995, p. 167).

Information services managers cannot know how good their services are until they ask the customers for whom the services have been designed. Such feedback is essential for the wellbeing of the information services operation, and there are four techniques that yield practical results. Direct customer contact, of course, is the main way of finding out what customers think. Equally helpful is the practice of distributing questionnaires and customer surveys and then analyzing the responses. Conducting interviews (both through the use of focus groups and in one-to-one discussions) is commonly accepted as a useful technique for determining customer attitudes, simply because, in most cases, people enjoy talking about their information-gathering activities. Analyzing complaints – often neglected in more traditional information services environments such as libraries and archives departments – is a feedback effort that provides immediate positive results. If done properly, a response to a complaint can turn a dissatisfied customer into an advocate and supporter of the information services unit, even if the original transaction continues to be unresolved. Why? Because the customer has been listened to, and responding to the complaint demonstrates to that customer that his or her opinion, even if negative, is important. A fifth technique, using formal and informal committees, ad hoc groups and special task forces to study and analyze particular information-related

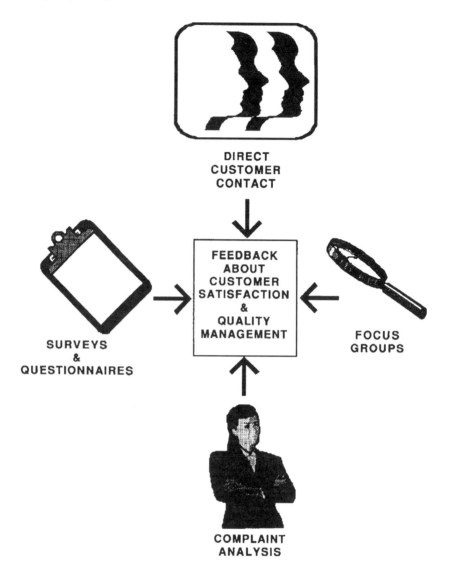

issues can also provide valuable feedback for the manager of an information services unit.

Direct customer contact

This feedback technique is found in two forms, the information transaction itself, and a direct follow-up immediately after the transaction has taken place, either before the customer leaves the information services department ('exit surveys') or with an immediate telephone call or e-mail query to the customer.

Using the information transaction itself as an immediate source of customer feedback is obviously a successful methodology in a single-staff situation (one-person librarians, for example, often comment that one of the things they like best about being solo is the opportunity it provides for immediate response about the quality of their work). In an information services operation with a larger staff, even of only five or six employees, most information practitioners have the opportunity to attempt to obtain feedback information, but without proper training and continual awareness-raising on the part of the department's manager the customer response effort can get bogged down in day-to-day work and in the fast turnaround often required in answering information queries.

Training is the best approach, and all staff should be given frequent opportunities to discuss their reference interview techniques and to build in the follow-up queries. It is not inappropriate for a departmental manager to conduct a series of one- or two-hour training courses in techniques for eliciting customer response, and certainly the many continuing education courses offered by professional associations and commercial training companies include customer feedback sections in their programs. Taking advantage of these learning opportunities proves worthwhile in any information setting.

Simply discussing the feedback process can also be useful. For example, in a staff meeting the departmental manager might lead off the discussion with an example of how he or she gained some typical feedback information at the end of a telephone conversation:

> Alan Simpson called to ask me to serve a term on the company's liability review committee. I accepted, but when I finished the call I commented that I hadn't seen him using the research library in a long time. He said that his assistant has found she doesn't much like coming to the library, and since she lives near the university, she goes to the Law School library to get the materials they need for his department. I was a little disappointed, and I thought we might talk about this today.

The meeting would then move to a conversation about the types of materials Alan Simpson's assistant might be seeking, whether they are available in the company's research library, whether there are barriers to her coming to the library ('Why doesn't she "much like" coming to the library?' it might be asked. 'Does anyone have any ideas?'), and whether Alan and his staff are, in fact, customers that the research library should be concerned about. After all, if their special information needs have to do with legal research, and the company's research library is not focused in that direction, perhaps they are better off to go to a law school library. On the other hand, if the mission of the research library is to serve all corporate customers, and if legal research is part of that mission, there is room for exploration and study in the fact that the legal staff are not using the research library.

A staff discussion can also be built around the employee's own sense of dissatisfaction at the outcome of an information interaction, even if formal customer feedback was not obtained. For example, the following paragraph might be distributed prior to a staff meeting, to encourage staff to discuss some awkwardness they might be feeling about their customer service approach:

> Can you describe a recent situation in which you felt you "failed" a customer who came to you for an information product or service? Why do you think you failed? What were the circumstances? Was the request a reasonable (or realistic) one? Could anyone else on the staff have responded differently (or better) than you responded?

Another useful technique that practically all information services managers practice is to spend time themselves in answering reference or research queries; certainly for the manager this is the most direct of any of the customer contact situations. Obviously the senior manager in a large information services unit is not going to be able to spend much time 'at the desk', as it were, simply because much of his time will be required for administrative and planning work. On the other hand, there is a coterie of information services workers who take great pride in spending an hour or two every other day or so working with the queries, and this, of course, provides ample direct customer feedback to those managers about the work being done.

One manager, in the information services department of a large New York bank, intentionally schedules herself to work with her reference services staff at least twice a week when she is in town (this manager also has international information services management responsibilities, so much of her time is spent in travel). She is not shy about what she learns from these occasions.

'I am the beneficiary of the action', she says. 'In fact, because the reference services staff is so much more skilled than I am in these matters, they end up being my teachers, so to speak (and so far they don't seem to mind!). Doing this gives me exposure to what's going on, and even if I don't become expert, permits me observe some of newer techniques that are coming along and, as important as anything else, clues me in on what people are asking.

'When I do this', she continues, 'one of the best results is the immediate customer response I get. Our customers seem to be surprised that I am answering the telephone or greeting them at the reference services desk. After all, this is a pretty big operation and my title – Vice-President for Global Information Services – is pretty off-putting! Nevertheless, once they hear me answer the telephone or meet me at the desk, the customers almost invariable want to talk with me about something more than what they came to the department for. It might be to tell me how good they think the staff is, or to detail a particular research request that was – or wasn't – properly handled. It might be a complaint, but more often it is a conversation about some of the subjects the customer is interested in and how we might fit into the work that the person is doing. It pays off, this being available first-hand to the customers. It pays off in spades. I just wish I had time to do it more often.'

Surveys and questionnaires

Using a formal survey instrument to determine customer satisfaction can be useful simply because it requires the respondent to take the time to express his or her interest in the workings of the department. Ideally, during the time the survey is being completed interviews are conducted with selected members of the organization or community, either one-to-one or in focus groups. When the surveys have been returned and the interviews completed, the results are then tabulated and interpreted in the light of departmental goals and, if the findings support a change in processes or procedures, recommendations about these changes can be made.

A cautionary note should be sounded about going overboard, however, for if customer satisfaction surveys become too routine their effectiveness will be weakened, as well as the level of participation. In some situations it is better to save the customer satisfaction surveys for 'special case' situations, so that there will be a level of seriousness connected with what is being measured. At Martin Marietta Energy Systems Inc., the team responsible for studying the customer satisfaction measuring system realized that too much of the same thing lessened the impact of the measure: team members 'unanimously agreed that an ongoing survey was repetitious and had a negative impact on the customer and on survey results'. To solve that problem, the Martin Marietta group moved to a two-part measure: 'biannual surveys of each measuring unit (specific service to be measured, e.g. online search service, document delivery service) would suffice and still provide a method of communicating satisfaction or dissatisfaction. Customer comment cards were designed to enlist customer feedback during the remainder of the year' (Schier 1990, p. 131).

In using questionnaires and other survey instruments to determine customer satisfaction, attention must be paid to the sensitivities of the information staff during the process. In some organizations a special committee or task force might be organized to review the returns and interpret the data, or another third party might be involved (an external consultant, say, or a management team). Care should be exercised to see that information staff are given every opportunity to understand the customer satisfaction evaluation procedure, and if necessary special training classes can be held to see that staff are so informed. For example, Schier reported that at her organization an independent third party is designated to receive the surveys and to prepare reports, which are then sent to the unit whose services are being measured for review and discussion (Schier 1990, pp. 133-134). Library and other information services managers who expect to use this or a similar process should recognize that this can be unsettling for some of the more insecure staff, who might think that the third party is meddling in the affairs of the unit, so caution is necessary.

Information services managers should bear in mind that there are several side benefits which contribute to the value of a customer satisfaction survey. First of all, during and following the survey the information services operation is perceived throughout the organization or community (particularly at the management level) as part of the enterprise-wide team, a management team concerned about the role of the information services department's work in relation to the organization or community as a whole.

Secondly, the customer satisfaction survey enables the unit to build good will, to raise awareness about the department and its products and services. One of the most frequent responses, particularly in the interviews, will be: 'Gosh! I didn't know you could do that for me'. Managers should be prepared. The department will find new customers and make new friends as the customer satisfaction survey is being conducted, and the unit's visibility will be significantly raised. People – customers and non-customers alike – will talk about the survey.

Finally, preparing for and conducting a customer satisfaction survey and the supplementary interviews provides a splendid opportunity for the manager of the department to review his or her own contribution to the organization or community. For many managers, the day-to-day activities, the routines that seem to occupy an inveterate amount of time, prevent them from looking at the larger picture. Not that they are disinclined to do this: this is not the case at all, and many managers would welcome the opportunity to think more about the information issues that affect them and their work, but they frankly don't have the time. A customer satisfaction survey (whether done by the information staff, by an in-house consultant, or by an external consultant hired specifically for the purpose) requires that the information services manager give attention to these matters, and in many cases enables him or her to reposition his or her role in the organization or community in such a way that his or her work is, in fact, more rewarding after the survey has been completed and the results incorporated into the work of the unit.

Focus groups and interviews

Whereas a questionnaire or other survey instrument will provide the hard statistics about customer satisfaction, the successful analysis of customer satisfaction data also requires impressionistic, subjective information which the information services staff can then analyze and interpret in order to make their own recommendations to link to the hard numbers. It is in the interview process that the information services manager gets the impressions and the subjective information that are needed.

As a first step the questionnaire is organized and distributed as previously described. At the same time, a certain amount of time and energy are set aside for the interviews. Or, if there is no time for the interviews to be conducted by internal staff, an external consultant is called in.

As the customer satisfaction study moves into the interview phase the information services manager must determine whether the interviews should be individual with specifically selected people or whether the process should include group interviews or, as they are popularly known, focus groups. This title is something of a misnomer, for a focus group is not exactly the same as a group interview, but it now seems to be common practice to refer to any group interview as a focus group.

Most successful customer satisfaction studies combine both types of interviews, depending of course on the circumstances of the organization in which the process is taking place. In some cases the departmental culture is such that a group interview would be disruptive, and in fact might bring forth more dissension than management wants to deal with. On the other hand, the employees of some departments work so well together (and the information services staff know this if they have worked with these people for any length of time) that a group interview would be very successful, and the people chosen for the group would be very open and supportive of the effort.

As for selecting the participants (whether for group interviews or for one-to-one meetings), the information services manager and his or her staff are the experts. No one else knows information usage patterns within the organization as well as they do, and no one else knows who does or does not use the information services department as well as they do, and this knowledge should be taken advantage of. The information services staff can be invited to prepare a list of people that they would like to speak with, and this list can be the basis for selecting interview participants.

Before the appointment for the interview is made, however, the manager should step back and take a look at the list. Are there any people who have been left out and who, for political reasons, should be included? Although many (if not most) senior management might not use the facility directly, shouldn't one or two of them be interviewed, just to get their views about their satisfaction with the department's activities? After all, they use information in one form or another in their work. Where do they get it? If it is not coming through the information services department, this needs to be recorded.

It is also smart to ask other management staff to suggest people to participate in the customer satisfaction process. And as part of the selection process, the questionnaire respondents be separated from the interview participants. Some managers would prefer that the interviews be conducted only with people who did not participate in the question-naire, but there is no time in the interview to ask the questions from the

The customer satisfaction study: suggested interview questions

These questions have been developed to provide impressionistic feedback about the satisfaction of information customers with the products, services and consultations they obtain through the information services department. Not all questions will be asked of all interviewees, and other questions will usually be developed as the interviews progress (especially if the interviews are group interviews or focus groups). The objective of the interview is to encourage the information customer to open up about his or her information use, and to provide substantive suggestions or comments about how the information the department is providing is (or could be) useful to him or her.

Briefly describe your job. What department do you work in, and what products and services are provided by your department?

How does your department relate to the organizational/corporate mission?

With regard to your specific role, what do you do and how do you use information in your work?

Describe briefly what you seek most in information products and services (things like quality, value, convenience, solutions to problems, cost, reliability, etc.).

How do the products and services you obtain through our department match these criteria to meet your needs?

How satisfied are you with the services of our department?

What do you like best about coming to us for your information?

Are there problems associated with your gathering information through our department? What are they? Be as specific as you can.

Where do you get information when you don't come to us?

In your opinion, does the company/organization/community need information products/services from our department?

Do you have any 'ideal' scenario regarding information services and products from our department? What 'ideal' information products or services do you wish existed?

survey as well as the interview questions, and the person conducting the interview runs the risk of wasting valuable time on the survey questions. So, interview participants should be encouraged to fill out the questionnaire before the interview. Not only does this ensure that they participate in the anonymous part of the study, but responding to the questionnaire sets them up to participate more fully in the interview process: they are prepared for the questions they will be asked.

The people conducting the interviews should adopt a businesslike manner in their approach: after the participants have been selected, they should be sent a memorandum giving them a brief idea of what the information services department is attempting to do with its customer satisfaction study, and requesting an interview (it should be pointed out that the interview is not expected to last more than 30 minutes). Several specific times might be suggested, but the total timeframe should not be limited to 30 minute blocks for they will undoubtedly find that for some participants 30 minutes is not enough and the interview schedule will run late. Rather than have that happen, it is best to schedule an hour for each interview. If the time isn't needed it can be used for other work, or for compiling notes from the previous interviews.

Complaints analysis

Certain basic questions must be addressed when the information services manager is considering how to establish a complaints analysis plan. First, how are complaints received in the department, and when they are received, how are they handled? What is the basic plan for dealing with complaints? Is there a plan?

If the answer to the last question is negative, this is the place to begin. Each information services unit should have a policy for dealing with complaints, and the policy should be published and distributed to every customer, either in an introductory package that is given to the customer when they first use the unit, or available to all customers when they use the facility.

Ideally, the wording in the complaints policy will be soft, not confrontational, and each staff member will conduct the business of the unit based on its commitment to follow the procedures as published. A complaints policy should have the following components:

1. A statement that a procedure for receiving complaints is in place (see sidebar for a sample policy).

2. Immediate response. A departmental procedure for handling complaints must be established, and the departmental workflow will include a time and place for dealing with complaints. The task may be assigned to one person, or it may be the responsibility of a team chosen because they have good interpersonal skills. In any case, no deviation from the 'immediate response' standard should be permitted. Any customer who is less than satisfied with the service he or she receives, and who has taken the trouble to complain, must be contacted immediately.

3.   Progress reports. If the problem cannot be solved immediately, a deadline for its solution is established and explained to the customer. If the deadline cannot be met, the customer is so informed.

4.   Each staff member should find a way to react positively. And privately. If the complaint is being made in person, the customer should be taken to an area where the discussion can be held without others hearing. If the complaint is made in writing or via e-mail, respond in the same way; or, if the response is by telephone, the conversation should be held in an office and not in the public area.

     Staff should be instructed to begin any response to a complaint by establishing empathy with the customer. Each staff member is instructed to put himself or herself in the customer's position, and no matter how irritated or angry the customer appears to be, to try to imagine how he or she would feel about the subject being discussed. Staff should be reminded to remember that most people are not as sophisticated as information services workers about information transfer, and many misconceptions and erroneous expectations can be expected to creep in to the customer's ideas.

     A negative reaction says to the customer that he or she is wrong (thus heightening the tension): 'You gave us an incorrect citation'.

     A detached reaction (or one which moves the blame away from the customer) neutralizes the encounter: 'This looks like it might be the wrong citation', or even, 'I think we might have misread the citation'.

5.   All staff should be instructed to eliminate the personal and avoid argument, regardless of the intensity of the moment. Whether we like to admit it or not, this is one of those moments where the customer is right, since any arguing or confrontation at this point would be counterproductive. If the situation appears to be getting unpleasant, the staff member should have a back-up position, either stating that he or she doesn't think he or she has the authority to handle the situation and then bringing in someone else, or explaining, very politely, that under the circumstances he or she cannot fix the problem and that it has a better chance of being fixed if the complaining customer will send his or her complaint, in writing, to the department's manager.

6.   Empathize. We are all human, and it's best to let the customer with the complaint know that the staff member understands what the situation is, has perhaps been in a similar situation herself, and that he or she will do whatever he or she can to see that action is taken quickly.

7.   Use the complaint. After the complaint has been responded to, every effort must be made to bring it to the attention of all staff members at the next staff meeting, to use it as a training case study or role-play scenario, and to ensure that a similar situation does not arise again.

More important than anything else, if the complaint can lead to a different way of providing information services, or if new and innovative procedures can be developed through studying and improving the situation that brought about the complaint, both management and staff should make every effort to see that new procedures are developed.

Committees, task forces, and project teams

When formal and informal committees, ad hoc groups and special task forces are organized to study and analyze particular information-related issues, they can play a valuable secondary role in providing important feedback for the manager of an information services unit. Whether or not there is a formal library committee, there are often opportunities when other members of the organization or community are brought in to advise on matters to do with information services. The manager of a library/records management unit in a large research institute, for example, might be in the final stages of selecting an external consultant to organize a process re-engineering project, and in order to ensure that all points of view are recognized, might put together a task force to work with him or her in the selection process. These four or five people are certainly going to participate in the work at hand, but as they do so they will get to know the manager and his or her staff, as well as one another, and they will be in a position to advise on the quality of the unit's services from their particular perspectives.

Of course, where there is a formal library or other information services advisory committee, the input is ongoing and can be very valuable to the manager of the unit. These people, on a regular basis, are in a position to let the information manager know what the organization or community is thinking about the quality of the information services, products and consultations delivered by the unit, and at the same time he or she can use them as an informal sounding board to go out into the organization or community to elicit responses about the unit and its operation. In either case, the committee begins to play a powerful role in helping the information services manager acquire the data he or she needs to know what the perceptions and expectations of the community are.

Effectiveness measures

Much of the emphasis in information services today is generated by a very reasonable interest on the part of senior management in understanding how resources invested in services are used, and what the benefits of those investments are. Of course management requires quantitative data, as has been discussed, and the number of database searches conducted,

Handling Complaints: A Sample Complaints Policy

To our customers and patrons:

Thank you for using the Spring Analysis Corporate Library and Records Services Department. We take our work very seriously, and we pride ourselves on the professional expertise we have in providing you with the information products, services and consultations you need for your work. We want you to understand what our role is, and we particularly invite you to let us know if we are not helping you in the manner you expect.

For the record, the mission statement for the Spring Analysis Corporate Library and Records Services Department is as follows:

The Spring Analysis Corporate Library and Records Services Department is a part of the Spring Analysis Company's Corporate Services Division. Its mission is to provide the scientists and engineers and other staff of the company with the information they require for conducting SAC business. The staff of the Spring Analysis Corporate Library and Records Services Department will search for and deliver external and internal information as required, using the expertise of the department's professional and support information services staff. All information transactions are conducted privately, and all information obtained is delivered to the requesting employee in strict confidence.

The Spring Analysis Corporate Library and Records Services Department has established procedures for ensuring customer satisfaction. Among these is the following complaints procedure. If you ask the Library and Records Service for information and do not obtain the information you require for your work, you are encouraged to refer to the following:

A procedure for receiving complaints is in place. All Library and Records Services staff are trained to deal with these in person, but if you prefer you may write to us with your complaint. Please address your comments to Marjory Livingston, Library and Records Services Chief. She can be reached at MS 496-LRS, or at her e-mail address (mliv-int@sac.com).

In all situations, including on-the-spot complaints, a written report will be made so that the complaint and the response to the complaint will not 'slip between the cracks'.

If you prefer, you may use one of the SAC Library and Records Services Customer Response Cards for your complaint. These are located throughout the 14th floor. The card will be treated exactly as any other complaint format would be treated.

If you wish, you may simply discuss the situation with a staff
member, who will bring it to the attention of the proper authority
within the department and will file a written report describing the
situation. Your concern will be attended to.

the amount of money spent on the acquisition of materials, on document
delivery and the like are all valuable data to be incorporated with all the
other quantitative data that describe the effectiveness and efficiency of
the organization in achieving its established mission. Nevertheless, with
respect to information services there is also a great interest in knowing
how the information products, services and consultations are used.
Although information services managers are quite good at describing the
efficiency of their department, the effectiveness of that department with
respect to organizational success is not so readily apparent. Yet that is
what management, particularly in the specialist libraries community,
wants to know:

- What is the *effect* of having this information services operation onsite?

- What is the *effect* of the information services, products and consultations emanating from this information services unit?

The term 'effectiveness measures' is beginning to be used more and
more in information services management and, as mentioned earlier,
Griffiths and King use the term in their work and offer examples of
effectiveness measures such as amount of use ('the more a center or its
services are used the more effective it is', Griffiths and King 1991, p. 17),
users' perceptions of services, and user expressed satisfaction, as discussed earlier.

Certainly these measures make sense, but the information services
manager must look further at the consequences of use, to think about how
the information benefits the customers, and to determine whether these
are mission-critical services that are being provided.

The difficulty comes, of course, in establishing any sort of meaningful
effectiveness measurement standards, for no one has yet come up with
a formula that can tell us what we need to know about how useful our
services are. In the medical libraries community efforts are being made
in this direction, and some hospitals are now able to establish what
might be called 'quasi-effectiveness' measures, but for most information
delivery operations establishing effectiveness measures seems a long way
off.

It is not difficult to understand why, with respect to information
services, most effectiveness descriptions must of necessity be anecdotal.

Since each information customer comes in with his or her own unique query, and since the analysis of that query in the information interview, together with the decision about strategies for procuring the information, are all individualized and unique steps in the information delivery process, it is practically impossible to establish a standardized measurement that will determine whether a service, product or consultation has been effective or not.

For example, many people come into or contact a corporate library with a request for some piece of fast-turnaround, 'ready-reference' information. This is delivered to them, and as far as the information provider is concerned that is the end of the transaction. Would it be appropriate for the information unit to approach that customer and ask how the information was used, whether it was what he or she required, or whether it enabled him or her to achieve the desired effect he or she was seeking to achieve? In such a situation the effort to collect the data would take far more time than had been required for the original enquiry, and most information services manager's would decide that gathering such data would not be worth the effort.

On the other hand, it might be worth developing a system for analyzing higher-level queries, those that require the information services worker to spend some time in research, or perhaps to discuss the query with others in the unit, in order to provide the highest quality service for that particular enquiry. With this level of query, the unit could then establish a follow-up mechanism so that the effectiveness of the information delivery could be determined. It would, of course, still be limited to an anecdotal response, and a system of codification would have to be established so that the data could be studied in such a way that they would have some meaning, but this would be at least a step in the direction of effectiveness measures.

References

Duston, Beth. 'IT in the OPL: the fugitive user.' *The One-Person Library: A Newsletter for Librarians and Management* 10 (2), June, 1993.

Carson, Paula Phillips, Carson, Keory David and Phillips, Joyce Schouest. *The Library Manager's Deskbook: 102 Expert Solutions to 101 Common Dilemmas*. Chicago, IL: American Library Association, 1995.

Griffiths, José-Marie and King, Donald, W. 'A manual on the evaluation of information centers and services' New York, N.Y.: American Institute of Aeronautics and Astronauts, 1991.

Schier, Lois M. 'Customer satisfaction surveys: measuring satisfaction and communication service in special libraries.' *The Information Professional: An Unparalleled Resource: Papers Contributed for the 81st Annual Conference of the Special Libraries Association, June 9-14, 1990, Pittsburgh, PA*. Washington DC: Special Libraries Association, 1990.

White, Marilyn Domas and Abels, Eileen G. 'Measuring service quality in special libraries: lessons from service marketing.' *Special Libraries* 86 (1), Winter, 1995.

Chapter Eight

The information services manager's role in building trust and teamwork

In information services management the establishment of a quality environment is obviously an appropriate step in the movement toward improved information delivery. Every information services manager who considers total quality management is quite comfortable with seeking ways to give more attention to continuous improvement, and adequate and results-oriented measurement, in one form or another, is an objective that library and information services managers have pursued for as long as anyone can remember. There is certainly a desire for quality, and the benefits of enthusiastic support from senior management are not to be dismissed lightly. And a recognition of the authority of the customer is, as all agree, the critical element underpinning the quality perspective.

If this is so, if an intense focus on customer service is the essence of total quality management in the information environment, then surely the route to achieving customer focus is the establishment of a workplace culture built on trust and teamwork. These are concepts and words that are frequently overused in our society, but the successful information services manager must be prepared to cut through the overuse and to accept, without cynicism and with the full knowledge of the importance of the notion, that it is the human relationship that makes any endeavor succeed.

This assertion is no less true in the management of information services than in any other discipline or activity. Indeed, if we are going to put forward a vision of information services management that is structured around and emphasizes quality service delivery, we must understand and take advantage of the empowering role that trust and teamwork bring to the information workplace. TQM is a management philosophy that brings much good to the workplace, but its successful application in an information environment is dependent on the full and frank acknowledgement that the TQM effort is meaningless if it does not recognize and build on the human side of organizational management.

In information services, TQM will succeed if the effort concentrates less on the TQM *process* and more on the analysis of workplace behavior, on the identification and analysis of the processes involved in the successful completion of information-related (and mission-critical) tasks, and on workplace outcome, outcome that is judged by and designed for the information customer. The role of human relationships in the workplace, particularly in the information environment, must not be underestimated or overemphasized, and as it is now clearly established that no single TQM formula is going to be applicable in every information services workplace, so it must follow that the elements of those TQM efforts that are going to succeed must be built on and recognize the validity of trust and teamwork.

This idea has, in various forms, been fundamental to the TQM scheme from the very beginning. Certainly Deming's 14-point plan includes serious allusions to the value of trust and teamwork (particularly in the points recommending that managers institute training on the job, that they adopt and institute leadership, and that they make every effort to 'drive out fear, so that everyone may work effectively for the company'). The manager who is attempting to instill a quality perspective into the information services unit does the organization, the information unit itself, and most assuredly the information customers, a serious disservice if the effort is attempted and the human side of TQM is ignored. The merit of trust and teamwork is so important that the formation of 'new work relationships' (as Michael Barrier has described them) based on trust and teamwork is now recognized as an essential element in the move toward a TQM-focused workplace. 'Central to TQM', Barrier writes, 'is empowerment, through which management gives employees wide latitude in how they go about achieving the company's goals' (Barrier 1992, p. 23).

How the building of these new work relationships can be realized is, of course, the purview of the information services manager. With the certainty that the effort will provide measurable benefits for the information unit, the discerning information services manager takes steps to move towards a specific workplace and organizational culture that recognizes the value of 'people' skills and relationships. The new culture recognizes the role of employee empowerment in effective information services delivery, and the importance of teamwork and team building is a distinctive characteristic of the workplace. At the same time, the culture builds on and expects ethical workplace behavior on the part of all those who are part of the information services picture.

Employee empowerment

In championing TQM as the 'expert solution' to library management problems, Carson, Carson and Phillips, like Michael Barrier, move strongly in the direction of employee empowerment: 'TQM programs in library organizations', they write, 'are based on three major principles: patron focus, process improvement, and employee empowerment', and this last involves, on management's part, 'efforts to utilize the talents of all staff members in the library' (Carson, Carson and Phillips 1995, p. 171). Employee empowerment is very much a fine art, for it involves a willingness on the part of managers and supervisors to 'let go', to allow a subordinate to exercise judgment and participate in the decision-making process that, for many, is the very reason they want to be managers and supervisors. These managers must learn to accept that, when they permit employees to be empowered, they are not giving up power themselves but positioning the newly empowered employees to commit to departmental success and to assume a cooperative role in the achievement of that success, a commitment which they themselves have presumably already made.

Also contributing to the delicacy of employee empowerment is the recognition that, when the empowered employees are given 'permission' to make decisions, these will often be made under conditions that are not necessarily conducive to thoughtful, well-organized decision making. When a hurrying executive, for example, insists to the front-desk clerk in the financial firm's library that he or she must take the reference book to his or her office and goes out the door with it, the clerk, not an information 'professional' per se, and not 'authorized' to make decisions about exceptions to the library's rules about the use of reference materials outside the library, finds himself or herself in an awkward and unsettling position. Yet he or she would be foolish indeed if he or she were to attempt to prevent the executive from going through the door. For the clerk to be empowered to bend the rules, to work within the library's structured organizational framework yet still provide services that acknowledge the customer's individual needs, recognizes that the employee's talents are a valuable asset that contribute to everyone's benefit.

Further complicating the employee empowerment picture, however, is the very natural resistance on the part of the information employee to being given such decision-making responsibility. Many employees who work in information services departments (file clerks in a records management unit, for example, or student assistants at the circulation desk in a university library) are simply not paid enough and/or have not had training in organizational behavior and customer service to succeed in that environment. To authorize them to take on such responsibility, or to position them so that they must assume it, is often perceived by the employees as being unfair. If they had wanted that responsibility, they will argue, they would have sought training and jobs at a higher level in the organization.

Finally, however, there is the certain disruption and unease that results when the lines of authority in an organization or a department are

EMPOWERING EMPLOYEES

**BUILD
CONFIDENCE**

**ESTABLISH
ACCOUNTABILITY &
RESPONSIBILITY**

**CREATE
TEAMS**

**RECRUIT FOR
CUSTOMER
CARE**

loosened. Training can be provided, and staff members can be taught the importance of having an empowered role in the delivery of information, but if the managerial structure becomes so loose that no one knows who is in charge (a frequent complaint in these circumstances), the problems soon begin to outweigh the benefits, and unless the manager of the unit is particularly skilled at getting ideas and directions back on track, the empowering initiative slips into oblivion.

It is thus not an easy task for information services managers to empower their employees. While they and the employees might make approving noises about the possible benefits of the effort, when reality clicks in and they are confronted with the necessity of giving up some of their own power (or to share it), or when staff members are forced to make decisions under the wrong conditions, or don't want to be 'involved', or when staff feel that the lines of authority are being compromised, the pleasures of employee empowerment begin to look less promising.

Employee confidence

The best way to establish an empowered ambience is to build employee confidence. In the situations described above there are specific procedures that information services managers can take without running the risk of having the empowerment effort fail. (The first situation is obviously the exception, for in that case it is the manager and not the employee who must find confidence.) For example, there is no better way to instill confidence than to let employees know that while power is being delegated to them, management will see to it that they have the proper training to understand their empowered roles and to learn how to use their newly acquired power. Open communication is the key here, and it is important that the employee understand that the rules of library organization are not necessarily there to prevent information customers from receiving the services they come to the library for. The desk clerk who is the only employee on duty when the executive announces that he or she is taking the reference book to his or her office, will have been trained to understand why the 'no-reference-books-out-of-the-library' rule came into existence, but also to understand that in a presumably uncrowded library there is not a high probability that anyone else is going to be needing the book. In his or her training he or she will be taught that certainly he or she is not to encourage library customers to take reference books away, but when one is taken away he or she is to make a note of the loan and leave it on his or her manager's desk so that the executive can be called the next morning if the book has not been returned.

Role modeling can play an important part in employee training, for if they learn that their own manager allows him or herself to soften the rules with certain customers, they will soon understand why the rules exist and how they can be relaxed so that customers get the services that they need. They will also learn that it is imperative that the borrowing employee be telephoned early the next day, to be informed that if the book is not returned, the borrower's day is likely to be interrupted when the library has to send another customer to their office to use it (and hopefully retrieve it for the library). What the information services manager is doing, of course, is training the employee in a positive and understanding atmosphere about the library's quality goals, to see that the customers get the services they need while at the same time establishing staff relationships that recognize the talents of the staff members and encourage them to interact in a positive manner with the customers. It is an information services operation that is organized around a 'pattern of reasonableness' which respects not only the rights and wishes of the customer those of but the employees as well.

Success in employee empowerment builds on the basics of performance evaluation, in which the expectations of the manager are clearly outlined from the beginning. In the first interview, the workplace is described and the employee is told that he or she has decision-making authority in customer-related situations, or in planning departmental improvements, or in whatever area the manager has established as appropriate for employee participation, with those situations clearly explained and the employee's role in the process identified. The employee is told what the minimum expectations are, and at the same time it is agreed that the employee will be compensated in some manner above the regular or advertised compensation for the job, to emphasize that his or her participation is valued. Again, open communication is the key, for the manager must make clear that the employee's participation is not only expected but valued, and the expectations must be clearly spelt out. The employee and the manager come to an agreement, and the employee is then given the opportunity to participate and to be an empowered member of the departmental staff.

The fear that empowerment contributes to workplace disruption, with 'no-one in charge', is unfounded, for most employees in a library or other information services operation will welcome the opportunity to play a more participative role in its management and in seeing that the departmental objectives are achieved. The information services manager, however, must work hard to ensure that all employees are trained for this participation, that they do not find themselves in a situation for which they are unprepared. Certainly working with staff in setting goals, making decisions and solving problems is the best kind of staff training the manager can offer, but there must also be formally organized training programs. When they have been so trained, taught to set realistic goals and given encouragement about their ability to handle the situations that come up, their confidence will grow and their willingness to participate increase.

Nevertheless, empowerment goes beyond simply training employees to participate: it should also involve real participation built on a workplace attitude that draws on improved attitudes on the part of the employees and an increased desire to be empowered. Staff members do their best when they understand the environment to be one in which reasonable standards of behavior are applied, by both the customers and the staff, and one in which their interests are taken seriously by the management. For example, in a small research facility, a non-graduate staff member serving in a paraprofessional position might show particular promise in an area generally reserved for the professionals, and be invited to undertake training in searching one or more of the database services to which the library subscribes. While giving this kind of work to a non-professional might seem to imply that the work of the professionals is being compromised, if there is enough work and if that employee's contribution makes the overall departmental workflow move more smoothly, why shouldn't that employee be trained and do that work? However, both the professional staff and the about-to-be empowered employee need to understand that this is a change in the usual situation which is being undertaken for a purpose, and that benefits will be realized throughout the department because of it.

The most common employee empowerment circumstance in most information services units continues to be dealing with customers who are disappointed in the service, a situation that has been referred to by Carson, Carson and Phillips: 'Action taken to alter the negative feeling of a patron is called "service recovery." The empowered employees in a TQM environment should have the authority and power to take immediate action to solve a problem or compensate the patron for an inconvenience. . . . Patrons want performance, not just polite sympathy. Therefore, staff members must be empowered to take service recovery action. For service recovery to be effective, library staffers must be able to "right a wrong" as soon after it occurs as possible' (Carson, Carson and Phillips 1995, p. 183). In other information services operations the circumstances are equally serious. In the records management department of a company that manufactures small household appliances, for example, the staff who deal with corporate records are specialists in that work, while the files pertaining to product research and development are organized and filed by a different group of employees, who have been trained in working with their particular materials. Because of the light volume of requests for records retrieval in the late afternoon, only one staff member is required to handle the reception desk and retrieve materials. While the two types of materials are quite different and are organized and stored according to different criteria, there are occasions when a customer returns to the desk with records with which he or she was provided on an earlier occasion, and which were not the records he or she was seeking. Prior to a departmental reorganization, if the customer returned material that was from the corporate records files and what he or she needed was from R&D files, he or she could make an 'even exchange' only if the staff member on duty was one who worked with corporate records, and vice versa. Otherwise, he or she would be told that the R&D files were not available until an R&D records staff member was available, which in most cases would be the next morning. When the departmental manager discovered the difficulty that this arrangement caused for the information customers, he or she set up a training program so that all retrieval clerks could be taught to retrieve materials from either collection. At first, staff resisted because the filing systems were different and they were concerned that they would be held responsible if materials being returned were refiled incorrectly. However, once they were assured that their role was limited to retrieving the materials and passing them on to the customers, and that when they were returned they would be refiled by the appropriate filing clerks, staff were willing to participate in the program and customer service improved dramatically.

Accountability and responsibility

The other side of employee empowerment, particularly from the managerial and organizational point of view, concerns the employee's accepting responsibility for his or her actions. Here again, building employee confidence through training and open communication, particularly in terms of management support, and the establishment of clear guidelines and expectations, will go far in positioning the employee for exceptional performance. In seeking to move to a total quality management environment, the information services manager makes a commitment to bring his or her entire staff into the quality picture, and in fulfilling that commitment, to encourage participation and full and frank discussion. To this end, the value of accountability and responsibility is recognized and is incorporated into the relationship between the information services manager and all staff in the department.

The process begins in the initial interview and continues throughout the training the employee receives in how to perform the duties to which he or she is to be assigned. In the interview, the information service manager emphasizes that the environment in the department is heavily focused on TQM, with the delivery of information built around the requirements of the customer and an open and honest attempt to seek continuous improvement in all steps in the information delivery transaction. The point is made that from the customer's first approach to the enquiry desk, until the information transaction has been concluded and the customer has been invited to comment on how well the information product, service or consultation met his or her expectation, the emphasis is on finding exactly what the customer is seeking. When appropriate, the manager will describe how the department makes follow-up surveys to determine how useful the information interaction has been for the customer and how it would affect the work or other activity for which he or she had sought the information.

To reinforce the message, it must be emphasized that each employee is responsible for the work that he or she does, and that all employees must exert all reasonable effort to see that their performance matches customer expectations or, if the customer's expectations are not realistic or appropriate, that all reasonable effort is made to assist him or her in determining how the required information might be obtained through another avenue.

With respect to accountability and responsibility, employee confidence is also built through open communication and through cooperation between the employee and other staff members in the department. Clear guidelines and expectations are required, and at each stage of the interview and training process (and as part of the departmental culture) employees are encouraged to ask questions, to enquire as to whether their understanding of the guidelines is correct, whether their role in the information transaction has been described clearly enough, and whether they need further information before they can proceed. Two effective procedures which do much to strengthen employee confidence in terms of their accountability and responsibility are participation in team-based information transactions (described below) and the assignment of departmental mentors. In the latter, each new employee is introduced to a designated fellow employee who will 'show him or her the ropes' and work with him or her in learning the departmental culture, with special emphasis on TQM. This employee, either through his or her own experience in the organization of the TQM program or through his or her own training, will be chosen because of enthusiasm for and commitment to the program, and also because, with his or her understanding of the types of information transactions that take place, he or she is in a position to bring the new employee into the program at a level that permits him or her to share this enthusiasm and commitment.

Finally, the strongest influence is that engendered through management support, as exemplified in the relationship that grows up between the employee and the information services manager as tasks are completed and new tasks assigned. Not only does the manager take his or her supervisory role seriously, he or she too takes on a mentoring role and sees to it that the employee is given complete and clear instructions, that he or she understands what is expected as far as performance is concerned, and that he or she understands that he or she is expected to perform in a manner that fits into the departmental quality tone.

Teams and teamwork

When a quality application stumbles it is invariably because the new work relationships based on trust and teamwork just did not get off the ground. There is something about the library/information services workplace that is uncomfortable with the concept of teams and teamwork, and while information managers work hard to develop an ambience that lends itself to using teams to move the information delivery process forward, the barriers – from both staff and management, as well as from customers – can be formidable. The information services manager should look to the information environment itself to determine why these barriers are put forward, so that they can be removed.

Resistance to teams and teamwork is not unusual in many work situations, but with respect to information services it most likely grows from the information-gathering act itself, which is usually private, involving a one-to-one interaction between the customer and the information provider. Customers understand the seeking of information as a private pursuit, and certainly many information services practitioners regard the discipline the same way. As a result, an information-gathering culture builds up around this arrangement, and the use of teams is not perceived as fitting with the culture.

At the same time, staff members in information services units see themselves as professionals or at least in some way different in that they are dealing with a commodity (information) and the products, services and consultations relating to that commodity are unlike anything else dealt with in the organization or community. Consequently, these staff members see themselves as having little in common with information customers and others in the organization. Because of this they discount the need for consultation and interaction when they proceed to do their work.

Within the organization, information services managers are often isolated from other managers because the information management function is often regarded as a standalone function, not particularly pertinent to the work of the organization. Thus, when team participation is considered, whether within the organization at large or in the information services unit itself, the fact that information employees are not automatically considered for membership in enterprise-wide team activities takes them out of the picture, and reinforces the idea that team participation offers no special benefits for the information services manager or his or her staff.

Despite this lack of a teamwork tradition, in information services, the advantages of the team approach, particularly in terms of quality management, are clearly evident and should encourage every information services manager to make some effort to establish teams and team performance in their units. There is no dearth of reasons why teams are good for an organization, and Deborah Harrington-Mackin has identified what some of the key benefits are. Teams lead, she writes, to a more highly motivated environment and a better work climate and – the goal of all information services managers – to shared ownership and responsibility. According to Harrington-Mackin, teams enable a faster response to technological change, require fewer, simpler job classifications, provide a better response to the less formal values of a younger generation of employees, and provide for the effective delegation of workload and an increased flexibility in task assignments. Teams assure a common commitment to goals and values, they encourage complete buy-in by all partners in the team, and they encourage a proactive approach to problems, leading to innovative and effective problem solving and improved self-worth. According to Harrington-Mackin, teams provide for increased communication (thus leading to better decisions) and skill development in staff, they offer the opportunity for cross-training in roles and responsibilities, and they provide an early warning system for problems (Harrington-Mackin 1994, p. 2).

In an information services environment, the advantages of a team approach are quickly evident. Using the benefits that Harrington-Mackin identified, it is easy to see how a quality focus is insinuated into the workings of a specialist library in a research institute whose scientists are oceanographers and marine biologists. If the library has a staff of five (a departmental manager, two qualified professional librarians and two paraprofessionals) and the manager has established a team approach to both management and the delivery of information, there is by definition a more highly motivated environment and a better work climate simply because all employees understand that their opinions are valued and that their understanding of the workings of the department will be put to good use. By establishing management teams, partnerships and a buddy system, the manager has given each employee shared ownership and responsibility with respect to management issues. For example, as the time for the departmental annual report draws near, each staff member is assigned a section of the report to develop, according to his or her particular job emphasis and identified skills. As the staff members work together to produce the several sections of the report, they confer with one another and plan strategies for the best ways to present the information, and each feels that the final report pertains specifically to the work that he or she does.

According to Harrington-Mackin, teams enable a faster response to technological change, a situation for which an information services operation is certainly a case in point. With respect to information services, however, the team focus goes beyond any particular information unit itself and moves into the organization at large, as the current move in many organizations and enterprises toward the integration of information demonstrates. In the example mentioned here, the oceanographic institute might very well have three or four units with information delivery responsibility, and the forming of teams to integrate their work and to provide a centralized information services operation will naturally require representatives from each of the departments involved. No such endeavor should ever be undertaken without this, and the involvement of employees from each unit in the very first feasibility study is essential to long-term success.

There are other benefits to the team approach. If staff are going to be working together in management and information delivery teams, Harrington-Mackin suggests that fewer job classifications will be required and they will be simpler, because much of the generalist language of the classifications will overlap. As to whether teams provide a better response to the less formal values of a younger generation of employees, the benefits of this can be seen in the way information services staff, when not required to do so, are interested in working in an environment in which cross-disciplinary tasks and customer contact are encouraged. In this environment, staff work together in determining how the workload is to be delegated and, as part of the quality perspective, they are in a position to not only spend time working with one another analyzing and determining the information-seeking strategy to be employed before they begin working on a complicated query or research request, but they can also work together in evaluating and analyzing customer feedback after the information has been delivered. Because all members of the team are working toward common goals (whether in terms of management or information delivery), the team approach, as Harrington-Mackin notes, encourages complete buy-in by all partners in the team, all of whom then have an interest in the success of the activity. Because of the small number of players involved in the team approach at the oceanographic institute, innovative problem solving becomes the order of the day, leading to an exciting and entrepreneurial management approach for all activities relating to information services.

It should nevertheless be recognized that, depending on the organizational environment and culture, there can be disadvantages to the team approach to information services. For example, as with any quality effort, the amount of time and resources that must be devoted just to establishing a program for a team approach can be daunting: team assignments must be made and agreed to, meeting times and venues must be scheduled, agendas prepared and approved, meetings and discussions held and strategy agreements reached, all before the actual work of the team can begin. For example, in the oceanographic institute that serves as the example here, if a team approach is applied in providing a group of marine biologists with the information consultations and materials it is seeking for a particular project, the research team must schedule a meeting, prepare the agenda, hold the meeting, discuss the scope of the project, identify some of the materials that might be germane to the project, and assign one or more team members to consult with the scientists to begin the research. During the course of the project, the team members must identify materials, analyze them for their appropriateness for the project, provide some level of interpretation (if that has been agreed upon as part of the process), deliver the materials, engage in further consultations, and meet with the scientists to determine the effectiveness of the materials used. Thus it becomes clear that there is no question but that time will be required, in the information delivery process, and the expenditure of time (and other resources) must be weighed against the benefits to be accrued to the institute through the participation of the information delivery team. For some projects (especially smaller ones) an individual rather than a team approach is a more workable procedure, but when the team approach can be applied it provides the benefits described above.

Recruiting and training for customer care

When information services managers discuss quality management and seek to link total quality management to the competencies required for employment in an information services environment, the customer service skills of current and potential employees are often overlooked. Yet these are the very skills which can determine, from the customers' perspective, whether the information unit is functioning successfully or not.

Part of the problem, of course, is simply one of awareness. Customer service concepts are expected to be so much a part of daily life in the service sector (especially in western countries, or those whose cultures were developed with European influences) that most managers and employees do not see any real need for discussing them. Yet in most cases, because good customer service is *expected*, the basic concepts of good customer service are recognized more in the breach than in the observance. So we have a conundrum: employees need to understand the importance of good customer service and practice its values in the workplace, and at the same time no attention is paid to customer service values because we all assume that everyone knows what good customer service is.

In the information services environment the solution is to embark on a formalized and structured plan to emphasize customer service in the workplace, and 'emphasize' is the key word here. Any manager with information delivery responsibility will tell you, in no uncertain terms, that the pressures they and their staffs are under just to provide the information prevents them from taking on additional responsibilities for emphasizing a part of the service function that the employees should know already. But customer service emphasis is as much a part of the overall information delivery picture as other basic skills, such as communication skills, computer skills, or even literacy skills. Certainly in most industries and disciplines, acceptable standards of performance and certain competencies are expected in these areas, so why not in the area of customer service?

To be fair, more attention is beginning to be paid in certain subsets of information services. For example, in one large specialist library serving the business community of a large metropolitan area, as the library was created specific attention was given to customer service skills, and applicants for jobs were expected to have proven customer service experience. Once hired, all staff were required to attend a minimum of two days' formal customer service training. Customer service, in this particular information environment, is not an option, and customer service standards and expectations are built into the information delivery *and* employment picture.

To actively incorporate a customer service focus into the information services picture, then, an emphasis on customer service standards must be incorporated into the recruitment and training procedures. Four factors drive the effort: job analysis, hiring for customer service experience, actively seeking customer service skills, and training and continuing education.

Job analysis

Early on, the question must be asked: Where does customer service fit into the job descriptions of the employees who work in the information services unit? In preparing or reviewing job descriptions of information employees, a customer service requirement must be written in. Whether or not the descriptions are for the positions of frontline employees, where the customers have their first interaction with the information facility, or for other employees, is irrelevant. All employees in the department are responsible for the effective and efficient delivery of information products, services and consultations that meet the information customers' specifically identified requirements, and all employees should be covered under the customer service 'insurance policy'. A sample line in a job description might read: 'Employees who have this position are expected to have demonstrated successful customer service skills in previous positions, and they are required to maintain a high level of excellence in dealing with departmental customers, however defined. Specific customer service standards are in place for this position and will be used to establish the success of the employee serving in this position'. Specific customer service standards and/or competencies can then be written into the job descriptions. Obviously, different standards will be developed for different specific positions, but the primary result is that a general expectation of customer service excellence will now be included in staff job descriptions, and an emphasis on customer service is part of the department's management.

Actively seeking customer service skills

Advertisements for jobs in the information services department should include a customer service requirement in the basic requirements for employment. Candidates for these positions are expected to address their customer service experience, and should be informed that they will be expected to provide evidence of successful customer service experience, either by themselves or through their references.

It should be noted that many job applicants will initially be uncomfortable with being asked to state their experience in customer service, and some of them will find themselves unable to respond very well. So managers and others interviewing these applicants will want to exercise caution as they 'ease in' to a discussion of customer service in the interview.

The raised awareness of the value of customer service in the information facility will bring to the staff's attention the need for including what might be called customer-service attributes in the information workplace. As these attributes become part of the expected employment framework, the information services manager finds himself or herself including them into their thinking, and employees will be expected to have the following customer service characteristics well in hand:

- Empathy and patience;
- Willingness to take on the customer's problem;

- Poise, confidence and a general feeling of being comfortable with customer service standards;

- Decisiveness and independent judgment, and a willingness to follow up about an information product, service or consultation that has been delivered;

- Energy, alertness, and grace under pressure;

- A true interest in providing the customer with what he or she is seeking – the traditional service frame of mind of information services practitioners.

Unfortunately, current professional standards and competencies in information services do not address customer service. Even in those diciplines where there is an examination or certification procedure the emphasis is, of course, on information-related competencies. The needs of the information customer are hardly addressed, and where attention is given to the user, patron etc., the emphasis is rightly on supplying them with the information product, service or consultation they came to the information unit for. If there is any mention of how the customer is to be dealt with, some lip service is provided but no formal recognition or competency is expected. In information delivery disciplines in which no certification, licensing or other formal requirement for meeting standards exists, no attention is given to customer service standards. This may change, however, for leaders in some professional associations are uncomfortable with their organizations' lack of concern in this area, and there have been attempts to incorporate at least a modicum of attention to customer service standards into programs of professional standards (*cf.* The Special Libraries Association's PREPS Commission Report 1992, pp. 10–12).

In the hiring process the information services manager can determine a candidate's appropriateness for a position by asking several specific questions, and these questions might also be used in staff meetings and in other interactions with current staff (as in preparations for performance evaluation):

1. How do you build a good working relationship with customers you come in contact with? Be as specific as you can, and feel free to give examples.

2. What work situations have required (or currently require) special tact and patience in terms of customer service?

3. What are some of the problems you have dealt with (or are currently dealing with) in working with customers?

4. How have you handled these problems? Again, feel free to be as specific as you can, and give examples if you wish.

The trust/integrity relationship

An information services operation builds trust by establishing an ambience in which customers and staff can interact productively with one another, and it is important that customers understand that staff members take the authority of the customer seriously. However, it is also important that the manager of the information services unit extends the concept of the customer to include all information stakeholders, so that the staff all understand that the 'trusting workplace' is not someone else's responsibility. What is happening, of course, is that with the TQM focus the customer/provider relationship not only becomes more stable and more productive (i.e. a *better* relationship), but the perceptions that others have of the relationships between the information delivery unit and its customers begin to match the realities of the information delivery interactions. More than anything else, the TQM focus builds on the integrity of the relationship between the information provider and the information customer:

> Integrity deals with the issue of trust. A company must instill trust in its customers in order to survive. If the company lacks trust from its customers, it cannot expect to serve them efficiently. Furthermore, if TQM is truly a customer-focused approach to quality, companies must be conscious of the way they are perceived by their customers (Madu and Kuei 1995, p. 4).

In moving toward a TQM environment information services managers must never lose sight of the fact that they are building a trusting relationship on a foundation that relies on two very necessary elements, the recognition of the importance of ethical behavior on the part of all information stakeholders, and an understanding of the human side of information transfer.

The ethical information services manager

When we think about trust in the information services environment we must connect it with a consideration of the good of the whole, and we must recognize that ethical behavior is expected in the workplace, whether it is codified and regulated or whether it is intrinsic in the relationships between customers and staff.

In his important work on ethics in the business community, Paul Hodapp (1994) raises the question, 'What are reasonable ethical rules for the society in which we live?' It's not a new question, and Hodapp is quick to take the discussion back to Hobbesian theory (which moves it neatly into the realm of free market economy, where most of western business practices originate). 'How is it possible', Hodapp (and Hobbes) asks, 'to have ethical rules in a society of persons who are primarily self-interested?'

In both business and the information services operations that support business this is the crux. The conventional wisdom is that business is concerned solely with profit, and that all other interests are subsumed to that interest. Hodapp plays with this in a manner that is compelling and at the same time provocative, for he describes the tension created in today's society by opposing moral viewpoints, one in which the businessperson must always 'choose between business and ethics' and the other in which 'the task of ethics is to discover and justify the appropriate principles of commercial society'.

Hodapp, along with many others, believes that today's society is grappling with the latter. Much work in this area was undertaken by the Special Libraries Association's PREPS Commission in 1991–1993. Although this work was specifically focused on specialist librarianship, its conclusions can be applied to nearly all information services operations, even those (such as medical librarians, for example) who already have an ethical structure and a professional code of ethics. In fact, the 'Statement of Professional Conduct' which the PREPS Commission recommended to the Special Libraries Association can quite comfortably be adapted by all workers in the information services, and is quoted here to provide a model to stimulate thinking about these matters for all information professionals:

> Members of the Special Libraries Association are employed in libraries and information centers which are integral parts of other organizations. As such, they are bound by their parent organizations' codes of ethics or other such statements with regard to appropriate professional conduct.
>
> Nevertheless, there are areas of conduct specific to the management of a special library or information center and the provision of information for that library/information center's defined user group which are appropriate for members as part of their affiliation with the Special Libraries Association. These areas require compliance with laws currently in force and include such professional components as competence, continuing education, confidentiality, self-protection, comprehensiveness, honesty, and reliability.
>
> Therefore, members of the Special Libraries Association agree to be bound by the following obligations of professional conduct:
>
> - To provide constituent users, as defined by the employer/organization, with the most current, accurate, and relevant information, regardless of personal beliefs or the possible uses to which the information might be put.
>
> - To protect the confidentiality and privacy of individuals requesting information.
>
> - To select and organize information resources responsibly to support highest quality information services for the organization, consistent with the mission of the organization.

- To avoid misrepresentation of the purpose for gathering information or the use to which it will be put, in order to gain information which might otherwise be withheld.

- To uphold and actively advise others to uphold all laws governing the creation, reproduction, and dissemination of information.

- To maintain high standards of personal professional competence in information services.

- To abide by the legalities governing the employing corporate structure. (Special Libraries Association's PREPS Commission Report 1992, pp. 6–8).

Many information services practitioners shy away from the subject of ethics. It's a big issue, of course, and for many information workers it's easier to deal with by avoiding it altogether. Besides, for most practitioners (especially those who work in specialized libraries) ethics is one of those issues that is generally handled by someone else. Staff members in information units do not usually have to be too concerned about making ethical judgments themselves, for the organizations and enterprises that employ them generally operate according to some already established code of professional conduct, code of corporate ethics etc. If there is not an established and clearly defined code, the issue is handled through the organizational culture, which is a powerful motivating and influential force, regardless of how it is or is not 'officially' recognized within the organization.

So, while it might be acceptable for ordinary workers to shy away from ethical concerns, the managers of information services departments have no choice. Almost daily, stories filter through the organizational grapevine which raise ethical questions. Here's an example: a high-ranking human resources employee informs the head of the company's records management unit that her fax number will be used to receive résumés for a position that has been advertised. Why? Because the position is in the human resources department, and the incumbent in the position hasn't yet been told he's being fired.

Or the reference librarian is being 'eased out' because the library manager has a candidate for the job and wants to bring that person into the organization. And on what grounds is the reference librarian being fired? She spends too much time doing clerical and routine work, and doesn't give the information customers the full benefit of her professional expertise. This is because a decision was made before the reference librarian was hired to discharge the clerical assistant in the reference unit. The organization needed to get rid of one clerical position, and the reference librarian's assistant was targeted and let go just as the librarian came to work. When she asked when there would be a clerical employee for the job she was repeatedly told that the position would be filled, but it never was. In the meantime, she was expected to see that the clerical tasks were performed as well as the professional tasks. When the work wasn't done to the library manager's satisfaction, the way was clear for him to get rid of the reference librarian, because she was judged to be professionally incompetent.

These are not pretty stories, but they demonstrate precisely why information services managers must have a good understanding of the ethical issues they will confront in the workplace. For those referred to as 'lower echelon employees', it's not a problem. For managers, dealing with ethical issues is part of the responsibility that they assume when they become managers. Ethics and management are strongly commingled, and it is the ethical component that moves management above the mere seeking of corporate success.

The information services manager is, in fact, already predisposed to accepting the ethical role as part of his or her management responsibility, simply because many who have been trained for work in information delivery are committed to providing service based on the identified needs of the customer. It is this service framework that has long characterized librarians and many others who deal with information delivery on a regular basis, in their service standards. Obviously for many workers this motivating impulse is frequently compromised, and it is here that the true conflict for many information workers takes place. When the best information delivery is prevented through organizational or enterprise bureaucracy, through managerial ineptness, through lowest-common-denominator standards of service, or through illegal or highly question-able practices on the part of those in authority, frustration is the result. Naturally, service to the customer suffers.

So, how is the ethical information services manager defined? What kind of manager can see to it that ethical behavior is the established norm in the information workplace? What standards does he or she rely on? Five characteristics shape his or her success:

1. **Integrity.** There is no single quick explanation of what integrity is. For most people it is an uncompromising adherence to a code of values or, as one description puts it, 'utter sincerity, honesty, and the avoidance of deception'. For information services managers it means establishing a standard of service and ensuring that that standard is adhered to in the delivery of information in the unit that he manages.

2. **Humaneness.** For lack of a better term, this will have to do. The information services manager, while performing steadfastly and loyally for the company or enterprise which supports the information unit, must understand and accept that it is in the human interaction that the information unit's success is established. She and her staff must understand (and must make sure that everyone else understands as well) that the organization is nothing more than groups of individuals interacting with one another. It doesn't matter whether

the interactions are between staff and management, between information providers and information customers, or between organizational employees and suppliers (or other external contacts). What does matter is that the relationships and interactions recognize the people-to-people construct.

3. **Professionalism.** The information services manager must establish professional standards of excellence for the delivery of information, and that delivery must be designed, organized and implemented to meet those standards. In fact there are those who define professionalism through its connection to a professed code or standard of ethical service, and it is this component of professionalism that positions information workers as the information leaders that they often become in their organizations. They perform, and they are expected to perform, well. Because they are the information deliverers, no one expects any less of them. It is a powerful and (sometimes) awesome responsibility.

4. **Fairness.** The ethical information services manager knows what fairness is and attempts to bring it into his daily interactions, regardless of where or with whom in the organizational hierarchy they take place. In the two examples described earlier, when the story of the reference librarian's plight is related the universal reaction is 'But that's so unfair!' Of course it is, and fairness and unfairness are understood by everyone. When a staff member is assaulted in this manner, the primary defense (regardless of the other circumstances

in the situation) is that the employee is not being treated fairly. People have a very strong sense of justice: they know almost innately what is fair and what isn't, and they consider it unethical for people to be treated unfairly.

5. **Excellence of service.** The bottom line, of course, is whether the information customers get what they come for, and if the information services manager has established standards of service, those standards must be met. Excellence, like much else in life, is in the eye of the beholder. The rub comes when the establishment is not seeking or expecting a standard of service that is as high as that of the information services staff. When that happens, it's time to go back to the table and agree upon another standard and, this time, perhaps more realistic standards. But this is a slightly different issue, and does not affect the basic premise of workplace performance: ethical behavior in the workplace attaches to service excellence, however that excellence is defined.

The human side of management

For an information services operation to truly function in an atmosphere of trust, where all information stakeholders are confident of the success of the operation, it is frequently necessary to go beyond the standard procedures that one clearly understands. While good management practices can be expected in the accomplishment of day-to-day activities, managers also must be prepared to operate in a crisis situation. On these occasions the human side of management comes to the fore, and everyone suddenly discovers how important it is to have the normal rules of managerial conduct in place, so that the work can continue to be done. In these situations, though, more is required, and it is here that the information services manager is reminded of how important it is to remember that people are simply trying to go about their lives and do the best work they can.

In 1995, Oklahoma City was devastated by a terrorist explosion that ripped apart the US Federal Office Building, killing some 165 people. The event horrified people all over the world, and a year later the bombing was back in the news as a location for the trial of the accused bombers was being determined. Carol Campbell, library manager for *The Daily Oklahoman* and *The Sunday Oklahoman*, both published in Oklahoma City, agreed to talk about her experiences as an information services manager working under the extreme circumstances brought about by the crisis. The interview, reprinted here from *InfoManage: The International Management Newsletter for the Information Services Professional*, describes how all managers must at one time or another remember their human role in the work that they do.

InfoManage: You manage a news library with an interesting mix of employees reporting to you. How does your work as a manager in this situation differ from traditional library management?

Campbell: So much of the information we maintain is in electronic format that the traditional checking in and out of information in any form is foreign to us. Not that we wouldn't like to do that with the actual books in our library!

Whereas in a more traditional library the word specialist refers to reference, cataloging, indexing etc., in this library (and in most newspaper libraries) those specialists are electronic text archive managers, electronic photo archive managers, online researchers, and that most evasive of all . . . at least one person who has an incredible memory!

InfoManage: How is the work your unit provides perceived by others at the company? By editorial staff? By management staff? By the public?

Campbell: This perception has improved vastly in the last few years. The library has access to many information avenues not available to the company as a whole. In addition to all the new and wonderful electronic information, we maintain a vast array of file cabinets filled with photos dating back to Oklahoma statehood (1907), and some older than that. We also store all the microfilm for our newspaper, which began in 1894. And there is a microfilm reader/printer available.

The editorial staff sees our library staff as part of the team. Library staff frequently is credited in our newspaper, and as library manager I attend all department head meetings and am encouraged to attend the daily news meetings.

As for the public, we offer research for a fee, and we are responsible for photo sales. We are now a profit center, and we become a more effective one each year.

InfoManage: Oklahoma City has been much in the news since the tragic bombing, and now that the decision has been made to move the trial there is again much interest in Oklahoma City. How has this situation affected your work as a manager, and what specific resources (emotional, professional, personal etc.) did you have to call forth that you hadn't expected to use?

Campbell: The bombing's effects on our entire community were (and still are) the same as in this company, in our newsroom, and on my staff. We became closer, everyone worked harder, and consideration for others was at a peak. As far as my work as a manager, it required all my emotional strength to hold myself together, and help other individuals, some in other departments, hold together also.

InfoManage: What kind of specific leadership did your staff need during the immediate aftermath of the bombing? How much of a team effort was required at the company as a whole? In your department?

Campbell: The leadership required was mostly being available to talk or cry with someone when necessary, to take some of the most disheartening work from someone else's shoulders, such as processing (for the electronic library) the obituaries of victims, especially the children. It seemed to go on forever, child after child. Heartbreaking.

And the team effort was incredible, throughout the entire company I'm sure, but I can speak directly about the editorial staff, including photo, art, library, features etc.

Many people did types of stories they hadn't done for years, or perhaps never: feature writers were at hospitals interviewing victims and victims' families. People refused to go home; many worked more than 20 hours at a stretch. Management had food catered twice a day, noon and dinner times.

Our management also provided psychological assistance to anyone who felt in need. In other words, everyone did absolutely anything and everything they could think of to make sure our stories were the best they could be and that we were indeed serving the community's right to know in the best sense of that cliché.

As to our organization's support, although I would like to quote the entire contents of a two-page letter our managing editor, Ed Kelley, wrote to the newsroom staff a few weeks after the bombing, I'll settle for the last paragraph:

"While plenty remains to be done, we can take great pride in what this newspaper has accomplished since April 19. The effort has been superb; so has the result. Please accept my deepest thanks, for I truly am fortunate to work with such a gifted and caring group of people. Some day all of us can look back and say we were in the newsroom of *The Oklahoman* in possibly its finest hour."

InfoManage: What advice would you give to other library/information services managers who find themselves confronted with such a horrific situation? Even though your building was not in the bomb blast's immediate area, obviously you and your people have strong reactions to the situation. What would you tell others to do in such a situation?

Campbell: My advice would be to try to stay focused on what's to be done and the job at hand. It was very difficult to do, and everyone had lapses. Hard-boiled police reporters cried. Meek-mannered editors cussed. But everyone worked together. That's the most important thing you can do, foster that sense of teamwork. In fact, the sooner you start the better, like right now. Be extremely nice to each other. Offer pats on the back, hugs if that's what's needed, whatever it takes. And after a few days of long hours and troubled sleep, try to stay patient and try to forgive those who can't be. Tempers tend to get a little short.

Practically speaking, the instant you know what happened, begin pulling photo files, doing research in microfilm and electronic text files. Information you can place into the editors' or writers' hands before they ask saves them that much time.

If you or anyone on your staff has reported or written before, volunteer to do so again. If someone has served as copy editor, tell the department heads the person is available. The same holds true for any facet of getting the newspaper published: layout, headline writing, proofreading etc.

Volunteer to compile a list of phone numbers and, if possible, do it all by e-mail.

Many of these suggestions should be done all the time, not just in crisis situations. If you need to build good will and foster the team feeling between the library and the newsroom, do these things now. I promise the payback will be better than you believed possible.

InfoManage: Thanks, Carol, for sharing your thoughts with *InfoManage* readers.

Campbell: And thank you for this opportunity to brag on our profession. And, secondly, the chance to air some of these bombing-related issues, which are much easier to write about than to talk about. It's difficult to discuss some things without stifling tears. We are not through grieving. Perhaps we will never be.

References

Barrier, Michael 'Small firms put quality first.' *Nation's Business* 80 (5), May, 1992.

[Campbell, Carol] 'Five minutes with Carol Campbell in Oklahoma City.' *InfoManage: The International Management Newsletter for the Information Services Manager* 3 (5), April, 1996.

Carson, Paula Phillips, Carson, Kerry David and Phillips, Joyce Schouest *The Library Manager's Deskbook: 102 Expert Solutions to 101 Common Dilemmas*. Chicago: American Library Association, 1995.

Harrington-Mackin, Deborah *The Team Building Tool Kit*. New York: American Management Association, 1994.

Hodapp, Paul F. *Ethics in the Business World*. Melbourne, FL: Krieger Publishing Company, 1994.

Madu, Christian N. and Kuei, Chu-hua   *Strategic Total Quality Management: Corporate Performance and Product Quality.* Westport, CT and London: Quorum Books, 1995.

Special Libaries Association. Presidential Study Commission on Professional Recruitment, Ethics, and Professional Standards (The PREPS Commission).   *Report.* Washington DC: Special Libraries Association, 1992.

Chapter Nine

Establishing a desire for quality and ensuring the participation of senior management

Wherever an information function has been established, its role relates – at least theoretically – to the mission of the parent organization. Yet as any information services practitioner can attest, there are often barriers to the successful delivery of information that can be strongly inhibiting to the successful linking of the information services mission to the organizational mission. It is in identifying these barriers and determining how to bring them down that the information manager's true organizational skills are put to the test.

Obviously the planning, organization, directing and control of the information unit's operations is going to be the framework on which success is built. If that framework incorporates a strong focus on customer services, a commitment to measurement, a commitment to continuous improvement, and new work relationships built on trust and teamwork, the department is well on its way to success in the quality delivery of information. Nevertheless, regardless of how many of the organization's information stakeholders need and desire information services, or how closely the information mission connects to the organizational mission, there are those other quality essentials that must be recognized and affirmed before quality in information services can be achieved. What the information services manager is really looking at is the organizational *attitude* to information. Until there is a desire for quality management in information services, and until the organization's senior management has enthusiastically agreed to participate in the total quality management initiative with respect to information delivery, the effort will be lukewarm and half-hearted, and all participants will recognize its limitations and quality success will be restrained.

This situation can be avoided, and even predicted and thus approached from a position of strength, but to do so certain questions should be asked. What, for example, are the elements of the organizational or enterprise culture that lend themselves to a quality perspective in the delivery of information services, products and consultations? Or, from a negative point of view, what are the elements of the corporate culture that inhibit the pursuit of quality? Is there an ambience within the parent organization that encourages quality service delivery?

Once the organizational ambience is understood, why must quality be desired? Cannot quality in information delivery just be mandated by management and then be put in place?

Clearly such important questions cannot be dealt with in such a simplistic manner, for the corporate culture relates to such quality attributes as customer satisfaction, interest in doing the job right first time, employee participation and buy-in, an avoidance of concentration on the process and deliverables, and an understanding of the human touch in all transactions and interactions between staff, management, customers and all other stakeholders in the organization or community. Significantly, an analysis of corporate culture also links to an identification and analysis of employee loyalty, or, as would be more appropriate in discussing quality management with respect to information delivery, the two-way loyalty between employees and management and vice-versa.

So, a first step is to think about how information as a commodity and as a resource that has value is regarded in the organization. That is, how information is *respected* in the organization. Is information a commodity that is essential to the successful achievement of the organizational mission, and if so is it perceived as such, or is information not regarded with any sort of particular interest or understanding, any particular *value* as far as the organization or community is concerned? In other words, is information as a commodity the recognized basis on which organizational success is established, or is its acquisition and use simply another organizational function that is taken for granted?

Certainly in most organizations and enterprises the information picture is somewhere between these two extremes, and in today's management environment the role of information is ostensibly recognized as critical to organizational success. Whether this is actually the case will depend much on how the organization uses information, but generally speaking, practitioners in the information services discipline can take comfort that as society changes, so does the value of information in the management community. What information managers must do is to recognize that the general information picture is changing, that information is now recognized as having a much higher value than has ever been the case in the past, and to relate this change to the work being done in the information services unit. Certainly Miriam Drake was moving in that direction when she wrote:

> Success in any organization depends on contribution to productivity, achievement of objectives and the bottom line. Success also depends on knowing customers, exceeding customer expectations, using information technology appropriately and delivering useful and valuable products and services that make a difference for the customer and the organization.

Continuous feedback and measurement of customer satisfaction are essential (Drake 1994, p. v).

These are, of course, the attributes that connect information services with quality management, and which provide the information services manager with a realistic and practical approach for establishing a desire for quality among all information stakeholders in the organization or community.

It has now become clear that the value of information within the organization is reflected in two criteria, which are hopefully connected: how senior management has positioned the information delivery function in the corporate structure, and the organizational staff's own attitudes to the role of information and information delivery. It is the juxtapositioning and interrelating of these two criteria that influence and determine the potential for success of the quality management perspective in information services, and whether there can, indeed, be a desire for quality within the organization.

The management role in advocating quality

It is commonly recognized that attitudes within the organization reflect attitudes 'at the top'. If senior management does not understand or relate to the information function, it is going to be difficult for the quality effort to succeed. On the other hand, those managers who know what they need with respect to mission-critical information will support such an effort, because they understand that for their work to go forward they must have quality information delivery. So the desire for quality must emanate from senior management, and quality efforts in information services must reflect management's need for quality information.

The requirement for enthusiasm and support on the part of senior management for a total quality management environment has already been alluded to. Sometimes the lack of such support is manifested in an organization's management development program, in which people not particularly qualified for management positions are promoted for the wrong reasons, and they bring with them an antipathy to quality efforts. In other organizations there are managers who are fully qualified and who do a very respectable job of planning, organizing, directing and controlling the units for which they are responsible, but when it comes to the organization of a quality effort they find that it is 'too much trouble', and they resist (or even refuse) participation. Finally, there are those managers who, even when expected to participate in an organization-wide quality program, will resist because they see such efforts as 'getting in the way' of what they perceive to be the 'real' work of the organization. In all of these cases there is little chance of success for a quality initiative, because these managers are unable to understand the benefits the effort will bring to the organization at large.

In many organizations and communities total quality management is an enterprise-wide commitment, and the various units or departments that comprise the information services function are part of the effort through their organizational placement. For these information services units participation in the quality program is not a matter of choice, and the relationship with the organization keeps the program going. In other organizations, however, the genesis for a quality effort springs from one of the subunits, and it is then the task of the employees of that unit, through its manager, to bring the organization or community's senior management into the picture.

When there is no interest in a quality program at the senior management level, or when the subject is dismissed as a frivolous exercise that 'wastes time and keeps the work from getting done', it then becomes the responsibility of the information services manager to raise their awareness, to see that these senior managers understand the value of information for the company or enterprise at large, and specifically the role that a quality management effort can play in ensuring that the information provided through the organization's various information services units matches mission-critical demands.

How is it done? How does the information services manager bring the organization's senior management into the TQM process? Five key attributes spell success:

1. **The management role.** Whether the information services manager has organizational ambitions or not, he or she must have a clear-headed and dispassionate understanding of the management role in the organization. It is no longer possible or appropriate to engage in a 'we-vs.-they' relationship with senior management, for the same methodologies that senior management use to plan, organize, direct and control the organization are used in managing the information services unit. When the information manager and senior management are partners, recognizing that they have the same organizational goals and objectives, the quest for a quality perspective in information services becomes part of the larger quality picture, and even reluctant senior managers understand that they must participate in working toward the same quality goals.

2. **Management's view of information services.** Although information services managers are quite willing to seek feedback from customers, suppliers and other information stakeholders, they are not so keen on determining what management thinks about the operation of the information unit. Why this is so is not particularly relevant at this point, but the clever information services manager will become adept at determining, either formally or informally, how management views

information and the department or unit specifically charged with managing it. At a minimum, senior management will expect the information services unit to understand its own role in the organization or enterprise, and what the information products, services and consultations it provides bring to the organization in its quest for success. Certainly a knowledge of the industry or subject discipline of which the information services unit and its organization are a part can be expected, and participation in enterprise-wide activities will do much in establishing a framework for discussions between management and information staff about the role of the unit. In some organizations, more knowledgeable senior management might expect professional qualifications; certainly they expect professionalism in information matters if they or those who report to them have been exposed to the success of other organizations as a result of excellence in information delivery.

Administrative competence within the information unit is also expected by senior management, although most managers at the senior level take this attribute for granted in professional staff. Finally, excellence in communication and high-level communications skills, both within the information services framework (with customers, suppliers etc.) and in the organizational framework, are expected by senior managers, and failure in this respect will do much to harm the cause of the information services unit within the organization. In brief, management is looking for efficiency, effectiveness and cost benefits, and if an information services manager can demonstrate that these will be achieved through the deployment and implementation of a quality effort, the move toward quality-focused management will be successful.

3. **An agreed-upon mission statement.** One of the basic elements of management success is a clear understanding of roles, and for the manager of an information services unit it is imperative that the mission of the unit match the organizational or enterprise mission. Similarly, agreement must be reached about deliverables to be provided by the unit, and the best way to reach agreement is to have a representative of senior management work with the information services management in a partnering relationship to develop and create both the mission statement for the unit and the performance standards on which the success of the unit is to be judged. By establishing such a partnership, two objectives are achieved. First, senior management takes ownership in the workings of the information services unit and assumes a more direct interest in its success. Secondly, as the department moves toward a quality initiative, with quality goals built in to the evaluative methodology, senior management is less inclined to resist and more inclined to understand the value of TQM in enabling the department to meet its

organizational or community objectives.

A caveat must be stated, however, and that is to caution information managers to be alert, in their workings with senior management personnel (especially in the development of a jointly devised mission statement) that their role and that of their staff is not compromised. It is all too easy for senior management to become very interested in the specifics of information services management and attempt to assume a role of dilettante librarian, which could be disastrous for the person who has real management responsibility for the unit. The 'interested' manager who wants to assume a management role for which he or she is almost universally unqualified, can seriously interfere with the proper management of the unit, and so information services managers must be on guard to ensure that they themselves retain their professional and managerial responsibilities and are not compromised by energetic and enthusiastic people who think they know all there is to know about being an information services manager but in fact know little or nothing. Particularly with respect to the development of the mission statement, the information services manager must be careful to see that he or she is recognized as the authority in determining the services that can or cannot be provided by the unit, and resist persuasion to provide services that are not appropriate or achievable.

4. **Shared communication.** In attempting to move the organization's senior management into adopting and participating in a quality initiative for the information services department, two guidelines can be helpful. The first is that the manager of the information services unit should recognize that most managers do not have his or her understanding of information matters, and most especially do not understand the jargon of information management. It is a losing battle to expect these people to know and understand the language that information workers use casually and indiscriminately with one another all the time. In fact, it is to the information manager's advantage to learn to speak with reference to organizational goals in an organizational context. Some leaders in the information services discipline advise that not only should information people become versed in speaking the language of management, with respect to the organization, but that all statements should be in financial terms, and the role of the information services unit in the organization discussed in terms of the return on investment that is provided. Sylvia Piggott (1996) in her Inaugural Address before the Special Libraries Association, identified several pieces of what she called the 're-engineered model of information services' that she expects to be in place in the very near future (it is already in place in many organizations and enterprises). All of these are attributes that senior management will react to, positioning information services

management for a leading role in the organization in terms of establishing quality efforts. Piggott leads off with the contention that intermediation through the information unit must provide a bottom-line impact on organizational success, and that collaboration at all managerial levels plays an important role. All future information services units, Piggott contends, must be flexible enough to make the required paradigm shifts as society changes with respect to information and self-empowerment becomes the critical attribute of the successful information services worker. Piggott's primary point, however, is a bit of good, old-fashioned business advice: if information, practitioners want to succeed in information services management, she says, they must speak the language of their bosses and they must stop talking about money spent. Instead, Piggott advises information managers to talk about 'resources invested', to put the entire information services transaction into a return-on-investment framework. It is good advice for information services managers seeking support for the development and implementation of a quality management initiative for their units.

A second guideline recognizes that managers and information services workers use different evaluation methods, and with respect to information services, organizational management often veers far from the very quantitative measures that are required of other units in the organization. As discussed earlier, effectiveness measures are often of more value in this connection, even though in other departments quantitative measures are expected. The reasons for this are varied, but as has been noted by Matarazzo, Prusak and Gauthier, what information services practitioners must understand is that information services managers judge their departments' performance by methodologies that were usually designed specifically for the type of information operation being studied (libraries, records management units, archives etc.); senior management in the organizations of which those units are a part use 'far different, and often subjective, evaluation criteria' (Matarazzo, Prusak and Gauthier 1990, p. 1). When information services managers recognize this difference and attempt to match their evaluation methodologies with those used in the rest of the organization or community, or with those that management is seeking with respect to information services, communication between information services and senior management is enhanced.

5. **Management-critical information.** In many respects, the most important vehicle for bringing senior management into the TQM process – with enthusiasm – is the provision of analysis and the delivery of critical information products, services and consultations *to* senior management. If it can be clearly established that senior management staff are information customers – that is, if the success and responsible achievement of their work is determined by the

information that emanates from the information services agency in question – these managers are going to be much more likely to understand and relate to the value of a quality information services initiative. Sometimes the marketing of information services to senior management is not as easy as it is with other identified customer groups, and of course special efforts must be made to ensure that the services offered match those that can be provided, but when services can be established as valuable (or even as indispensable) to senior management, their quality will be of interest to these people and will elicit from them an equal interest in determining how those services should be offered and evaluated.

Staff attitudes

However committed to the development and implementation of a TQM operation the manager of the information services department might be, the effort requires the support and enthusiasm of senior management to succeed. Significantly connected with this support is the commitment of all staff in the information unit, for simple participation is not enough. These people, too, must enthusiastically embrace the quality standard in their work, and they must share their enthusiasm with other workers if the TQM initiative is to have a recognizable effect on the delivery of information.

It is of course impossible to mandate a concept as nebulous as enthusiasm. No serious manager would attempt such a thing, but any information services manager who is interested in attaining a quality framework for information delivery, and who has obtained the support and enthusiasm of senior management, will move ahead with a plan to influence workers, to encourage them to join in with the departmental (and, it is hoped, organizational) quality effort.

As touched on earlier, if libraries and other information services operations are to offer quality products, services and consultations for their defined customers, there must be an honest desire on the part of the service providers to provide that quality. When there are staff who resist the service ethos, it must be made clear to them that the delivery of information requires a change of heart, for in a quality environment information delivery must match customer expectations, and when it does not the manager must organize and implement initiatives that will ensure the match.

Among these initiatives is a commitment from the information services manager himself or herself, for honesty and openness – the elements of trust – must be in place for the manager's efforts to be taken seriously. It is a phenomenon that LeRoy Thompson has identified, and certainly it is one that affects how information services employees respond to management leadership:

Employees can tell when there is a genuine commitment by top management to change the culture of the workplace from one based on internal competition to one based on consensus decision making and shared values. These new values can be instilled . . . but only with premeditated action (Thompson 1994, p. 91).

What premeditated action can move employees into a new way of thinking about the organization, a commitment to quality in information delivery? To arrive at a satisfactory answer means conveying to staff members what happens in a quality-based information services environment, for once they understand that the workplace is *better*, for the customers, for themselves, indeed for all information stakeholders, it makes sense to determine to participate.

So, to change staff attitudes the information services manager begins with the hiring process, determining to ensure that as they are interviewed potential staff are told clearly about the department's quality commitment and how they would be expected to perform their work with the same level of commitment. The criteria for quality-focused information delivery are laid out for them, and they are examined to determine that they understand what is expected of them in relation to quality information delivery.

In Berlin, Frau Dr. Claudia Lux, who manages the Berlin Senatsbibliothek, has established her organization's criteria for new staff. When asked about how she deals with new hires, what criteria she has established for the people who work in this information operation that services the many and various departments of the Berlin city government, Dr. Lux came up with what, in brief, might be the formula for the information worker of the future. With new systems being put in place, would Dr. Lux and the Senatsbibliothek be seeking any special skills? Will she be looking for, say, traditional library skills in the people who come to work at the Senatsbibliothek?

'When we look for new hires', she said, 'we look for people who are flexible, creative and without fear, because they will have to work a lot with bureaucracy, government employees, and a very wide range of different problems and situations. As for "library skills", we may want some of this, at least along the lines of "information management methods", but what we really need is flexibility, and an ability to work well with other people, someone who cares about the future development of services, and is practical in their approach to information delivery.

'What we really must have are people who not only have ideas, but who talk about their ideas, who like working with clients, and with their colleagues, and who have fun in their work and don't fear responsibility' ([Lux 1996], p. 4).

In addition to establishing performance expectations for quality information delivery early on, a second management responsibility has to be communication with employees and between employees and management. For example, much attention and effort in the quality information workplace is given to communicating with senior management and the customers, but there are many times when information staff are simply expected to know what is going on, the assumption being that because they have had experience in a similar workplace, or are professionally qualified, or for some other reason, employees will naturally just pick up what is expected of them. It does not always happen, and the fact that communication is important should not be ignored. Even the group of management specialists (led by Ron Ashkenas) advocating the move to 'the boundaryless organization' recognize the value of ensuring that employees know what is going on:

> In nearly every employee attitude survey, communication is listed as a problem. Employees generally feel they are not informed enough or are actually misinformed about organizational goals and initiatives. Without information, they know they cannot keep customers in the loop of product changes and development, service procedures, or pricing. They find it difficult to take empowered actions on their own or to find they have a voice in the firm (Ashkenas et al. 1995, p. 74).

The same statement could be applied to the management of the information services unit, and the successful movement toward a TQM framework in information services is going to depend strongly on how management has conveyed to staff the objectives and goals of the effort. Ashkenas and his colleagues offer five specific actions for the successful communication of the organizational mission in the larger organizational construct, and they can be transferred successfully to an information services unit:

- Align channel and message.
- Share good and bad news.
- Use both cognitive and emotive news.
- Make messages both complex and simple.
- Use information to encourage change (Ashkenas et al. 1995, p. 74).

As part of the communications effort, information staff should be made aware that a basic premise of TQM is that people will open up, and for the department or unit to successfully establish a quality framework for its work employees are encouraged and indeed expected to participate in full and frank discussions about the issues affecting information delivery. The manager brings this about by demonstrating, at every opportunity, that it is to each employee's advantage to participate in quality thinking about departmental issues, and that a quality philosophy is the standard by which each and every employee does his or her job.

As part of this encouragement, the information services manager makes every effort to eliminate fear on the part of the employees, since, going back to Deming's original 14 points, eliminating fear is one of the basic goals of TQM. In fact, the information services manager will make every effort to encourage staff in positive ways, using reinforcement whenever possible and avoiding blame altogether. With respect to frontline staff in their relationships with customers, the avoidance of blame is one of the critical elements of the quality management program, and each staff member should feel that he or she is never going to be blamed for failures in information delivery when the failure is beyond their control.

A commitment to teamwork goes far in establishing an atmosphere in which staff look toward a desire for quality. Open discussion with staff about the department team and its approach to information services management can play an important role in establishing a quality-focused workplace, and all members of the department should be given provocative and thoughtful opportunities to think about what Thompson has referred to as the most critical issue in quality management:

> It would be hard for anyone who has been part of any group to deny that teamwork isn't a wonderful attribute. What is interesting, though, is to probe exactly what we mean by teamwork, and how it looks in the workplace. Technically, *teamwork* refers to a cooperative effort to achieve a common goal. But what is the goal, and how do we express *cooperative*? In practice, both are interpreted on an individual basis, so there is room for tremendous differences in interpretation. Being able to create a single definition is the most critical issue in quality management (Thompson 1994, p. 92).

Ensuring that all employees understand the mission of the department and how their work relates to the mission of the organization as a whole encourages the openness and departmental spirit that moves them towards a quality workplace. At the same time, such emphasis cuts out fiefdoms and 'turf' problems, those bastions of internal protectionism that are so endemic in information services, and which provide the most difficult barriers in the establishment of a TQM framework. A good example is the simple records audit: it is not uncommon for staff members to resist mightily when the information services team attempts to put together a records audit, to determine what records people need to retain in their offices and what can be discarded or moved to the organizational archives. Why there is so much resistance is not hard to determine, since most people simply do not want anyone else to know what's in their files (the old 'information-is-power' buffer); even more simply, they don't want anyone to know how badly their files are managed. Whatever the reason, for the beauty of a team approach to quality information delivery establishes an atmosphere in which such protectionism is unwarranted and, in most cases, moved beyond, by both employees and managers.

Finally, we look to a quality-focused department to provide an ambience in which staff can express their creativity, both in the delivery of information and in creative problem solving; in thinking about the delivery of information from the customers' point of view; in committing to a customer service process that enables the customer and the staff member to recognize that they are working together in a partnership, seeking a common and clearly identified goal. When staff members feel that they are operating in such an environment, in a workplace that respects them for their contributions and at the same time empowers them to provide the services they have determined are required by the customers, the desire for quality becomes a practical and achievable objective.

References

Ashkenas, Ron, Ulrich, Dave, Jick, Todd and Kerr, Steve. *The Boundaryless Organization: Breaking the Chains of Organizational Structure*. San Francisco: Jossey-Bass, 1995.

Drake, Miriam A. and Matarazzo, James M. (eds.) *Information for Management: a Handbook*. Washington DC: Special Libraries Association, 1994.

[Lux, Claudia] 'Claudia Lux at the Senatsbibliothek Berlin: Looking at information services with a political eye.' *InfoManage: The International Management Newsletter for the Information Services Professional* 3 (9), August, 1996.

Matarazzo, James M., Prusak, Laurence and Gauthier, Michael R. *Valuing Corporate Libraries: a Survey of Senior Managers*. Washington DC: Special Libraries Association, 1990.

[Piggott, Sylvia] 'Special Libraries Association breaks records in Boston: new President Piggott spells out her agenda for the future of information services management: an *InfoManage* value-added report.' *InfoManage: The International Management Newsletter for the Information Services Professional* 3 (8) [Supplement], July, 1996.

Thompson, LeRoy Jr. *Mastering the Challenges of Change*. New York: American Management Association, 1994.

Part 3

Bringing quality management to information services

The quality background

The background of the quality emphasis in management is fairly recent, going back only to the early years of the second half of the twentieth century. Although some elements of what would later become a quality focus were identified and implemented earlier in the century (such methodologies as Frederick Taylor's 'scientific management' and G. S. Radford's quality control predate the Great Depression of the 1930s, for example), it was the move toward the US Army's statistical quality control in World War II that captured the attention of management leaders. After the war, in the 1950s, Dr W. Edwards Deming used his own quality methods to help Japan move into the global competitive marketplace. It is Deming and Joseph M. Juran who are generally recognized as the two primary thinkers in the quality management community, Deming for his belief that a company or organization can achieve a quality framework through a radical organizational transformation, and Juran for his theory that organizations can be managed for quality. In the Juran approach to quality management, three conditions must apply: commitment and action from top management, training in TQM, and quality improvements at an unprecedented rate (Capezio and Morehouse 1995, p. 89).

Other names which should be familiar to information services workers instituting a quality management program are Armand Feigenbaum, Philip Crosby, Karou Ishikawa and Genichi Taguchi. In related fields of study, management leaders and scholars such as Tom Peters and Peter F. Drucker continue to influence quality planning in companies and organizations, and their thinking, and that of business leaders such as Karl Albrecht, is particularly useful in moving to the quality approach in the service sector, where it can be studied and applied to the workings of organizations created specifically as service providers, such as information delivery departments units.

Deming's 14-point management plan, which he developed in order to seek management's commitment to quality performance, can be adapted for the information services arena. It fact, it has already been demonstrated to be of working value in an academic library (Mackey and Mackey 1992, pp. 57–61). Other appropriate models can be found in Jurow and Barnard's (1993) work, and for the public library community a recent work published by the American Library Association offers an excellent and eminently practical approach to quality management in that environment, including an entire 21-page chapter devoted to the subject and its practical applications for librarians (Carson, Carson and Phillips 1995, pp. 163–184).

One of the features of the Carson, Carson and Phillips TQM chapter is that it lists Deming's 14-point management philosophy and offers suggestions about how the points might be applied to libraries (see sidebar).

Certainly that library-focused list can be of benefit to any manager with information services responsibility, and the values implicit in the suggestions that the authors make for adapting Deming's 14 points to library management should be transferable to other types of information delivery operations. It is, however, equally instructive to think about the 'Seven Deadly Diseases', for which Deming has received almost as much attention. 'W. Edwards Deming was a realist', wrote Richard L. Williams, 'and he knew that in bringing his quality philosophy to America he would be met with significant cultural and organizational opposition. He maintained that US organizations were afflicted with seven deadly diseases, any one of which could spell doom to quality improvement' (Williams 1994, pp. 11–12). By identifying these 'diseases', these barriers to quality, in advance of undertaking a quality initiative, the information manager is already on the way to a more creative and more productive management scenario, and even if some of these barriers are, as Williams has noted, obvious negative statements of some of his 14 points, giving them some consideration *before* we attempt to inculcate a quality perspective into information services management has practical advantages. Deming's Seven Deadly Diseases (as taken from Capezio and Morehouse 1995, pp. 82–83) when applied to information services are:

1. **Lack of constancy of purpose.** When there is no mission statement for the library or other information services operation, staff, users and organizational management do not have a clear picture of what the unit's role in the organization or community is. When that departmental mission statement does not match or is organized separately from the organizational mission statement, the place of the information services operation is unclear. Example: At a county agricultural training station, a management decision to store records older than five years at an offsite storage facility is not communicated to the staff. Every time a staff member who has been employed there longer than five years retires or changes jobs, office records and other papers are not sorted, and all are sent to the records management unit for disposal.

Deming's 14 points adapted for libraries

1. Establish constancy of purpose for service improvement. Libraries should avoid short-term 'band-aid' solutions to quality problems. Instead, long-term planning at the board and administrative levels must consider how quality service delivery can best be achieved.

2. Adopt the new quality philosophy. Those who work in libraries must adopt a philosophy in which negativism and poor service are unacceptable. Unhappy patrons not only cease visiting libraries (which reduces the need for staff), but also resist tax hikes and avoid making financial contributions to support the library.

3. Cease dependence upon mass inspection. Continuous improvement – not quality assurance – is the key to excellent service. With a quality assurance approach, staff members will assume their errors will be detected by others, and thus may underemphasize the importance of doing things right the first time. Quality breakdowns are more difficult to fix after than before the fact.

4. End the practice of awarding vendor business based on price alone. Rather than constantly searching for cheaper suppliers, long-term relationships should be established with vendors. For example, when choosing a CD-ROM service, more than price should be considered. The capabilities of the system and service support will be important to the librarian.

5. Improve constantly and forever every system of service. TQM is not a one-time effort, not even something that is ever accomplished. Instead, it is a journey. Once this journey is embarked upon, management is obligated to continually improve the library. Because of the high level of inter-dependency among organizational members in a library, a team approach is required for making decisions about quality improvements.

6. Institute training procedures. Staff members often learn their jobs from colleagues who were improperly trained themselves. When this occurs, new members cannot adequately perform. Instead, organization members should receive proper training through activities such as in-services, professional conferences, and continuing education.

7. Adopt and institute leadership. Managers should go beyond telling employees what to do and actually lead by example. Leadership means discovering and removing barriers that prevent individuals from taking pride in their work.

8. Drive out fear so that everyone can work effectively. Library staff members must feel secure if quality is to improve. They must be able to ask questions, report quality problems, and take a firm position on necessary improvements without fear of reprisal.

9. Break down barriers between departments. One department's goals can interfere with another's. Therefore, departments must be able to communicate with each other. Departmentalism must be replaced by an identification with the mission of the entire library.

10. Eliminate slogans, exhortations, and targets for the workplace. Management slogans (such as 'if it's worth doing, it's worth doing right') can breed resentment among staff members as these messages (erroneously) imply that improvement will follow increased effort on their part.

11. Eliminate numerical quotas, including management-by-objectives. Work standards place a cap on productivity, since very few will be motivated to produce beyond the expected level. Moreover, numerical quotas do not focus on quality issues. In fact, Deming feels that the emphasis on numbers by American management impedes quality improvement more than any other single factor.

12. Remove barriers that rob people of pride in workmanship. Barriers such as outdated equipment, substandard materials, and authoritarian managers stand in the way of quality improvement. Annual ratings and merit pay heighten conflict and competition. The humanity of the workforce must be fostered through true delegation and autonomy – not through pseudo-participation.

13. Institute a vigorous program of education and self-improvement for everyone. Management, professionals, and nonprofessional staff members should be continually educated. People are important assets, and they must acquire new knowledge and skills to keep up with changing technology and advanced in the field of librarianship.

14. Create a new structure that puts everybody in the organization to work accomplishing the transformation. Administrators must

communicate a new vision for the library. They should be accessible to organization members and provide a structure in which people can contribute to the quality mission.

Source: *The Library Manager's Deskbook: 102 Expert Solutions to 101 Common Dilemmas*, by Paula Phillips Carson, Kerry David Carson and Joyce Schouest Phillips. Printed with permission of the American Library Association, (50E. Huron St., Chicago, IL 60650), © 1995.

2. **Emphasis on short-term profits.** Most information services organizations are not in the profit mode, but they nevertheless have certain goals and objectives that they seek to achieve, and by constantly emphasizing immediate or quarterly results, larger goals are not given their full attention. Example: A small law firm has no information policy and information-related matters are handled by the Managing Partner who, being a lawyer and naturally more committed to practicing law than managing the office, refers matters to the individual staff member he thinks is best positioned to deal with it. Thus information decisions are made in haste and without attention to organizational goals.

3. **Evaluation of performance by merit rating or annual review of performance.** Obviously some agencies in the government sector have no choice in the matter, for they are required by government to compensate employees, including information services employees, according to merit ratings and annual reviews. For those organizations that have an option, other, more service-oriented compensation should be considered. Example: In the company offices of a large retailing operation, customer service staff are constantly 'on the line', for they are the people who deal with the public through walk-in visits, telephone calls, faxes, electronic mail etc. Accounting staff and human relations staff are not required to present a corporate image, and indeed have few interactions with external visitors. Yet both groups are compensated according to the results of an annual performance review, which includes no feedback from the customers who have been attended to by the customer service staff.

4. **Mobility of management.** Two problems surface here: the promotion from within, which moves line staff to middle management positions as a reward, with no additional training for management work, and the tendency of management staff to move from organization to organization, thus destroying corporate loyalty and, more significantly, corporate memory. Example: An archives manager

moves from company to company, in each one organizing and implementing short-term projects that have high visibility and which can be used to demonstrate on her résumé her managerial skills. Unfortunately, all she can bring to each new position is skill in archives management. She has no subject memory that can be transferred from job to job.

5. **Running a company on visible figures alone.** The deadly sin which is the bane of every library or records manager's existence, for these are the organizations where the quality or level of the service provided by the information services unit is irrelevant: all management wants is increased productivity in number of materials circulated, number of files transferred, number of literature searches performed. Example: The database manager of a large publishing company is constantly reporting the numbers of databases installed in various departments throughout the company, and because the numbers keep going up her department is perceived by management to be performing well. In fact, of the new databases installed, many are temporary systems put together for a particular project or activity, and not maintained when that activity is completed.

6. **Excessive medical costs for employee health care that increase the final costs of goods and services.** Although this is hardly the domain of the information services staff, the manager of the unit is in a position to influence organizational or community policy in these important matters. Through his participation in enterprise-wide management meetings, he can see that his staff are encouraged to maintain good physical and mental health. Example: Senior management in a manufacturing company institutes a new health plan for all exempt (i.e. non-unionized) employees, which includes all information staff. Based on the assumption that exempt employees are higher paid, the deductible figures for medical care are increased, thus saving the company a considerable amount of money in premium fees. Unfortunately, the information services staff are included in this group, and the information services manager must see to it that the new health plan is revised so that it is fairer to those employees.

7. **Excessive costs of warranty, fueled by lawyers who work on the basis of contingency fees.** Again, although somewhat remote from the specifics of this 'deadly disease' (as most information services units are not involved in warranting, or otherwise accepting liability for the information products, services and consultations they provide), the concept can be applied in an information setting as managers attempt to instill in their staff the requirement that information delivered be accurate and timely. In the private sector liability can extend to the information provider, particularly if faulty decisions are made based on information provided by the

information services unit. Example: The marketing staff of a large advertising agency plans to build a campaign to acquire an account that one of the oldest executives remembers the agency having years ago, perhaps as long as 30 years ago. The records department and the archives manager search for evidence of the account, but none is found and the agency moves forward with its plans. Fortunately, before too many resources have been invested in the work, the executive finds evidence of the campaign in his personal scrapbook and the work is cancelled. Had the materials not been found, the company could have found itself in an embarrassing position, as well as having expended considerable resources to move the project forward.

Deming's 'deadly diseases', then, are obviously traps that information services managers want to avoid as they attempt to incorporate the quality perspective in their operations. When considered in connection with the 14 points that lead to quality success, a handy program for the development of a TQM framework for an information services operation falls into place, and the information services manager is now in a position to consider thinking about how TQM can be made to work in his or her department:

1. **Create constancy of purpose toward improvement of product and service, with the aim of improving competitive position and staying in business and providing jobs.** The organization or community of which the information services unit is a part must undertake the creation of a strategic plan, including an enterprise-wide information policy, that relates the role of information to the organizational or community mission. Example: A large engineering firm creates a strategic planning team to guide its corporate direction for the next five years. Members of the team include a representative of senior management, a senior engineer from one of the departments, a representative of the research and development section, and the firm's chief records officer. This last member is specifically appointed to ensure that all information-related matters are considered from a corporate-wide perspective, and not from the point of view of the individual subunits of the company.

2. **Adopt the new philosophy.** Quality management cannot be incorporated into an organizational management philosophy by osmosis. Specific efforts must be made, with the support and enthusiasm of senior management, to ensure that all company employees and those with whom they have company-related interactions understand the role of quality services in their organization. Example: In the office of a municipal transportation authority, the person with senior management responsibility for information

delivery assigns all middle management staff to review the information transfer process and to offer suggestions for the integration of all information activities in the company, meaning that the distinctions between external and internal information must be identified, and avenues explored for exploiting those areas wherein the information units share similar methods, products etc.

3. **Cease dependence on inspection to achieve quality.** In this area other information services might part company with library-centered quality programs, for quality assurance programs have been shown to succeed in records management and archives situations. Instead of an emphasis on 'mass inspection', the information services manager might look to creating a quality assurance team to study customer satisfaction rather than processes, to determine whether the customers are getting information that is appropriate to their needs (and their requests). Example: In a research institute connected with a major university, the staff procuring technical reports have in the past reviewed each information query, fitting it to match a standardized information request form and each query is discussed with a supervisor before it is filled and checked after it is filled to verify that the correct document was sent to the scientist requesting it. Instead of reviewing each information request, the manager of the technical reports section might institute a procedure for calling randomly chosen information customers, to discuss their query with them and to ensure that the information (or document) they received was exactly what they required.

4. **End the practice of awarding business on price alone. Instead, depend on meaningful measures of quality along with price and move towards a single supplier for any one item, on a long-term relationship of loyalty and trust.** Information services managers and their staff should enter into working relationships with suppliers, to ensure that the vendors understand the department's needs and can anticipate them, as well as adjusting prices and service standards as required, to fit the specific needs of the department. Example: A specialist library in a consulting firm has traditionally relied on one supplier for journals and magazine subscription fulfilment. However, prices have continued to climb, and success with such exceptions as claims, special pricing situations with publishers and so forth, is not as good as it should be. Incorporating service standards into the contract with a different supplier, or renegotiating the contract with the current supplier, will permit the library to have a relationship with the vendor that encourages the vendor to offer better service and, at the same time, spells out exactly what the requirements for service are.

5. **Improve constantly and forever the system of production and service, to improve quality and productivity, and thus continually decrease cost.** In an information services department a quality study team can embark on a process review and improvement program which works with various departmental staff to review all processes, establish which steps of each process are mission critical, and proceed from there to determine the most effective ways in which to move the process along. For this activity, a variety of tools have already proven useful in the information services discipline. The Shewhart Cycle, flowcharts, cause-and-effect diagrams, Pareto charts, control charts and benchmarking, all described in detail by Jurow and Barnard, can be useful for an information services operation (Jurow and Barnard 1993, pp. 117–124).

6. **Institute training on the job.** Except for one-person management operations, every information delivery facility can be structured to offer on-the-job training for staff. The arrangement can be formal or informal, and it can be built around offering training within the information unit, among the different members of the information staff on matters relating to information delivery, or it can be outside the unit and relate to organizational or community matters. In either case, the emphasis is on ensuring that information staff have the best opportunities to increase their knowledge of techniques, tools and information delivery methodologies so that the information interactions between themselves and their information customers are enhanced. Example: In a firm which has several manufacturing plants scattered throughout a relatively compact geographical area, the records managers for the various plants meet on a regularly scheduled basis for courses in records retention methods, in order to return to their individual departments and share that training with their own staffs and with administrative staff who have document storage responsibilities in the various departments of each plant.

In the information services environment, training issues also relate to the training of customers and to the determination of how information is obtained by them. There is much talk in the information services discipline about whether or not its practitioners are information educators or information providers, and the truth of the matter is that in most organizations and institutions they are both. If the customer has in his own office the tools to procure the information he needs, once he has had initial training there may be an arrangement whereby he can refer to the information services unit for additional guidance when he has reached the limits of his own skills. On the other hand, such advanced training may be provided, both for him and for the information services staff, through a contractual arrangement with the vendor. In either case, training is available so that the information can be delivered as needed.

7. **Adopt and institute leadership.** It must be recognized that, as in all other management situations, information services employees and customers require guidance and leadership from those who have managerial responsibility for the work the department provides. Leadership in TQM terms derives from an understanding of collaboration in the workplace, and one of the best analyses of the collaborative environment is that provided by Edward M. Marshall in his work on the collaborative organization, work that transfers appropriately into information services. A study of Marshall's basic ideas about collaborative leadership offers useful guidelines for information services managers:

> In the collaborative workplace, the organization is led and managed by people working in teams, building on the symbol of the circle rather than the pyramid. In this organizational design, there are four basic kinds of collaborative teams that need the leadership function:
>
> - *Strategic leadership team.* Provides overall strategic direction and guidance to a company, department, or unit.
> - *Functional team.* A standing group that has a designated functional responsibility and is tied into the strategic leadership team. Functional teams may also have subgroups called "natural work groups". These are groups of people clustered by geography or task in manageable units.
> - *Project team.* A temporary grouping of people who are working together on a specific task. It may last from a few days to a year or more. Often, members have more than one team responsibility.
> - *Cross-functional team.* A temporary or permanent team of people who come together across the boundaries of specific departments to focus on a customer need or concern common to the entire organization (Marshall 1995, p. 77).

Marshall's description of leadership and teams in the collaborative workplace continues with useful job descriptions for the leader, descriptions which can be transferred appropriately to the information services environment as the quest for a quality management operation continues:

> - *The leader as sponsor.* The sponsor of any team, particularly a leadership team, provides air cover and strategic direction for the team; provides the resources, initial charter, and boundary conditions for the activity; provides coaching support for functional team leaders and monitors the process to ensure its success; helps maintain the integrity of the team's operating processes; and makes necessary interventions.
> - *The leader as facilitator.* The facilitator ensures that meetings, team dynamics and interpersonal relationship function effectively; provides meeting design and implementation services, manages preventions

and interventions; ensures internal coordination of activities among team members; protects the integrity of the team process; and works with the sponsor if there are problems.

- *The leader as coach.* This function requires objectivity about individuals and their roles in the team/organization. It is a supportive role, one that involves providing guidance and being a sounding board.
- *The leader as change agent/catalyst.* This function requires a very great level of objectivity about the organization, teams, and team members. It requires the ability to hold individuals accountable for their actions, to make unpopular observations, and to energize a group to action, enabling breakthroughs where possible.
- *The leader as healer.* Most organizations have a lot of pain stored up in them about broken relationships and broken processes. In this role, the leader plays the role of mediator and catalyst in bringing people together, ensuring integrity in work relationships, and making necessary interventions.
- *The leader as member.* At one or more points, even "natural leaders" will simply serve as members of the team, taking full responsibility for the success of the team; actively participating in its activities; nurturing and supporting the team's development, doing the work; and living up to the team's governance processes.
- *The leader as manager/administrator.* This traditional role involves the daily administrative responsibilities, processes, and systems essential to managing the boundaries with the larger organization or key stakeholders. It may also involve administrative action affecting individuals if coaching and mediation do not work (Marshall 1995, p. 77).

8. **Drive out fear, so that everyone may work effectively for the company.** In information services, there is often a level of fear associated with the work - fear, perhaps, that organizational management may seriously reduce support for the information operation, fear that the information provided is not of a standard expected by the customers, fear that jobs may be lost, fear that some customers' unpleasantness with respect to specific information interactions might explode into a great cause that could harm the information unit or the organization as a whole. For most information services managers, the best approach to reducing fear among staff is simply to instill a 'worst-case' philosophy, giving staff to understand that in all circumstances the question to be asked will be: 'What is the worst thing that will happen if this action is pursued?' In most cases, the worst thing is something that can be lived with, and of course the worst-case level is seldom reached. Example: Senior management in a midsize museum determines that the archives and registration functions for the museum's acquisitions will be restructured, and the staff who perform those functions will now be linked to the museum's various libraries (the general museum library, the

educational library, the slides and reproductions library etc.) and all of these functions will report to the museum's Vice-President for Financial Affairs. All staff in all of the units affected are very nervous that, in losing their autonomy, the various departments will be expected to provide services that do not match their original missions. In fact, after studying the situation and thinking about the change in terms of a worst-case scenario, the managers of the different information units recognize that the worst thing that can happen is that the various departments will now be required to organize the different information functions according to type of information requested. However, the fact that all of these functions are dealing with information in one form or another, and different types of information that can be better provided to information customers through an integrated information operation, quickly changes the worst-case scenario into a best-case scenario.

9. **Break down barriers between staff areas and departments.** In information services today much is written and said about the value of partnering and collaboration between various departments and subunits within the parent organization, and cross-departmental and cross-disciplinary approaches to information management are now recognized as positive forces in the field, moving the different departments toward the successful achievement of organizational goals. While cross-departmental partnering is now widely perceived to be advantageous to the organization as a whole, the concept has taken on particular strength in information services, where the specific advantages of partnering between the different departments and functions that have to do with information delivery have been given attention.

   Four steps for partnering with other information units can be identified. It does not matter whether the units are information *providing* units, such as a specialized library or a records management unit, or a *servicing* unit, such as a computer department or MIS unit, for information services managers thinking about how their departments can have a more rewarding relationship with other information-focused units in the organization, the following can be helpful:

   • **Identify an advocate.** No information services manager can accomplish change (especially cooperative arrangements with other departments in the organization or community) alone. No matter how good the information services operation and its staff are, they require the support and enthusiasm of others in the organization, preferably senior management. Preferably those people will be information customers, but what is really important is that they support the work of the information services unit and are willing to 'champion the unit' when required.

- **Establish rapport.** Rapport is required not only with advocates, but with other information managers in the organization or community. It's hard to think of an improvement or enhancement to current information services that doesn't affect the organization at large, and the information services manager should speak with other information personnel in the organization. It's often surprising to discover how much of what happens in one information unit relates to and affects work that is going on in another information department.
- **Use specific projects.** There is often benefit to be gained from departments working together on specific activities. For example, when the corporate library, the MIS department and the company's archives unit wish to develop a program for the electronic retention of certain information, it should be done cooperatively. In fact, if the different units share the responsibility and the credit, all of the units will benefit when the project succeeds.
- **Identify concerns/issues.** If the financing of certain information products is too much for one unit alone, it might be appropriate to invite another department to be the primary beneficiary if such a product is installed. In many cases, the head of that department will not even know the product exists and will be happy to participate in a shared-cost arrangement, when the information services unit provides the service, works with the vendor etc., and the other department has primary access.

The partnering does not have to be limited to department staff, however, and Marisa Urgo has written about the importance of senior management in the partnering activity, particularly in terms of establishing a workplace ambience that encourages collaboration between those who work in information services and those who work in information technology. 'Every information professional's manager is different, like a fingerprint or a strand of DNA', Urgo has written. 'Nevertheless, there is one dilemma that all information professionals face, in varying degrees of severity, whether they work in information services or in information technology. Specifically, it has to do with the ignorance of people who are not in information work, but who have management responsibility for those who are.' Urgo goes on to describe a survey in which, among some 1,000 managers, randomly chosen, only about twenty per cent knew 'a lot' about general information technologies such as computer networks, and she used this fact as a springboard to express some of her ideas about the need for partnering that builds on the support and encouragement of senior management:

> As the rate of change seems to stretch a manager's time and learning curve, both information services staff and information technology professionals are increasingly finding themselves in the same awkward position. While it might be hard for some practitioners (of both groups) to believe, the fact of the matter is that sooner rather than later they will need to ally with each other. There is going to be a need for both information services units and information technology staff to communicate with one another and learn from each other, especially within the organization in which they are both employed.
>
> If they are going to do their jobs with any level of expertise and effectiveness, information services professionals must be required to be aware of IT fundamentals and be able to understand new developments in their proper context. At the very least, they should be *above* the learning curve of their organization's general population and everyone in the organization should know that they are above the learning curve. Conversely, IT professionals need to understand the importance of communicating new developments to their managements and to their information customers within the organization, primarily because, as the information technology specialists in the organization, they have the expertise and the experience to demonstrate what IT can do for the enterprise.
>
> What management has to do, then, is to encourage (require, in fact) information services professionals and information technology practitioners to promote their expertise throughout the organization and, above all else, to promote it with one another. Neither of them is going to *replace* the other, but if they can be encouraged by management to *partner* with one another in bringing a raised awareness of the role of information – in all its varieties – to the enterprise as a whole, the abysmal ignorance of staff and managers alike will be reduced.
>
> And if it's not happening fast enough, it's not all management's fault. One information systems professor believes that managers feel a "sense of confusion" about technology, because, as he puts it, "the technology side has often been oversold, has frequently disappointed, and has generated its own kinds of confusion. . . . " It's a sentiment that is echoed by one of the designers of the survey referred to above, who indicated that managers feel lost when they are exposed to new technologies, "until they see how others use it [and] they can envision it."
>
> For information services professionals and practitioners in information technology, this learning gap is an opportunity to improve information delivery within their organizations. If senior managers in the organization or community know they aren't receiving the information they need to make better decisions, then providing that information can be an excellent mechanism for improving communication between them and their expert information employees. And as the need to add value to services increases,

opportunities like this one will further blur the line among information professionals – to their benefit (Urgo 1996, p. 7).

10. Eliminate slogans, exhortations and targets for the work force; don't ask for new levels without providing methods to achieve them. Although there are information services operations for which some public relations-type slogans might prove useful in pointing out to their various customers what the facility can provide, in most cases the workplace exhortations so popular on the factory floor only generate cynicism in the employees to whom they are directed, and the same is true in an information services environment. Since staff consider such exhortative management techniques as foolish gimmicks, it is better for management to concentrate its efforts on open and honest communication, determining what department goals are expected to be and working to achieve those goals. When that is the case, information services managers will not be required to resort to the dishonesty and hypocrisy that such slogan-based management engenders. This is a condition that was given some attention by Herbert S. White when he wrote about participative management. White noted that when staff have reason to believe that no matter how hard they try, success is not possible, defeatism and indifference become 'great demoralizers'. Addressing his comments to library managers, White contends that it is this issue, rather than participation in the greater overall process, that probably poses the greatest challenge and opportunity for library managers:

> . . . .We must provide an environment in which individuals can reconcile their personal objectives (diverse as those are) to organizational objectives. Most subordinates are willing to meet us more than halfway, because they accept the premise that in order to be paid they and their co-workers ought to do something productive.
>
> Organizational objectives, unlike goals, we are reminded, are finite targets of short duration. They must be important, and *they must be accomplishable*. If that accomplishment requires money, staff, space, time and equipment, and these resources are not available, then the objectives must be adjusted to reflect what can be done. If not, hypocrisy reigns, and employees have no difficulty in spotting that sort of environment.
>
> Libraries, to a greater extent than other political units, embrace or allow themselves to be coerced into accepting objectives for which there are no resources, no plan, and no hope of success. We tell our staff members to "do the best they can," thereby clearly absolving them of responsibility but also depriving them of any hope of success and of ultimate celebration. In other words, the objectives are gibberish, and nothing really matters (White 1989, p. 163).

11. Eliminate numerical quotas for the work force and numerical goals for management. Although most operations concerned with information delivery are going to continue to use quantitative measures, the emphasis must be on effectiveness measures. From the point of view of senior management and customers, the true value of an information services operation is drawn from the effect that it has on the organization, community or enterprise that supports it and of which it is a part. It is not enough to suggest that a medical librarian in a hospital performs *x* literature searches during a given time period. For that library's value to have any meaning, attention must be given to what was done with the information obtained through those literature searches: was a proposed surgical procedure avoided? Was a hospital admission postponed? Was a newly approved medication utilized? The point of the exercise is not to perform the searches: it is the *effect* of the search that has value to the institution, not the *fact* of the search.

12. **Remove barriers that rob people of their right to pride of workmanship and eliminate the annual rating or merit system.** There continues to be great controversy in the library/information services profession about the value of annual ratings and merit systems, because they have the potential to remove pride of workmanship and move the information transaction to a robotic performance. For the information services manager it becomes important to recognize that the human side of information delivery is what customers seek, and when staff are discouraged from performing in a way that customers can react positively to, the entire information services operation suffers. As for the role of performance evaluations and merit ratings in an information services environment, Paul John Cirino has provided a provocative and worthwhile essay on the subject in his guide to public library management; the context can be shifted to any information services operation with ease:

> The purported purposes of performance evaluations are (1) to provide employees with adequate feedback concerning their performance, (2) to serve as a basis for modifying or changing behavior towards more effective working habits, and (3) to provide managers with data which they may use to judge future job assignments and compensation . . . (Cirino 1991, p. 89).

Having said that, however, Cirino goes on to discourage information services managers from employing performance appraisals:

> Performance appraisals are almost unanimously disliked and mistrusted by management and employees alike. Despite this widespread repugnance, personnel specialists expend thousands of hours trying to devise new and ever more intricate evaluation systems. Personnel officers will claim they are needed to improve efficiency, or to evaluate people for promotion, although they almost never accomplish their stated goals.

Some of the reasons for their failure are:

1. Managers see little or no direct benefit to be derived from the time and energy spent in the process. (They're right.)
2. Managers dislike face-to-face confrontation. (Unfortunately, face-to-face confrontation is the usual modus operandi.)
3. Most managers are not sufficiently skilled in the use of performance evaluations. (An understatement.)
4. The level of standards, biases, and subjective judgments that vary from rater to rater seriously damage the validity of any rating system.
5. The judgmental process required for evaluation is in conflict with the helping role that should be a leader's prime objective.
6. Appraisals are usually conducted as a once-a-year activity, and they often resemble a formal legal case in which the supervisor documents the evidence instead of conducting a helpful motivational discussion.
7. Employees don't like to hear negative comments, especially long after the supposed offense has taken place.
8. Appraisals are often used by supervisors as a form of disciplinary procedure.
9. Where real disciplinary proceedings are necessary, appraisals can also work against the best interests of the employer.

Operating a successful business or a successful library requires that the leader take on the role of parent–coach. Like good parents, leaders want their followers to mature, and eventually to be able to function as independently as possible (Cirino 1991, pp. 90–91).

13. **Institute a vigorous program of education and self-improvement for everyone.** Although similar, this admonition of Deming's is not quite the same as his sixth point, which requires quality-directed managers to institute training on the job. At this stage in the history of information services management, the manager who expects to encourage quality performance from all staff and all information stake-holders is required to recognize that all training and all self-improvement does not necessarily happen in the workplace, and networking, conference attendance, release time for formal educational endeavors, sabbaticals and the like are all now recognized as standard elements in the professional information delivery environment. The days are long past when senior managers looked on conference attendance as a perk that should be counted against the employee's compensation; such activities, even on the international level, are now recognized as bringing prestige and recognition to the employing organization as well as providing the employee with tools and methodologies that he or she would not be able to obtain in the workplace. Example: In a small government agency, the chief of the records management section has been invited to be nominated for the presidency of an international association of records managers. If she allows herself to be nominated and wins the election, for three years

(as President-Elect, President and Past-President) she will be required to travel extensively, speaking to chapters of the organization throughout the world, to preside as the Chief Executive Officer of the organization during her presidency, and to represent the organization in public forums, Congressional hearings and the like. Her organization will be required to provide an additional employee (at least half-time) on a temporary basis to assist her in her usual managerial responsibilities. When she approaches the agency's senior management officer for permission to proceed, he is fully supportive, recognizing that the agency will gain much more in good public relations, in her prominence in the profession, and, not to be too altruistic about it, in the advanced skills that she will have acquired during her term of office. Needless to say, the agency head approves, and she goes on to permit her name to be submitted in nomination for the election.

14. **Put everybody in the company to work to accomplish the transformation; create a system to push every day on the above 13 points.** In many respects, this last of Deming's points is simply a strong injunction to encourage information services managers to undertake a total quality program. The creation of a TQM culture, the organization of a TQM-focused strategic plan for information delivery, the creation of a TQM-directed mission that links to the mission of the parent organization, and the development of TQM methodologies for operations, staff training, marketing, customer service, information delivery and information follow-up, all combine to create a system that positions the information services department to do what a well-managed information operation is supposed to do: to provide the information products, services and consultations that the information customers require, and to do it as well as it can be done.

References

Capezio, Peter and Morehouse, Debra *Taking the Mystery Out of TQM: a Practical Guide to Total Quality Management*, 2nd edn. Franklin Lakes, NJ: Career Press, 1995.

Carson, Paula Phillips, Carson, Kerry David and Phillips, Joyce Schouest *The Library Manager's Deskbook: 102 Expert Solutions to 101 Common Dilemmas*. Chicago: American Library Association, 1995.

Cirano, Paul John *The Business of Running a Library*. Jefferson, N.C.: McFarland, 1991.

Jurow, Susan and Barnard, Susan B. (eds.) *Integrating Total Quality Management in a Library Setting*. New York: Haworth Press, 1993.

Mackey, Terry and Mackey, Kitty ' "Think quality" the Deming approach *does* work in libraries' *Library Journal* May 15, 1992, pp. 57–63.

Marshall, Edward M. *Transforming the Way We Work: the Power of the Collaborative Workplace.* New York: American Management Association, 1995.

Urgo, Marisa 'Information services and information technology: can management make the partnering make sense?' *InfoManage: The International Management Newsletter for the Information Services Professional* 3 (9), August, 1996.

White, Herbert S. 'Participative management is the answer, but what was the question?' *Librarians and the Awakening From Innocence: A Collection of Papers.* Boston: G.K. Hall and Company, 1989.

Williams, Richard L. *Essentials of Total Quality Management.* New York: American Management Association, 1994.

Developing and implementing the quality plan: a checklist for information services

It's all well and good to have a theoretical understanding of total quality management, with plenty of anecdotal references to describe how others have implemented TQM in an information environment. What most information practitioners need, though, is a practical, 'hands-on', step-by-step guide to developing and implementing a quality initiative in the library or any other department that has information delivery responsibility. So, in fairness to any information services manager who is thinking about moving forward with a quality initiative, it is important to understand (and to ensure that other information stakeholders in the organization or community understand) that the endeavor is a serious one, and that the investment of energies, effort and resources is being considered and hopefully undertaken in order to provide information delivery that is *as good as it can be*. Any other motivation or interest stirred up by the TQM approach must be secondary to this goal.

A useful model exists, and while it was not created specifically for the information services environment, strategic total quality management includes much that transfers appropriately into the management of information services. As put forward by Christian N. Madu and Chu-hua Kuei (1995) in their study of corporate performance and product quality, STQM begins with the two essentials that we have now determined as critical to the endeavor: there must be a desire for what Madu and Kuei refer to as a 'total transformation' of the organization (or the information services unit of the organization), and the support and enthusiasm of senior management must be firmly established before success can be achieved:

> Achieving total quality is not simple. A firm must undergo a transformation to change from its traditional management approach to total quality management. This transformation must be initiated by top management and be strategic in scope (Madu and Kuei, 1995, p. 1).

There are those who work in information services who will wish to initiate the quality effort in their own departments without waiting for or seeking senior management's participation and approval, and while this approach can be taken it should be remembered that beginning the endeavor without the prior commitment of senior management simply makes the task that much more difficult. So the wise information services manager aims to get the support and enthusiasm before the quality initiative gets started.

More important, however, is to think about what the goal of the effort is to be. Certainly the broader goal stated above - to achieve an information services operation in which information delivery is *as good as it can be* - is the primary focus of the effort. Having stated that, however, the information services manager is immediately asked, '. . . but what does that mean?' Again, a useful point of departure can be provided in the Madu and Kuei model, in which the quality management program in an information services unit will include most, if not all, of what they call the 'dimensions' of strategic total quality management. With respect to the delivery of information, the purpose of the quality initiative will be to look at the following:

Customer needs
Capabilities and weaknesses
Design specifications (or, in the case of information delivery, specifications for the services, product and consultations that will be delivered to the information customers)
Appropriate process technology
Management commitment
Organizational vision and mission
Management of change
Organizational flexibility
Multidisciplinary background
Teamwork
Employee motivation and organizational cultural change
Training and retraining
Education
Continuous improvement philosophy
Environmental sensitivity
Benchmarking
Cost analysis of quality
Organizational commitment to employees
Image building and social responsibility
Communication among workers
Human input in work
Supplier relationship
Reduce gap between top management and least paid employees
Strategic information system
Functional strategies

> Focus on value strategy
> Redesigned business (or services) processes
> Redesigned business (or services) network
> Working smarter
> Organizational learning and sharing
>   (Madu and Kuei 1995, pp. 7-13).

Realizing these objectives, pieces of the more broad-based goal, so to speak, requires an unsentimental and no-nonsense point of view about the role of the information services unit in the organization or community. It also requires a constant emphasis on mission-critical information, with a coldly objective rejection of those products, services and consultations that are nice to have but which cannot be demonstrated as being critical to the organizational goals. Once the mission of the information services unit has been established, and refined to link with the organizational mission, every   question, query and information interaction must be responded to in terms of whether the answer moves the organization forward towards the successful   achievement of the organizational mission.

To plan and begin the implementation of a total quality management initiative in an information services operation, certain questions must be asked. The following pages offer a set of questions which can serve as an introductory framework, an outline, as it were, for the establishment of a TQM program. As each question is discussed (and answered, if a specific answer can be given), the response can be used to stimulate further discussion within the information services unit and to provide a structure for the development of an action plan relating to that specific element of the quality process. This means, of course, that each question is as important as all the other questions, and that none of them can be 'glossed over' simply because the response would seem to be obvious or self-evident. For example, the first question asks if there is a desire for quality. Certainly no-one is going to say that there is *not* a desire for quality, since quality is a desirable and positive entity. But within the question is another, more implicit question ('Is there *really* a desire for quality?'), indicating that in the asking there is a realization that, if quality is going to be pursued, it may very well cost something, in time, in money, in discomfort, in job security, in inconvenience etc. Having now asked the question more directly and more bluntly, and having added to the question as presented here some 'coloring' or bias that will affect the way it is answered, it becomes clear that there are no quick or easy answers. Each question is expected to provoke serious thinking about the role of quality in the specific information services unit and to generate beneficial as well as practical discussion among all information stakeholders.

The desire for quality

Is there a desire for quality?

What is the corporate (organizational/enterprise/community) culture?

What is the approach to quality in the delivery of services (or products) in the other departments or organizational subunits?

Is the pursuit of quality a defined goal in the organization, community or enterprise?

If so, how is this goal defined and communicated to organizational stakeholders?

If not on an enterprise-wide basis, is there a formal, codified quality effort elsewhere in the organization?

Is there a strategic management plan for the organization or community?

Has an organizational strategic plan been provided to those with managerial responsibility for information services?

Did anyone with information delivery responsibility participate in the creation of the organizational, community or enterprise strategic plan?

Is there a strategic management plan for the information services operation?

Is there an organization-wide TQM or other quality-focused management concept in place, or being considered?

If not, what is the organizational readiness for total quality management?

Is there an awareness of TQM or other quality efforts within the organization, enterprise or community? Do organizational stakeholders know what a quality management effort means, what the benefits of a quality effort are, and what is required for the achievement of quality in the organization?

Why is TQM or any other quality-focused management concept being discussed?

What issues have brought the interest in quality management forward? What is the motivation?

Has an organizational or managerial desire for quality been established?

Is there a specific historical or 'circumstantial' reason for TQM consideration (e.g. a new CEO who is 'quality conscious')?

Is a quality effort being thought about because there are specific problems to be addressed? Have the problems been defined, or is there simply a sense that something wrong is afoot in the organization?

What was the basis for connecting a move toward a quality effort to the resolution of the problems that are affecting the organization or the information services unit?

What is the connection between organizational leadership and the organization's workers, with respect to quality?

Is there staff interest and support, or is the concept of quality too far removed from the day-to-day work that most employees must be concerned with?

What is the history of formalized quality efforts within the organization? Have there been in the past a quality improvement team, quality circles, or other organizational efforts to move toward quality?

Is there a TQM awareness with respect to information services?

What is the history of formalized quality efforts within the information services sector? Has there ever been an attempt to move toward quality, with respect to information delivery, in the past?

Support of senior management

How does the organization, community or enterprise *at large* deal with change?

Is organizational change a fundamental motivator in the organization? What is the organizational perspective on change and change management?

What is the management culture with respect to change management efforts? If employees refuse to participate, even after help and training has been provided, are they permitted to stay on as employees, or are they asked to leave?

Does the concept of total quality management (or one or a combination of its various related quality management methodologies) have enthusiastic support from senior management in the organization, community or enterprise?

If not, can senior management be brought into the quality picture?

If yes, should the information services quality effort be connected to the organizational effort?

If no, can support and enthusiasm for a free-standing TQM effort in the information services unit be expected? Will the organizational culture support such a quality program, even if it is department focused and not an enterprise-wide activity?

Is there an awareness, at the management level, that quality delivery can provide a competitive edge for the organization, community or enterprise?

What is the communications framework within the organization? Is communication top-down or does senior management respond to initiatives communicated up?

Is open communication standard within the organization? What about within the information services unit itself?

What are the barriers to senior management support to a quality initiative within the organization?

Are resources available for a quality effort?

Is there an understanding by management of the organizational benefits of TQM?

What are the barriers within the information services unit to a quality initiative?

Are resources available for a quality effort?

Do the managers of the various information services units have a clear understanding of the departmental benefits of TQM?

What is the leadership/educational/motivational role of management within the organization?

Are feedback mechanisms in place so that management hears from staff on substantive matters?

Customer service

What is the present customer-service picture in the enterprise or the community? Is the information services unit a customer-focused operation?

Who are the information customers?

What is the size of the identified customer base? Has the identified customer base been segmented by major groupings (e.g. by department, demographic categories, level of information products used etc.)?

Have all information customers been identified, or are there potential customers who should be using the facilities of the information services unit but are not?

What are the information needs of the identified information services customer base?

Has an information audit been conducted? Do customers require from the information services unit internal information, external information or some combination of both?

Is there communication between the organization and its customers?

Is the communication one-way, or is it a dialogue?

What is the 'first-impressions' picture with respect to the customer? How does the customer gain an image of the information services unit? [For example, does the information services manager ever call the unit, to see how the telephone is answered?]

Is there communication between the information services unit and its customers?

Is the communication one-way, or is it a dialogue?

What are customer expectations with respect to information services?

Is quality of service in information delivery defined by the information services staff or by the information customers?

Does the organization at large have quantified performance standards for customer service?

Does the information services unit have quantified performance standards for customer service?

What tools are used to determine customer satisfaction? What is done with the information that is obtained through using these tools?

Is there a systematic methodology for measuring customer satisfaction?

Are regular customer satisfaction reports and analyses prepared by the organization at large?

Are regular customer satisfaction reports and analyses prepared by the information services unit?

Is an information marketing system in place, to capture information relating to customer needs, profiles etc.?

In the organization, community or enterprise at large, does information technology contribute to excellence in customer service?

Does the organizational information technology strategy include a clearly stated reference to quality and customer service matters?

How are the products, services and consultations of the information services unit marketed?

If the information services operation is to move to a customer-driven culture, can staff be trained to take ownership of customer service?

What are the barriers to staff ownership in customer service? Can the attitudes and behavior of employees be changed to move to a customer-driven culture?

If bureaucracy prevents good customer service in the information services unit, is there a mechanism for eliminating the bureaucracy?

Do information services staff have authority to use their own judgment to satisfy an information customer?

How many points of contact does a customer have to make in order to complete an information services transaction? How many of these can be eliminated?

How customer friendly is the information services unit? Is it easy to come to the information services unit with a request for information, or is the information services unit avoided except when necessary?

Continuous improvement

Does the organizational, community or enterprise culture permit a move toward process improvement in information delivery?

Is there an awareness of continuous improvement in the information services unit? Can information services staff recognize opportunities to improve processes?

What formal and informal procedures are in place for the effective deployment of continuous improvement in the information services workplace?

Do information services staff (and management) understand what a process is? Do they understand what a critical process is?[1]

What are the services that the information services unit offers? Have they been identified and listed?

What are the processes that are required for the delivery of each product, service or consultation emanating from the information services unit? How is this process done today? What are the steps of the current process?

What is the established evaluation criteria in the delivery of each information product, service or consultation? Is there a gap between what is being delivered and what is desired?

For each process that is considered for evaluation, what is its importance to the information services unit's customers?

What is the objective for evaluating the process? Are there problems? Have they been identified (or will they be identified as the process is reviewed)?

Will changing the process save money, staff time, eliminate waste? What is the expected outcome of changing the process?

For each step in the process, why is the step done? What is gained?

Is something being repeated (data entry/rewriting/recalculating) that has already been done by the information customer or in another department? If so, why is the step being repeated?

Within the process, are there bottlenecks that must be examined?

Does the process flow well, without backtracking to the same people?

Is there significant dead time, that is, time when nothing is happening? If so, can two tasks be handled concurrently?

Are tasks being done manually that should be automated? Is automation required for some steps which would be better performed manually?

---

[1]For more on this, see Barnard: Every organization is made up of separate but usually interrelated processes which help determine how work is organized and how customer needs are met. A process is "a flow of work that progresses from one person or one activity to another." A critical process is "an important process, defined by customer need, that is a major part of the mission of the organization." Identifying and evaluating the critical processes that drive an organization is vital to the continuous improvement of systems fundamental to TQM (Barnard, 1993, p. 66).

Are, for example, three spreadsheets being created (one for orders, one for subscriptions, one for statistics) that could be combined into one?

Are the right people doing each task? (Spiegelman 1994, pp. 110-112).

Are there specific goals, timeframes and measures for implementing each improvement?

Measurement

How are information products, services and consultations measured?

Are procedures in place for inspecting, measuring and testing processes?

Are results tabulated, charted and distributed (or displayed) for all information stakeholders?

Are the measures easy to apply and use? Are they expensive to administer? Are they customer-oriented?

Do the measures link to the information unit's mission? Do they link to the organizational, community or enterprise mission?

Are the following considerations made with respect to information services measurement?

1. The complexity of the instrument

2. The ease of administration and analysis of results

3. Its orientation to overall performance quality or to quality of specific services

4. Its usefulness for predicting overall variance

5. Its usefulness for providing diagnostic information

6. Its usefulness for providing a basis for comparisons across a range of types of libraries other service organizations. (White and Abels 1995, p. 41)

Do all information stakeholders understand the distinctions between input cost measures, output measures and service domain measures?

How significant are effectiveness measures in the organization, community, or enterprise?

Is the effect of an information service, product or consultation important to senior management?

Is the effect of an information service, product or consultation important to the information stakeholders?

Does the measurement of information delivery include usage statistics? If so, how accurately do these statistics reflect overall value?

What performance indicators are in place in the information services unit? How are they used, and how are the results delivered to management and other information stakeholders?

Is benchmarking used as a measurement tool for the information services operation?

If so, are information services, products, and consultations benchmarked against similar operations within the organization at large?

Are information services, products and consultations benchmarked against other information units that are not part of the organization, community or enterprise of which the information services unit is a part?

What is the role of the information customer in the measurement process? Are customers asked to rank the value of the products, services and consultations?

What is the role of information staff in the measurement process (particularly frontline staff dealing with customers on a regular basis)? Are staff members asked to rank the value of the information unit's products, services and consultations?

Trust and teamwork

Are systems in place for the development of trust and teamwork in the information services operation?

Is there a culture within the organization, community or enterprise at large that will support a team-based information services operation?

What are the communications enablers and barriers within the organization? How many of these are in place in the information services unit?

What methodologies have been identified for ensuring the effective flow of information within the organization? Are these same methodologies in place in the information services unit?

Are the employees of the information services unit empowered to participate in a team-oriented approach to information delivery?

What is the level of acceptance for each of the following elements of a team-focused unit:

- Trust
- Commitment
- Shared vision (and an understanding that it is shared)
- Openness
- Non-judgmental participation.

Follow-up, review and ongoing quality

Is there a strategic plan for total quality management in the information services unit?

Is there a quality planning team with responsibility for planning and implementing a quality program within the information services unit?

Who are the members of the quality planning team, and what authority do they have in the organization and management of the quality process?

Have the staff with management responsibility for information services attended educational/training programs in quality management?

Do the information services staff (the information practitioners) attend educational/training programs in quality information delivery?

References

Barnard, Susan B. 'Implementing total quality management: a model for research libraries.' *Journal of Library Administration* (The Haworth Press Inc.) 18 (1/2) 1993.

Madu, Christian N. and Kuei, Chu-hua *Strategic Total Quality Management: Corporate Performance and Product Quality*. Westport, CT. and London: Quorum Books, 1995.

Spiegelman, Barbara M. 'Total quality management: how to improve your library without losing your mind.' In: *Information for Management: A Handbook*, edited by James M. Matarazzo and Miriam A. Drake. Washington DC: Special Libraries Association, 1994.

White, Marilyn Domas and Abels, Eileen G. 'Measuring service quality in special libraries: lessons from service marketing.' *Special Libraries* 86 (1), Winter, 1995.

Quality in information services: Two case studies

Georgia Institute of Technology Library and Information Center Atlanta, Georgia, USA

Miriam A. Drake, Dean and Director of Libraries

The Georgia Institute of Technology is the nation's most intensive engineering university. Three-quarters of the Institute's 13,500 students are majoring in science or engineering. In addition to supporting the Institute's instructional programs, the library and information center supports the Institute's US$180 million programs in sponsored research. The Library's collections are 80% science and technology and reflect campus priorities.

Background

Georgia Tech is an innovative campus. The Institute installed a campus network in the early 1980s. It is computing and networking intensive and students and faculty are sophisticated computer and network users. When students register at Georgia Tech they receive an identification and password for campus computers. New employees also receive identification and passwords as part of orientation. Quick issuance of identification gives students, faculty and staff quick access to the library, to e-mail, to campus information and to the Internet.

The library has been equally innovative. In 1975 the card catalog was replaced by microfiche, which was distributed to all academic departments, enabling faculty to view the catalog in their departments. Delivery services to faculty offices were begun when the catalog was distributed. Reference service at that time was reactive and traditional, and users did most of the work of information finding by themselves. The staff provided direction and standard bibliographic instruction. As in other traditional libraries, there was little concern for added value, evaluation, appropriateness or reliability of information.

The Library began offering services to off-campus users for a fee in 1968. In the early 1970s, online searching for off-campus users was implemented. During the 1970s, off-campus users received more responsive service than students and faculty.

Change of mission

In 1985 the library began a continuing strategic planning process, which involved environmental scanning, identification of trends, definition and segmentation of the customer base, and the formulation of a mission statement for the library. The library's mission had been implicit and was collection based. Staff viewed their purpose as acquiring, cataloging and maintaining the paper and microfiche collections needed by students and faculty. Staff doing online searches believed that their job was done when they delivered a list of citations: their jobs did not involve content, substance, answering questions or problem solving.

Initially, many staff viewed strategic planning as a fun exercise that would not result in any significant change. It was considered an episodic event rather than a serious program for change. The change of mission and goal setting did not mean that operations would change automatically. Many staff members were wary of new services. Some staff resisted. Some staff resigned. Others were enthusiastic and wanted to learn all they could about ways to enhance their value to the customers. The change in culture was significant and staff had great uncertainties about their ability to work in an environment where content, context and problem solving were more important than the volumes on the shelves.

Staff were concerned that customer focus would shift power to the customers. The success of a collection-based approach depends on having materials available, not on how well those materials satisfy a customer's needs. Success was measured by number of circulations and uses of materials. In the new culture, success would be measured by customer productivity and satisfaction.

GTEL®

In 1985 the library implemented the Georgia Tech Electronic Library (GTEL®) to provide campus-wide and remote access to the library's catalog and locally provided databases. GTEL® changed the culture of using the library. Students and faculty could access the system from their offices, dormitories or homes. Faculty used formatted e-mail to request items to be delivered to their offices. Materials are delivered twice daily via truck, fax and e-mail.

As new resources became available via GTEL® and its gateways, it became apparent that the library staff needed to think about value-added services and how their knowledge and expertise could be marketed.

TQM INITIATIVES
AT THE GEORGIA INSTITUTE OF TECHNOLOGY

 Redefining the library's mission

 Implementation of Georgia Tech Electronic Library

 Input from users and staff

 Staff training

 Service awards

 Information consultants

TQM initiatives at Georgia Institute of Technology

In 1989, Florida Light and Power Company won the Deming Prize and the Milliken Company won the Baldridge Award. In 1990, John Hudiburg of FLP and Thomas Malone of the Milliken Company presented a seminar on total quality management to the Georgia Tech administration, faculty and alumni. This seminar was the kickoff to the Institute's program in continuous quality improvement (CQI) and was followed by a trip to Milliken to learn about that company's TQM processes and strategies. Four librarians went to Milliken. After learning about the Milliken TQM program they had the challenge of translating TQM processes from manufacturing to services, and from a profit-making business to a not-for-profit academic institution.

The challenge of CQI for the library was to create an environment that supported customer satisfaction, employee involvement and innovation. A committee of five people was appointed to develop a plan of quality improvement. Elements of the plan included staff involvement, improving customer satisfaction, increasing opportunities for feedback and communication, providing value-added services, and identifying staff training needs. The committee utilized several techniques.

The library adapted Opportunity for Improvement forms from the Milliken Company, which were designed so that employees could recommend improvements that they believed would make a difference. The suggestions were reviewed by the quality group and referred to the appropriate manager for review. Initially there were many suggestions. Some ideas could be implemented quickly; others involved items not controlled by the library. During the next two years the forms were used less and less. Now staff suggestions are made in a variety of ways. For example, three years ago a staff member used a travel report to recommend two innovations, 'Ask a Librarian' and InfoFair. 'Ask a Librarian', an online reference, was incorporated into the GTEL Home Page and has been very popular. In the autumn of 1994, a week-long InfoFair was held to introduce students and faculty to new systems and information services.

Brainstorming has been used in the library for more than ten years. These sessions provide opportunities for staff to contribute ideas to a specific problem. They also help identify problems that may not have been apparent to managers. Staff have had brainstorming sessions on customer service, GTEL®, physical facilities, signage and programs for a library addition. As a result of these sessions, signage was improved, the physical layout of terminal clusters and service areas has been improved, glare-free screens for computer monitors are available to all staff, and ergonomic chairs have been purchased for staff. Brainstorming on the library addition gave staff the opportunity to look into the future and project the type of facility needed for a twenty-first century library and learning center.

Staff were surveyed on their development and training needs early in the CQI process. Staff continue to suggest topics for development. Workshops were held on handling customers, managing multiple priorities, the Internet, diversity, teamwork, and a variety of personal productivity software packages. More recently, workshops were held on using the World Wide Web, various Internet search engines and the Galileo system implemented by the State of Georgia in late 1995.

Staff who attend campus workshops often recreate those workshops for other staff members who may be interested. In this way, staff are trainers as well as learners.

Service awards

Each year, library staff nominate individuals who have provided outstanding or extraordinary service to internal or external customers. Winners are selected by the senior management of the library. A special staff recognition day is held each May. The recipient of the service award receives a cash gift and his or her name is added to a plaque, which is publicly displayed.

Recently, two endowments were established to provide two service awards to be given for the first time in spring 1998. The Price Gilbert Award and the Frances Kaiser Award will be given to staff members for outstanding service. The Frances Kaiser Award is named for the late Frances Kaiser, who gave extraordinary service to students, faculty, alumni and local business, and who pioneered in the application of information technology.

Information consultants

In 1993 the library formalized the role of information consultants. These librarians were assigned responsibility for the provision of information and instructional services to specific academic departments. Their duties include marketing services, performing research for faculty, working with graduate students on theses and dissertations, collection development, and providing instruction for specific classes upon request of the faculty. In order to carry out these responsibilities, consultants need to learn about the curriculum, the literature and current developments in the field, current research projects, and research areas to be stressed in the future.

This program is growing and improving. Information consultants work together and learn from each other. When appropriate, they may form an ad hoc team to work on problems for faculty members. For example, the information consultant for civil engineering may invite a government information specialist and a geographic information systems person to a meeting with a faculty member. The purpose is to ensure that the talents necessary to solve the problem are present and part of the team.

During the last few years the library has recruited information consultants with experience in marketing and providing value-added services. These staff members have made significant contributions in raising awareness of opportunities, how to add value and how to market services. As staff gained experience and became more comfortable with marketing, research and working in partnership with faculty, their confidence increased. They have richer jobs because they can see how their work contributes to better instruction and successful research.

The future

Three important lessons have been learned from the CQI initiative.

First, it is essential that processes be adapted to each organization. Processes that work in one setting may not work in another.

Secondly, experimentation, outcomes and results should not be sacrificed for process. In any organization there are people who are reluctant to change. They want recipes and endless meetings to discuss potential problems. These staff need to be assured that it is acceptable if an experiment fails or a client contact is not as successful as anticipated. People who value process at the expense of outcomes need to be kept focused on results and supported in risk taking.

Thirdly, real change takes time, patience and energy. Organizations and people change slowly. New values and goals need to be integrated into the existing culture. Staff need to make judgments and decisions in a new context and be supported in their efforts.

The challenges for the future are continuous improvement within the changing program and priorities of the Institute and its faculty, a different student population, and the changing context of information finding and use. The Georgia Institute of Technology library and its staff held two brainstorming sessions in early 1996 to talk about the future and the issues that will need to be addressed.

Among the trends identified by staff are an older student population, the need for lifelong learning, distance learning, more interdisciplinary research, more interinstitutional research, the need for knowledge navigation and management skills, and the need for more instruction and training, for both staff and customers. The library staff envisages closer working partnerships with faculty and the Office of Information Technology. Assigning information consultants to be physically located in academic departments may be desirable. In the next year, staff will be working closely with the Office of Information Technology in designing courses to help students with personal productivity software, information finding, evaluation and use, and ethics. The staff predict more multimedia instruction, more reliance on the Web for classroom teachers, and more electronic publishing.

During the brainstorming sessions there was great energy and enthusiasm in the room. Staff raised questions about developments and changes that would be best for the customers. They recognized challenges in a 'can-do' way, rather than as obstacles to be overcome. Staff were candid in their assessments, concerns and recommendations for improvement. They raised legitimate concerns about the space, resources and support they need to do their jobs.

CQI is now deeply rooted in the Georgia Tech Library. Staff have greater confidence in themselves and their abilities. Perhaps the most telling comments come from visitors, who report on staff's knowledge, confidence and enthusiasm for their work.

Westinghouse Electric Corporation Energy Systems Technical Library, Pittsburgh, Pennsylvania, USA

Based on the author's interview with Barbara M. Spiegelman, Manager, Technical Information and Communication, Westinghouse Electric Corporation.

There are still consumers who think of light bulbs when they hear the word 'Westinghouse', but they couldn't be more wrong. Westinghouse Electric Corporation now consists of several diverse industries, including broadcasting, power systems for electric utility plants, its Thermo King Division (which manufactures refrigerated transport control equipment for trucks, containers, buses and railcars), a Government and Environmental Services Division, and a communications and information systems operation. With some 68,000 employees Westinghouse is a major player in the international business community, and those responsible for information services management in all its many forms – special libraries, records management, corporate archives, and a variety of other information delivery units – participate fully in corporate efforts for evaluating performance and service delivery.

The management environment at Westinghouse has for many years been recognized for innovative, out-of-the-box thinking, and this characterization continues to be valid. As the company continues to re-invent itself, looking at new products and new markets (for example, in October 1995 Westinghouse bought CBS, and in June 1996 purchased Infinity Broadcasting, making Westinghouse the largest broadcaster in the US), the emphasis continues to be on innovation, creativity, and entrepreneurial thinking.

Background

Total quality management has been an important part of the company's history, and as early as 1981 the company developed a program called '12 Conditions of Excellence' to guide its move into a quality environment. It was not necessarily a new approach though, for quality, without being emphasized as such, had always been part of the Westinghouse culture, and certainly as the company moved into the production of diverse products and even more diverse markets, the emphasis continued to be on corporate success. Attention to the successful development and sale of products that bring profit to the company is the reason Westinghouse, like all companies, is in business, and an attention to quality had always been part of that business picture.

In the 1980s, however, the move into a quality environment was made more formal, and although the TQM procedures that were developed have now evolved into a more fluid, competency-based performance system, the decade and a half when Westinghouse was actively pursuing a company-wide quality practice was remarkably distinguished. In fact, so fundamental to the quality technique were those 12 Conditions of Excellence developed in 1981, they were eventually adapted to become the seven criteria of the now-famous Malcolm Baldridge Award (and the effort came full circle in 1984, when the Commercial Nuclear Fuel Division at Westinghouse became one of the first winners of the Malcolm Baldridge Award).

Barbara M. Spiegelman has management responsibility for technical information and communication for the Energy Systems Business Unit, which includes the ESBU technical library. The library has participated in the company's quality program all along, either as part of the formal initiative or, more significantly, because quality in the delivery of information products to the company's identified customer base is expected by the customers and provided by library staff who themselves expect to offer a quality service.

Total quality at Westinghouse

Spiegelman, who has been affiliated with the Westinghouse information operation since 1974, describes succinctly and with considerable enthusiasm the progress of – and now the slight move away from – the more formal total quality effort at Westinghouse. In fact, she has done so in two published articles[1] and numerous presentations before groups of fellow information services professionals. Now, as a member of the company's training force working worldwide to help staff master the perplexities of change management, Spiegelman is well qualified to offer other information services managers advice about quality management and the program she has in place at Westinghouse.

The program at Westinghouse is built on a pyramid or triangle of four 'imperatives' (as they're called at Westinghouse): customer orientation, employee involvement, process improvement and management leadership, with these four imperatives divided into 12 criteria: the basis of the pyramid is management leadership, which includes the criteria of culture, planning, communication and accountability. The next row in the pyramid – process improvement – emphasizes products, processes/ procedures, information and suppliers. Employee involvement includes participation, development, and motivation. Customer orientation, the final imperative, has of course no further components, for that is exactly what it is: customer orientation. (These imperatives, criteria, and the further 49 subcriteria that make up the Westinghouse total quality framework, are illustrated in Figure 1 and described in the 'George Westinghouse Total Quality Achievement Award Evaluation Criteria' in the appendix.)

The first thing you learn from Spiegelman about the TQ initiative at Westinghouse is that it is now solidly ingrained in the corporate culture. Without apology, Spiegelman states that the company is moving away from the more traditional emphasis on total quality, and she is quite

---

[1]'Total quality management in libraries: getting down to the real nitty-gritty.' *Library Management Quarterly* 15 (3), Summer, 1992, and total quality management: how to improve your library without losing your mind, in *Information for Management: A Handbook*, edited by James M. Matarazzo and Miriam A. Drake. Washington DC: Special Libraries Association, 1994.

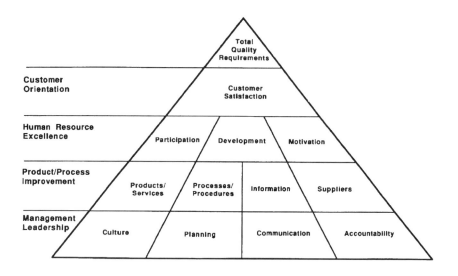

deliberate in explaining that the move toward competency-based performance is a natural outgrowth of the TQ experience. If employees come through total quality at Westinghouse, the concepts and underlying philosophy of TQ become part of their strategic thinking.

TQ Audits

The quality process at Westinghouse is built on a series of total quality audits. These included such specific applications as the total quality fitness review, developed by the Westinghouse Productivity and Quality Center, and the TQ self-assessment, an internal process designed to involve the actual group in the evaluation experience. External audits, in which an outside consultant was brought in to assess a department or division's success in achieving its stated mission, were also used by some managers, but they were not required and individual managers had the option of determining themselves whether they felt the external audits were necessary. As would be expected, each of these audit tools had particular advantages, but taken together they provided a fairly comprehensive picture of the organization's quality status at any given time. The TQFR and the TQ self-assessment audits are built on the 12 Conditions of Excellence, and participants use them to compare the quality status of a plant, division or organization in order to identify the successful aspects of the operation and, of course, to identify improvement opportunities. Not surprisingly, the external audit, while not specifically using the 12 Conditions of Excellence as such, refered to the concepts, even as the department or unit is being examined.

The specific characteristics of the audits demonstrate how each of them has a separate focus, but at the same time related to the organizational quest for quality. The TQFR, for example, was confidential, focused on strengths and areas for improvement, was voluntary ('If you're not looking at "Total Quality," Spiegelman says, 'you don't belong in the company'), operated through a team made up of qualified managers and led by a PQC (Productivity and Quality Center) mentor/consultant, worked on criteria that applied to line staff and the services provided by the unit, and was part of the overall organizational quality effort. The self-assessment audit used the same basic process as the TQFR (and the same scoring structure), but was developed for internal use within the immediate department or section. The external quality audit, which was included in the technical library's quality program, brought in an outside consulting firm to evaluate the strengths and weaknesses of the unit and looked at such key departmental elements as staff evaluation, training and equipment, departmental procedures and processes, marketing, organizational barriers, and similar issues that affect the effective delivery of information.

Management support for the development and implementation of a quality effort is essential, of course, and at Westinghouse it has been in place since the company first began to look seriously at quality issues. When the TQ effort was rolled out in the early 1980s, major resources were devoted to its development and implementation, and much time and energy was devoted to staff training, to putting the quality focus to work within the company. In recent years, with the move away from a more formal TQ effort, some business units of the company are giving it less attention whereas others, such as the energy systems technical library, continue to use those elements of TQ that continue to work for them.

'I tend to be a little more focused in this direction', Spiegelman says, 'for I still think it is important to have that matrix out there, and it is still part of my routine reporting.'

Certainly, as Spiegelman has pointed out, the quality idea is now so much a part of the Westinghouse culture that it doesn't matter whether there is a mandated total quality focus or not. The level of formality or codification of the quality process can now be decided in each managerial section, depending on the needs of the particular unit. It is an approach that could only be successful in an enterprise where the quality focus has become an accepted element in the organizational culture, and where all staff, management and line, are comfortable with the quality emphasis.

Staff participation

Such an acceptance of total quality is in evidence at Westinghouse, and certainly employee involvement, as one of the four imperatives that the TQ program is built on, is given due emphasis in the company's energy systems technical library. Nevertheless, for things to go smoothly, a certain sensitivity on the part of management is required. One of the predictable problems with any quality effort (and one Spiegelman recognizes) is that early on in the general development of the quality approach the language was not well refined. Consequently, most efforts to get staff involved run into an immediate – and very natural hurdle: the very act of organizing a quality effort seems to imply the opposite, that the work already being done is *not* quality work.

This is not a message to be sent to staff members, Spiegelman says, especially if management expect them to participate in the effort. In the management community, as attempts at organizing quality programs were beginning, staff perceptions about what was being done were sometimes lost in the commotion. ('We kind of got off on the wrong foot', is the way Spiegelman puts it, meaning that in any total quality management attempt, not just the effort at Westinghouse, the perceptions of staff about why the effort is being made are as important as any other component in the activity.)

If that mistake is made, and it usually is, it has to be corrected quickly, and that is exactly what happened at Westinghouse. One approach, Spiegelman suggests, is to focus on the continuous improvement element in the quality package, to put the emphasis on the processes that can be improved, and to pull back – wherever possible – in placing blame or finding fault with the employee's work. The other approach, which should be built into any management scenario, is to recognize the important role that the staff play in the information transaction. Because this role is so important, staff are critical to the success of the quality effort.

'It's the staff, the people who are providing the service, who know what the customers need', Spiegelman says, 'and it's the staff who serve as our biggest watchdog, finding out for us what the customers need at any given time.' In fact, the staff and the teamwork they engage in is one of the things Spiegelman is proudest of, when she describes the TQ initiative at her library. 'The staff members are very dedicated in their work', Spiegelman says. 'Most of them have had more than three-quarters of their careers in the library. And there are no whiners or complainers. That sort of thing doesn't work in our library. After all, we had a 50% downsizing in 1990, and we went from a staff of 12 to a staff of 6. We simply couldn't have done this without re-engineering processes, and, at the same time, putting together a team that was willing to pull together. When there are only 6 people, everybody's job touches everybody else's.'

The teams are a big part of the TQ process at Westinghouse, but team assignments, at this point, are not a structured process at the energy systems technical library. In fact, people are not really selected, as such, for teams any more because so many of the teams come together routinely, springing up on their own to work on a particular piece or phase of a process, project or activity. And the people who come on to the teams are interested in what is being done. Spiegelman is a strong believer in having people assigned to teams where there is a natural interest, a project or a process they work with. If team participants are not interested, or the work of the team is not germane to their work, their inactivity will hold the team back, and they are best discouraged from being on the team.

So, it would appear that it's the staff who are driving the TQ effort in the library, but when the point is raised, Spiegelman contradicts it.

'That's where we've come to', she says. 'As we've moved away from the more formal TQ activity, we don't need a specific program in place. So I wouldn't say the staff are driving the TQ effort, because it doesn't need to be driven any more. The staff have taken ownership, and the quality focus is now built in to the work that they do.'

But management has a role, too. A couple of times a year, for example, Spiegelman takes a real leadership initiative with her staff and in all-employee meetings uses an overhead transparency to display the technical information and communication mission and vision ('We've done this often', she says with a laugh. 'It's time for a new overhead!'). Then she and the staff discuss what parts of their work match the mission, about what processes or elements of their work are moving them toward the successful achievement of the mission. And she also asks, very seriously, what isn't matching, if there is something they are doing that doesn't match the department's or the company's vision, for she needs to know, and she and the staff need to discuss it, so they can fix it.

Finally, though, it is the results that count, and at the energy systems technical library at Westinghouse there is a record of exceptional service. It has happened because Spiegelman, her staff and her managers all worked hard to take the results of their total quality efforts and move them into a framework that builds teamwork ('Meaning', Spiegelman says, 'that all our work reflects on all of us'). It's this teamwork that leads to the successful delivery of information, but it also means that everyone who is part of the team must be willing to give some thought to change and to the role of change management in their work. The teams will not succeed unless the members of the teams understand the value of working together, and for some people, that means looking at the work they do – and the company they work for – in a different light.

It also means, in undertaking a total quality management initiative, that information services managers must seek to ask their staff how they can expect to make a difference.

'The staff member has to ask', Spiegelman says, "What is *my* effect on the company's bottom line?" "Where will *I* make a difference?" "Where can I save time, money, materials?" "Can I do anything that will affect the business and business success?" '

These are not easy questions to ask or to answer, and for some staff they pose major barriers against participating in a quality initiative. However, they are barriers that can come down, for the supportive manager, sensing that the fundamentals of trust and teamwork are in place, can lead the staff into understanding and recognizing the value of the quality effort, and it is in that understanding and recognition that the benefits of the quality emphasis can go forward, perhaps even to the extent that it has moved forward at Westinghouse, where all staff, now thoroughly committed to quality practices, simply provide quality service as part of what they do.

Chapter Ten
Moving information services into the quality culture

Just as some of the books of this series begin with quotations that set the tone for some of the issues being addressed, so it is appropriate for this work about total quality management in information services to end with a quotation that expresses exactly what is happening in the general management community, and can be expected to happen in the information services environment as well:

The modern corporation is a thing of the past. The twentieth-century enterprise was defined by Alfred P. Sloan, the legendary chairman of General Motors and the most influential professional manager of our time. His classic opus, *My Years with General Motors*, articulated a management philosophy that has dominated American corporations for decades. The success of the vast modern company, he argued, was based on efficiency and economics of scale – he never once mentioned the words creativity or flexibility. Large, efficient organizations, Sloan theorized, must decentralize manufacturing while centralizing corporate policy and financial controls in hierarchical structures.

For decades, that model remained intact – even as managers ranging from the brash conglomerateurs of the 1960s to the nimble entrepreneurs of the 1980s challenged, debated, and refined it. But by now, so many management gurus and corporate executives have abandoned Sloan's tenets that they're increasingly speaking of a "paradigm shift" in management thought – a dramatic change in the way we think about business problems and organizations. And, in large part, the quality movement is responsible for this change.

This new paradigm values teamwork over individualism, seeks global markets over domestic ones, and focuses on customers, not short-term profits. It views time, rather than a single-minded focus on costs, as the key competitive advantage. It recognizes the value of a multicultural work force in an increasingly diverse labor pool and customer base. The new form of organization is based on a network of alliances and partnerships, not Sloan's self-sufficient hierarchy. It is governed by an independent board with a broad view of the company's constituents, who include not just shareholders, but also employees, suppliers, customers, and the local community. Workers, previously expected to be self-sufficient, can now aspire to personal growth on the job. An autocratic leadership has given way to an inspirational one. And quality, once constrained by what was affordable, is no longer compromised for any reason (Byrne 1994, p. 201).

Certainly that is the goal of any information services operation, to provide the highest standards of information delivery that can be provided, and to do so without compromising quality for any reason. It is a noble endeavor, and it is what draws those with management responsibility for information services operations to the TQM methodology. Anyone working in the delivery of information wants to provide the best information that their identified customers can get, and to do so they are more than willing to embrace TQM techniques to ensure that such high standards are embraced. And today's information services practitioners are well aware that they are living in a time when enabling technology provides them with the means for meeting these standards, and they take on the challenges with enthusiasm and spirit.

The beauty of the quality approach to information delivery is in its adherence, without apology, to the authority of the customer. By building on this critical framework, TQM and its many variations provide a unique vehicle for moving information practitioners back into the customer-focused emphasis that the profession has always purported to have. Now, with enabling technology, with the application of quality methodologies to information delivery, and with a new emphasis on the role of the customer, the people who deliver information to those customers can finally do what they've been saying they wanted to do for generations. With a TQM focus in the information services unit, staff and customers come together to achieve what they had meant to achieve all along. Without damaging in any way the relationship between the information customer and the information provider, a quality framework sets up a basis for mission-critical information delivery, which is all the customers (and presumably the staff) want anyway.

In many respects, a good review of what this book attempts is to look at the 'top management strategies for quality improvement' that Madu and Kuei put forward as the new focus of management in the new managerial environment, and to attempt to link some of them to the information services environment. Just as management paradigms are changing, so are information services paradigms (as has, been the theme of much of this book). Madu and Kuei (1985), in their look at strategic total quality management (pp. 13–15) contend that certain management strategies will lead to management success in the general business community. Four of these, if incorporated into the strategic planning and thinking for information services management, can lead to success in information delivery:

1. *Management development, employee retention and leadership.* 'Top management should take the lead in the strategic total quality management transformation process. The "critical mass" (the workers) at the floor level must be taught the importance of organizational change and transformation. They must consider their stakes at risk and view the success and survival of the organization as theirs. They must be made aware that their performance and their contributions to the organization are significant in shaping its future. By management taking steps to include and value the responsibilities of its employees, a linkage is established between STQM and company vision. An STQM culture is developed to motivate employees from within.'

   For information services managers it becomes a matter of considerable urgency that all staff be encouraged to participate in the organization's and the information services unit's efforts to develop a quality focus. It becomes essentially a matter of trust, but it goes beyond trust in assigning responsibility and accountability to all employees for the value of the work the unit produces. The enthusiastic acceptance of the corporate vision becomes more than a matter of corporate/staff loyalty: it becomes (or *should* become) the standard by which information services workers keep their job. If they are interested in and committed to providing the highest levels of service, they continue to be employed in the department. If they are not, they and the information services manager should agree to part company.

2. *Total customer focus.* 'Process changes should always be viewed from the perspective of the customer. How will change in technology or work process improve services delivered to the customers? These may be in terms of product satisfaction, reduction in the emission of dangerous gases, or building of trust and confidence in the firm's services. If these are not achieved, the organization is not purely customer focused.'

   In an information services operation, unlike a production facility, the information worker has the opportunity to deal directly with the value and effects of the services, products and consultations he or she is providing to the customer. Although there are naturally some barriers to the implementation of an ongoing and direct follow-up from customers (they may be in a hurry to leave the unit, for example, or they may take the information they need via an electronic or other delivery format, which means that they are not in physical proximity with the information worker, etc.), every effort should be made, and built in to the unit's operating procedures, to include some methodology for follow-up. Additionally, part of the clerical or backstage administrative work of the unit must be devoted to analyzing and interpreting the customers' perceptions about the service they receive, so that when it is necessary to move to a new phase of study of processes, or to review the effectiveness of one or another process, the customers' point of view will be represented.

3. *Entrepreneurial spirit.* 'Workers must be motivated to think positively about change – change that will enhance their work and make them more productive. Generally, people are reluctant to change especially when they are used to routines. However, if they are to be more productive and continuously improve as suggested by the STQM definitions, change will be inevitable. It is more important to implement new ideas with potentials to improve organization performance than to rely on experiences that make only marginal contribution. Top management must therefore encourage workers to develop the entrepreneurial spirit.'

When information services workers are permitted to take risks, and when they understand that failures will be treated as learning experiences (for the department as well as for its employees) and not as personal or professional failures, that punishment is not inflicted because this or that calculated risk was taken and failed, the level of innovation rises and all information services employees, especially frontline staff, become enthusiastic and, more important, *interested* in providing exceptional service for information customers. But they cannot achieve this level of participation if they are not encouraged by their managers, so the encouragement of an entrepreneurial spirit is required.

4. *Implementation focus.* 'Organizations often fail in their TQM transformation because they lack appropriate implementation. The *check* stage of Deming's plan-do-check-act cycle should be the focal point for evaluating any process of change.'

For the information services employee and the quality team that he or she will belong to, every process review and every innovation will include a routine step where the team will stop to ask if they are achieving the results they expect to achieve and, especially important, if the information being brought forward can be acted upon. At this stage the hidden barriers must be brought out into the open, and the quality process cannot proceed unless the team has determined that the barriers can be overcome.

In total quality management terms, then, how do you build an information services operation that *works*? In Chapter 2 of this book reference was made to Lucy Lettis and her three criteria for success in information delivery: the information customers are getting is what they need, the information services unit is contributing to organizational success, and the information services staff are happy and proud of the work they are doing.

In the same interview, Lettis was asked what she would say if someone came along and asked her the secret of a successful information services operation. She identified five key elements in the management/success formula, and putting them together creates an information services operation that is built on a quality-focused foundation:

1. **Find supportive management.** This is key, but working with management is also a two-way street. Yes, management has to be interested in what is going on in the library or information center, but the information practitioners must also recognize what senior management's information needs are and how they can be served. Catering to the decision makers is not a choice, it's a requirement.

2. **Build a top-notch staff.** No matter how good a manager you are, you can't do it all yourself. You simply must find the best people, see that they are trained (and that they continue to be trained), compensate them properly, and let them do their work. Trust them and they won't let you down.

3. **Keep up.** As the manager, you yourself must keep up, by reading, by participating in professional organizations, by going to conferences, by doing all you can to learn all you need to know. And you don't limit yourself to information issues: you're a manager, and you have to keep up with what's going on in management as well.

4. **Understand marketing.** You must recognize that you're not just marketing a department or an organizational unit, but yourself and your staff as well. Don't hide your light under a bushel. If you've reached a management level of responsibility, your talents are too good to be hidden away, and so are those of your staff and your department.

5. **Work hard – and be fascinated by the work.** Being the manager of a successful information services unit is not easy. Long hours are required, and while an obsessive/compulsive personality is not necessarily called for, having some tendencies in that direction can provide serious motivation. More important, however, is the requirement that you be really excited by the situation: not necessarily the content of the information being delivered or the subject specialty of the organization, but the process of managing an information unit. It's that fascination that spurs you on to try newer and better things, to look for even more demanding challenges.

In information services, what we are seeking is really not very complicated: we want to provide our users and our customers with the best information services, products and consultations that we can. We want to do this in a framework that builds on their authority as customers, and we want them to take the information they acquire from our efforts and put it to work effectively, so that they accomplish what they started out to accomplish. If we are to succeed, total quality management in information services is no longer something we can choose or not choose to implement. TQM and the quality focus are now essential elements of our work in information services we recognize that we must demand quality management in information services in order to succeed as information services providers, the sooner we will be delivering what our customers expect from us. We do it through the establishment and implementation of a serious quality program in our information services operations, and we do it because we have a desire for quality, because we have the enthusiastic support of our management, because our services are customer-focused, because our measures are valid, because we are continuously improving our processes, and because we are an information services unit built on a foundation of trust and teamwork. When these all come together, as they do in a quality-focused information services unit, the unit and its employees are judged successful by all information stakeholders.

References

John A. Byrne. 'TQM in the twenty-first century: paradigms for post-modern managers,' in *The Quality Imperative: A Business Week Guide*. New York: McGraw-Hill, 1994.

[Lettis, Lucy]. "Determined?" "Driven?" Perhaps even "Relentless?" At Arthur Andersen in New York, success in the company's business information center connects with Lucy Lettis's own career path.' *InfoManage: The International Management Newsletter for the Information Services Executive* 3 (5), April, 1996.

Madu, Christian N. and Kuei, Chu-hua. *Strategic Total Quality Management: Corporate Performance and Product Quality*. Westport, CT. and London: Quorum Books, 1995.

Selected bibliography

Abram, Stephen A. 'Adding value . . .' *InfoManage: The International Management Newsletter for the Information Services Executive* 3 (3), February, 1996.

ACLIS (Australian Council of Libraries and Information Services). *Benchmarking, Best Practice, and Quality Management: What's it All About?* Canberra, ACT, Australia: Australian Council of Libraries and Information Services, 1996.

Aguilar, Francis J. *Scanning the Business Environment*. New York: Macmillan, 1967.

Albrecht, Karl. *At America's Service: How Corporations Can Revolutionize the Way They Treat Their Customers*. Homewood, IL: Dow Jones-Irwin, 1988.

Albrecht, Karl. *The Northbound Train: Finding the Purpose, Setting the Direction, and Shaping the Destiny of Your Organization*. New York: American Management Association, 1994.

APQC (American Productivity & Quality Center). *The Benchmarking Management Guide*. Portland, OR: Productivity Press, 1992.

Ashkenas, Ron, Ulrich, Dave, Jick, Todd, and Kerr, Steve. *The Boundaryless Organization: Breaking the Chains of Organizational Structure*. San Francisco: Jossey-Bass, 1995.

Ashworth, Wilfred. *Special Librarianship*. London: Clive Bingley, 1979.

Auster, Ethel and Choo, Chun Wei. 'Environmental scanning: preliminary findings of interviews with CEOs in two Canadian industries. In *Proceedings of the 56th Annual Meeting of the American Society for Information Science held in Pittsburgh, PA, October 26–29, 1992*, edited by Debora Shaw. Medford, NJ: Learned Information Inc., 1993.

Australia Department of Finance. *Quality for our Clients: Improvement for the Future*. Canberra, ACT, Australia: Australia Department of Finance, 1995.

Balm, Gerald J. *Benchmarking: A practitioner's Guide for Becoming and Staying Best of the Best*. Schaumburg, IL: Quality & Productivity Management Association, 1992.

Barker, Joel. *Paradigms: the Business of Discovering the Future*. New York: HarperBusiness, 1993.

Barrier, Michael.'Small firms put quality first.' *Nation's Business* 80 (5), May, 1992.

Blewett, Laurel A. 'Part of the team: profile of a pediatric librarian.' *The Best of OPL II: Selected Readings from The One-Person Library: A Newsletter for Librarians and Management, 1989-1994*.Washington DC: Special Libraries Association, 1996.

Bovet, Susan Fry. 'CEO serves as chief communicator of TQM program.' *Public Relations Journal* 50 (6), June/July, 1994.

British Standards Institution. *Quality Vocabulary: Part 2. Concepts and Related Definitions*. (BS 4778: Part 2: 1991), quoted in Brockman, John R. 'Just another management fad? The implications of TQM for library and information services.' *Aslib Proceedings* 44 (7/8), July/August, 1992.

Brockman, John R. 'Just another management fad? The implications of TQM for library and information services.' *Aslib Proceedings* 44 (7/8), July/August, 1992.

Burk, Cornelius F. Jr. and Horton, Forest W., Jr. *InfoMap: A Complete Guide to Discovering Corporate Information Resources*. New York: Prentice Hall, 1983.

Byrne, John A. 'TQM in the twenty-first century: paradigms for post-modern managers,' in *The Quality Imperative: A Business Week Guide*. New York: McGraw-Hill, 1994.

[Campbell, Carol] 'Five minutes with Carol Campbell in Oklahoma City.' *InfoManage: The International Management Newsletter for the Information Services Manager* 3 (5), April, 1996.

Capezio, Peter, and Morehouse, Debra. *Taking the Mystery Out of TQM: A Practical Guide to Total Quality Management*. 2nd edn. Franklin Lakes, NJ: Career Press, 1995.

Carson, Paula Phillips, Carson, Kerry David, and Phillips, Joyce Schouest. *The Library Manager's Deskbook: 102 Expert Solutions to 101 Common Dilemmas*. Chicago: The American Library Association, 1995.

Choo, Chun Wei. *Information Management for the Intelligent Organization: The Art of Scanning the Environment.* ASIS (American Society for Information Science) Monograph Series. Medford, New Jersey: Information Today Inc., 1995.

Clausen, Helge. 'ISO 9000 and all that: is the information sector ready for the big quantum leap?' *Online Information 94 Proceedings.* London: Learned Information, 1995.

Crosby, Philip B. *Let's Talk Quality: 96 Questions You Always Wanted to Ask Phil Crosby.* New York: Penguin, 1990.

Crosby, Philip B. *Quality is Free: The Art of Making Quality Certain.* New York: Signet, 1979.

Crosby, Philip B. *Quality Without Tears.* New York: McGraw-Hill, 1984.

Cundari, Leigh, and Stutz, Kara. 'Enhancing library services: an exploration in meeting customer needs through total quality management.' *Special Libraries* 86 (3), Summer, 1995.

Curzon, Susan C. *Managing Change.* New York: Neal-Schuman, 1989.

Davenport, Paul. *Process Innovation: Reengineering Work through Information Technology.* Cambridge, MA: Harvard Business School Press, 1993.

Davidow, William H. and Malone, Michael S. 'Rethinking management.' *The Virtual Corporation.* New York: HarperCollins, 1992.

Deming, W. Edwards. *Out of the Crisis.* Cambridge, MA: Massachusetts Institute of Technology Center for Advanced Engineering Study, 1986.

Dinerman, Gloria. 'The information professional: a portrait of progress.' *The SpeciaList* 19 (5), May, 1996, pp. 1, 11, 14.

Drake, Miriam A. 'Libraries, technology, and quality.' *Advances in Library Administration and Organization.* JAI Press, 1993.

[Drake, Miriam A.] Mimi Drake at Georgia Tech: ten years online and the future is NOW!' *InfoManage: The International Management Newsletter for the Information Services Executive* 2 (6), May, 1995.

Drake, Miriam A. and Stuart, Crit. 'TQM in research libraries.' *Special Libraries* 84 (3), Summer, 1993.

Drucker, Peter F. *Managing in a Time of Great Change.* New York: Truman Talley Books, 1995.

Drucker, Peter F. *Managing the Non-Profit Organization: Practices and Principles.* New York: HarperCollins, 1990.

Duncan, William L. and Luftig & Warren International. *Total Quality: Key*

Terms & Concepts. New York: American Management Association, 1995.

Duston, Beth. 'IT in the OPL: the fugitive user.' *The One-Person Library: A Newsletter for Librarians and Management* 10 (2), June, 1993.

Duston, Beth. 'Technology changes customer focus and customer service.' *The One-Person Library: A Newsletter for Librarians and Management* 10 (11), March, 1994.

Ettorre, Barbara. 'Managing competitive intelligence.' *Management Review* (October, 1995).

Fahey, Liam and Narayanan, Vadake K. *Macroenvironmental Analysis for Strategic Management*. St. Paul, MN: West Publishing, 1986.

Ferriero, David S. and Wilding, Thomas L. 'Scanning the environment in strategic planning.' *Masterminding Tomorrow's Information – Creative Strategies for the '90s*. Washington DC: Special Libraries Association, 1991.

Fine, Sara. 'Research and psychology of information use.' *Library Trends* (32).

Franklin, Brinley. 'The cost of quality – its application to libraries.' *Journal of Library Administration* 20 (2), 1994.

Fredenburg, Anne M. 'Quality assurance: establishing a program for special libraries.' *Special Libraries* 79 (4), Fall, 1988.

[Ginsburg, Carol]. 'The information independent organization: Carol Ginsburg's bold approach.' *InfoManage: The International Management Newsletter for the Information Services Executive* 1 (1).

Gohlke, Annette. 'Reinvention effort provides model for libraries.' *Library Benchmarking Newsletter* 3 (1), January/February, 1996.

Griffiths, José-Marie, and King, Donald W. *A Manual on the Evaluation of Information Centers and Services*. New York: American Institute of Aeronautics and Astronautics, 1991.

Hammer, Michael and Champy, James. *Reengineering the Corporation: A Manifesto for Business Revolution*. New York: HarperCollins, 1993.

Hammer, Michael, and Stanton, Steven A. *The Reengineering Revolution: A Handbook*. New York: HarperBusiness, 1994.

Harari, Oren. 'Think strategy when you think quality.' *Management Review* (March, 1993).

Harari, Oren. 'Mind matters.' *Management Review* (January, 1996).

Harrington-Mackin, Deborah. *The Team Building Tool Kit*. New York: American Management Association, 1994.

Hayes, Robert M. *Strategic Management for Academic Libraries: A Handbook.* Westport, CT: Greenwood Press, 1993.

Hodapp, Paul F. *Ethics in the Business World.* Melbourne, FL: Krieger Publishing Company, 1994.

Hodgetts, Richard M. *Implementing TQM in Small and Medium-Sized Organizations: A Step-by-Step Guide.* New York: American Management Association, 1996.

Horton, Forrest Woody. *Extending the Librarianis Domain: A Survey of Emerging Occupation Opportunities for Librarians and Information Professionals.* Washington DC: Special Libraries Association, 1994.

Imai, Masaaki. *Kaizen, the Key to Japan's Competitive Success.* New York: Random House, 1986.

Ishikawa, Kaoru. *What is Total Quality Control? The Japanese Way.* Englewood Cliffs, NJ: Prentice-Hall, 1985.

Jauch, Lawrence R. and Glueck, William F. *Business Policy and Strategic Management.* New York: McGraw-Hill, 1988.

Juran, Joseph M. *Juran on Planning for Quality.* New York: The Free Press, 1988.

Jurow, Susan, and Barnard, Susan B. eds. *Integrating Total Quality Management in a Library Setting.* New York: Haworth Press, 1993.

Kahaner, Larry. *Competitive Intelligence.* New York: Simon and Schuster, 1996.

Kushel, Gerald. *Reaching the Peak Performance Zone: How to Motivate Yourself and Others to Excel.* New York: American Management Association, 1994.

[Lawes, Ann] 'Ann Lawes: thinking about the information manager as change agent.' *InfoManage: The International Management Newsletter for the Information Services Executive* 3 (1), December, 1995.

Lester, Ray and Waters, Judith 1989. *Environmental Scanning and Business Strategy.* London, UK: British Library Research and Development Department, 1989.

[Lettis, Lucy] ' "Determined?" "Driven?" Perhaps even "Relentless?" At Arthur Andersen in New York, success in the company's business information center connects of Lucy Lettis's own career path.' *InfoManage: The International Management Newsletter for the Information Services Executive* 3 (5), April, 1996.

Lewis, David W. 'Eight truths for middle managers in lean times.' *Library Journal* September 1, 1991.

[Lux, Claudia] 'Claudia Lux at the Senatsbibliothek Berlin: looking at information services with a political eye.' *InfoManage: The International Management Newsletter for the Information Services Professional* 3 (9), August, 1996.

Mackey, Terry, and Mackey, Kitty 'Think quality! The Deming approach *does* work in libraries.' *Library Journal* May 15, 1992.

Madu, Christian N. and Kuei, Chu-hua. *Strategic Total Quality Management: Corporate Performance and Product Quality*. Westport, CT. and London: Quorum Books, 1995.

Marshall, Edward M. *Transforming the Work We Do: the Power of the Collaborative Workplace*. New York: American Management Association, 1995.

Matarazzo, James M. *Corporate Library Excellence*. Washington DC: Special Libraries Association, 1990.

Matarazzo, James M., Prusak, Laurence and Gauthier, Michael R. *Valuing Corporate Libraries: A Survey of Senior Managers*. Washington DC: Special Libraries Association, 1990.

Matarazzo, James M. and Drake, Miriam A. eds.. *Information for Management: A Handbook*. Washington DC: Special Libraries Association, 1994.

McFadden, Laurie. 'AT&T Bell Laboratories creates a quality team to study technical reports.' *Special Libraries* 85 (1), Winter, 1994.

Megill, Kenneth A. *Making the Information Revolution: A Handbook on Federal Information Resources Management*. Silver Spring, MD: The Association for Information and Image Management, 1995).

[Megill, Kenneth] 'Relaxed at the revolution: Ken Megill takes us into information resources management.' *InfoManage: The International Management Newsletter for the Information Services Executive* 1 (10), pp. 1-4.

[Molholt, Pat] 'Pat Molholt's bold CHIPS project.' *InfoManage: The International Management Newsletter for the Information Services Executive* 1 (2), pp. 1-5.

Orna, Elizabeth. *Practical Information Policies: How to Manage Information Flow in Organizations*. Brookfield, VT: Gower, 1990.

[Park, Mary] 'Mary Park thinks "partnering" is a good idea – if the partner is senior management.' *InfoManage: The International Management* Newsletter for the Information Services Executive 3 (2), pp. 1-5.

Parris, Lou B. 'Know your company and its business.' *Information for Management: A Handbook*. Edited by James M. Matarazzo and Miriam A. Drake. Washington DC: Special Libraries Association, 1994.

Paul, Meg. 'Improving service provision.' *The Australian Library Journal* February, 1990.

Penzias, Arno. *Ideas and Information*. New York: Touchstone, 1989.

[Piggott, Sylvia] 'Special Libraries Association breaks records in Boston: new president Piggott spells out her agenda for the future of information services management: an *InfoManage* value-added report.' *InfoManage: The International Management Newsletter for the Information Services Professional* 3 (8) [Supplement], July, 1996.

[Piggott, Sylvia] 'Sylvia Piggott at the Bank of Montréal: reengineering information services for the 2nd era of the information age.' *InfoManage: The International Management Newsletter for the Information Services Executive* 2 (3), pp. 1–4.

Piggott, Sylvia E.A. 'Why corporate librarians must reengineer the library for the new information age'. *Special libraries* 86 (1) 1995, 11–20.

St. Clair, Guy, ed. 'Benchmarking, total quality management, and the learning organization: new management paradigms for the information environment.' *Special Libraries* 84 (3), Summer, 1993.

St. Clair, Guy. *Customer Service in the Information Environment*. London and New Brunswick, NJ: Bowker-Saur, 1993.

St. Clair, Guy. *Entrepreneurial Librarianship: the Key to Effective Information Services*. London and NY: Bowker-Saur, 1995.

St. Clair, Guy. *Power and Influence: Enhancing Information Services Within the Organization*. London and NY: Bowker-Saur, 1994.

St. Clair, Guy. 'TQM in the one-person library.' *The One-Person Library: A Newsletter for Librarians and Management* 9 (5), September, 1992.

St. Clair, Guy. 'TQM in the one-person library: a further look.' *The One-Person Library: A Newsletter for Librarians and Management* 9 (5), September, 1992.

St. Clair, Guy and Berner, Andrew. 'Thinking about . . . how insourcing changes the role of the one-person library.' *The One-person Library: A Newsletter for Librarians and Management* 13 (4), August, 1996.

St. Clair, Guy and Williamson, Joan. *Managing the One-Person Library*. London: Butterworths, 1986.

Schier, Lois M. 'Customer satisfaction surveys: measuring satisfaction and communication service in special libraries.' *The Information Professional: An Unparalleled Resource: Papers Contributed for the*

81st Annual Conference of the Special Libraries Association, June 9-14, 1990, Pittsburgh, PA. Washington DC: Special Libraries Association, 1990.

Senge, Peter M. *The Fifth Discipline: the Art & Practice of the Learning Organization.* New York: Currency Doubleday, 1994.

Senge, Peter M. 'The leader's new work: building learning organizations.' *Sloan Management Review* 32 (1) Fall, 1990.

Senge, Peter M. 'Microworlds and learning laboratories.' *The Fifth Discipline Field Book.* Peter Senge et al. New York: Currency Doubleday, 1993.

Shapiro, Eileen. *Fad Surfing in the Board Room: Reclaiming the Courage to Manage in the Age of Instant Answers.* Reading, MA: Addison-Wesley, 1995.

[Siegel, Ira] 'LEXIS-NEXIS executive focuses in on the ninth wave for information services.' *InfoManage: The International Management Newsletter for the Information Services Executive* 3 (5), April, 1996.

Special Libraries Association. Presidential Study Commission on Professional Recruitment, Ethics, and Professional Standards ('The PREPS Commission'). Washington DC: Special Libraries Association, 1992.

Spiegelman, Barbara M. 'Total quality management: how to improve your library without losing your Mind,' in Matarazzo, James M., and Miriam A. Drake, eds. *Information for Management: A Handbook.* Washington DC: Special Libraries Association, 1994.

Spiegelman, Barbara M. 'Total quality management in libraries: getting down to the real nitty-gritty.' *Library Management Quarterly* 15 (3), Summer, 1992.

Szilagyi, Andrew D. *Management and Performance.* Glenview, IL: Scott, Foresman, 1988.

Tees, Miriam. 'Is it possible to educate librarians as managers?' *Special Libraries* 75 (6), July, 1994, (173-182) .

Thompson, LeRoy Jr. *Mastering the Challenges of Change.* New York: American Management Association, 1994.

Urgo, Marisa. 'Information services and information technology: can management make the partnering make sense?' *InfoManage: The International Management Newsletter for the Information Services Professional* 3 (9), August, 1996.

Victoria. State of Victoria Office of Library Services. *Measuring*

Performance: a Guide to the Use of Benchmarking for Public Libraries. Melbourne, V: State of Victoria Office of Library Services, 1995.

White, Herbert S. 'Participative management is the answer, but what was the question?' *Librarians and the Awakening From Innocence: A Collection of Papers.* Boston: G.K. Hall and Company, 1989.

White, Marilyn Domas and Abels, Eileen G. 'Measuring service quality in special libraries: lessons from service marketing.' *Special Libraries* 86 (1), Winter, 1995.

Williams, Richard L. *Essentials of Total Quality Management.* New York: American Management Association, 1994.

Younger, Jennifer. 'Total quality management: can we move beyond the Jargon?' *Central Ohio Bulletin Special Libraries Association* 27 (2), February, 1992.

Zeithaml, Valarie A., Parasuraman, A. and Berry, Leonard L. *Delivering Quality Service: Balancing Customer Perceptions and Expectations.* New York: Free Press, 1990.

Zeithaml, Valarie A., Parasuraman, A. and Berry, Leonard L. 'Reassessment of expectations as a comparison standard in measuring service quality: implications for further research.' *Journal of Marketing* 58 (1), January, 1994.

Appendix

The George Westinghouse Total Quality Achievement Award Evaluation Criteria
(Reprinted with permission)

Evaluation Criteria Summary

		max. pts.
1.0	**CUSTOMER ORIENTATION**	**225**
	Subcriteria:	
1.1	External Customers' Perceptions	50
1.2	External Customer Focus	50
1.3	Values Comparisons	40
1.4	Internal Customers	30
1.5	Employee Customer Awareness	30
1.6	Customer Commitment	15
1.7	Public Safety and Health	10
2.0	**PARTICIPATION**	**100**
	Subcriteria:	
2.1	Management Involvement	40
2.2	Employee Involvement	40
2.3	Departments	20
3.0	**DEVELOPMENT**	**75**
	Subcriteria:	
3.1	Development Process	25
3.2	Needs Assessment	15
3.3	Awareness	15
3.4	Skills Training	20
4.0	**MOTIVATION**	**50**
	Subcriteria	
4.1	Climate and Environment	30
4.2	Recognition	20
5.0	**PRODUCTS AND SERVICES**	**75**
	Subcriteria:	
5.1	Value to Cost	30
5.2	Definition of Requirements	20
5.3	Continuous Improvement	15
5.4	Review and Verification	10
6.0	**PROCESSES AND PROCEDURES**	**100**
	Subcriteria:	
6.1	Integration	20
6.2	Organization Support	20
6.3	Verification and Management	20
6.4	Error Prevention	15
6.5	Technology and Innovation	15
6.6	Safety, Health, and Environment	10

		max. pts.
7.0	**INFORMATION**	**50**
	Subcriteria:	
7.1	Information Quality	20
7.2	Information Improvement	15
7.3	Customer and Process Requirements	15
8.0	**SUPPLIERS**	**50**
	Subcriteria:	
8.1	Requirements	15
8.2	Product and Service Quality	15
8.3	Supply Processes	10
8.4	Supply Accountability	10
9.0	**CULTURE**	**50**
	Subcriteria:	
9.1	Organization Beliefs	15
9.2	Change Leadership	15
9.3	Total Quality System Description	10
9.4	Pride	10
10.0	**PLANNING**	**75**
	Subcriteria:	
10.1	Strategic Imperative	30
10.2	Total Quality Improvement Plan	30
10.3	Organization Plan	15
11.0	**COMMUNICATIONS**	**50**
	Subcriteria:	
11.1	Policy and Requirements	15
11.2	Two-Way	15
11.3	Actions Versus Words	15
11.4	Public Responsibility	5
12.0	**ACCOUNTABILITY**	**100**
	Subcriteria:	
12.1	Performance Trends	35
12.2	Reports and Diagnostic Techniques	20
12.3	Progress Reviews	20
12.4	Departmental Measures and Objectives	15
12.5	Employee Objectives	10
MAXIMUM TOTAL POINTS		**1000**

EVALUATION CRITERIA

1.0   CUSTOMER ORIENTATION
225 points

Satisfying customers through meeting their requirements and value expectations is the primary task of every employee.

1.1   External Customers' Perceptions
50 points

Describe how products and services are perceived by customers to be first in Total Quality.

Areas to Address

A.   Customer perception of products or services: measured; perceived first in Total Quality.
B.   Customer feedback: documented; tracked; improvement action taken; timely; distributed internally and to customer; lost business analyzed; management regularly visits customers.
C.   Direct Sales Force/Distributors/ Dealers/ Agents: selected; trained; evaluated; visit and participate in customer feedback.
D.   Evidence that market share or competitive position enhanced by Total Quality efforts.

1.2   External Customer Focus
50 points

Describe how meeting customer requirements is the primary objective of all employees.

Areas to Address

A.   Customer needs: how determined; policy to meet or formally change requirements; communicated to organization.
B.   Communications to customer: quality of proposals; presentations; ads and brochures include Total Quality.
C.   Customer complaints: documented; tracked; corrective action taken; timely; distributed internally and to customer.
D.   Easy to do business with: organization permits easy access for information and assistance; employees empowered to resolve problems; follow-up to assure satisfaction.

1.3 Value Comparisons   40 points

Describe how the organization's value (as perceived by customers) is compared with competitors' value (as defined by customers) and is used to gain competitive advantage.

Areas to Address

A.   Customer value is defined, measured, benchmarked to competitors, used for improvement.
B.   Value/Price ratio: understood; competitive; improving trends.

1.4 Internal Customers   30 points

Show how internal customers' (the next person or department in the process) perceptions of performance are measured, evaluated and reported to responsible functions.

Areas to Address

A.   Internal customer concept: understood; applied; performance measures reflect understanding of concept and are improving.
B.   Response to internal customer requests followed; response time tracked; feedback obtained as to response adequacy.

1.5   Employee Customer Awareness
30 points

Describe what the organization does to actively seek ways to make all employees aware of customers and their needs.

Areas to Address

A.   Customer awareness: employees receive feedback about customer perceptions; personal contact with the customer is encouraged.
B.   Employees aware of customer's value system and performance measures and their role in satisfying the customer.
C.   Customer contact employees: defined, measurable standards; trained; empowered.

EVALUATION CRITERIA

1.6 Customer Commitment   15 points

Describe product or service guarantees or warranties and data concerning customer views.

Areas to Address

A. Guarantees and Warranties: viewed as appropriate; competitive; improving trends.
B. Other Commitments to promote trust and confidence.
C. Trends during last three years.

1.7 Public Safety and Health   10 points

Describe goals and requirements for the safety and health of customers and the community. Describe procedures for compliance with health and safety standards.

Areas to Address

A. Appropriate formal safety program for customers and the community. Clarity and completeness of safety documentation (i.e., safety manuals, warnings, and training, etc.)
B. Collection and use of safety-related data from customer. Timeliness of response to customer complaints about safety.
C. Compliance with federal and state safety regulations, i.e., CPSC, DoT, FTC, etc.

2.0 PARTICIPATION   100 points

All employees participate in establishing and achieving Total Quality improvement goals.

2.1 Management Involvement   40 points

Describe how managers are personally and effectively leading the Total Quality Improvement Process.

Areas to Address

A. Meetings: staff and workplace; regularly planned and scheduled; results communicated; judged effective; all functions represented.
B. Managers visibly involved and committed: open door policy exists.
C. Managers lead by example: hands-on; daily involvement; up/down/peer participation.
D. Decision-making is at the lowest practical level in the organization.

2.2 Employee Involvement   40 points

Describe how employee contributions to improvement are actively encouraged by management and implemented when Total Quality improvement will result.

Areas to Address

A. Measures/Goals: all employees involved; consistent with Total Quality.
B. Opportunities for participation: suggestions encouraged and prompt response given; *multifunctional* quality improvement teams active, growing and showing *results*.
C. Receptivity: different opinions sought; all views considered; no detectable 'Not Invented Here.'

EVALUATION CRITERIA

2.3 Departments   20 points

Summarize how all functional departments contribute to developing and implementing Total Quality Improvement Process.

Areas to Address

A.   Total Quality Improvement Process has input from all departments; involves appropriate departments in implementation.
B.   Interdepartmental relations: cooperative and mutual advantage sought.
C.   Evidence of successful interfunctional activities is available.

3.0 DEVELOPMENT   75 points

People are recognized as key strategic resources. Development opportunities are provided to assure that each employee understands, supports and contributes to achieving Total Quality.

3.1 Development Process   25 points

Describe how all employees are developed as key strategic resources.

Areas to Address

A.   Commitment: employees are seen as a major source of competitive advantage; career development is emphasized; guidance and counseling provided; employees have a leading role in their own development.
B.   Process: employee development is a defined process; goals are set; progress is measured; plans are revised and continuously improved. Includes classroom training, lateral/rotational assignments and other activities responsive to global business and individual needs. Management is accountable tor the development process. Employees view the process as credible.

3.2 Needs Assessment   15 points

Describe how development and training needed to support Total Quality improvement are objectively assessed and documented.

Areas to Address

A.   Development and training needs assessments: are conducted objectively: anticipate change; support Total Quality improvement.
B.   Employee development and training plans: documented; implemented; reviewed regularly and updated.

EVALUATION CRITERIA

3.3 Awareness   15 points

Describe how awareness training is provided to assure that each employee understands, supports and contributes to achieving Total Quality.

Areas to Address

A. Employees attitudes: beliefs are evaluated; are improving; reflect positive climate; are changed through training and management actions; support achievement of Total Quality.
B. Awareness: Total Quality understood; vision, mission, policies communicated; quality improvement strategy communicated; specific improvement projects identified; Total Ouality orientations conducted.

3.4 Skills Training   20 points

Show how each employee receives sufficient training in techniques and job skills to support the Total Quality Improvement Process.

Areas to Address

A. Techniques: training conducted in areas such as value (defined by customers) measurement; quality measurement; quality plan; product and process integration; information systems; diagnostic techniques.
B. Job skills: key skills identified; upgraded through training and self-development.

4.0 MOTIVATION   50 points

Employees are motivated to achieve Total Quality through trust, respect and recognition.

4.1 Climate and Environment
30 points

Describe evidence of management beliefs that employees want to do a good job.

Describe how a positive atmosphere of trust and respect between management and employees has been created.

Areas to Address

A. Climate for resolving problems: asks 'what' and 'why,' not 'who.' A positive atmosphere is encouraged by people who listen.
B. Organization provides equipment materials and information to do the right things right the first time.
C. Change is viewed positively. Disincentives to change are minimized.

4.2 Recognition   20 points

Describe how managers personally, regularly and fairly recognize individuals and groups for measurable contributions to Total Quality.

Areas to Address

A. Objective: based on measurable contributions to quality; is widely communicated; goes beyond immediate supervisors.
B. Regular: personally given by managers; promptly follows achievements; occurs frequently.

EVALUATION CRITERIA

5.0   PRODUCTS AND SERVICES
75 points

Products and services are appropriately
innovative and are reviewed, verified
produced and controlled to meet customer
requirements.

5.1 Value to Cost   30 points

Summarize how value/cost ratios are known
and are globally competitive.

Areas to Address

A.   Value/cost: compared to others; is one
      of best; is improving.
B.   Quality costs: decreasing.

5.2 Definition of Requirements
20 points

Describe how customer requirements as well
as world-class internal product/service
standards, are defined.

Areas to Address

A.   Product/service development guidelines
      available and used; customer and all
      departments involved; compared to
      world-class standards; requirements,
      processes and facilities compatible;
      meet customer and internal
      requirements.
B.   Product/service: value-centered;
      simplicity stressed; key and critical
      characteristics emphasized, e.g.,
      producibility, reliability, availability.
C.   Standards are established for
      appropriate products/services,
      verification and controls.

5.3 Continuous Improvement
15 points

Describe ongoing programs to improve
products and services through measurement
and analysis of feedback data and
incorporation of new technology.

Areas to Address

A.   Customer and internal feedback:
      reports exist; Total Quality measures
      used effectively; effective problem
      response; improvements achieved.
B.   New technologies: assess new product
      or service capabilities; use where
      appropriate for competitive
      advantage.
C.   New developments: monitored for
      effectiveness and timeliness.

5.4 Review and Verification   10 points

Describe how formal reviews and/or
verifications are accomplished to assure that
products and services meet all requirements.
Show how products and services are verified
before delivery.

Areas to Address

A.   Review: continuous; value and costs
      assessed; use independent, formal
      reviews especially at conceptual
      stage.
B.   Verification: conformance to
      requirements verified before delivery.

EVALUATION CRITERIA

6.0 PROCESSES AND PROCEDURES
100 points

Processes and procedures used throughout the organization to create and deliver products and services are developed as an integrated, verified and controlled system using appropriate technology and tools.

6.1 Integration 20 points

Describe how processes and procedures and the products and services created by them are jointly designed as an integrated system. Show how cycle time reduction is a driving force.

Areas to Address

A. System approach: any changes consider all processes; system-related inhibitors are minimized; overall cycle time is improving dramatically.
B. Product/service and process: match product/service and process capabilities for high value; globally competitive.

6.2 Organization Support 20 points

Describe how the organization structure supports the processes and procedures as an interactive system.

Areas to Address

A. The organization: supports processes and procedures; provides for functional interaction.

6.3 Verification and Management
20 points

Describe how all processes and procedures are verified before use, thoroughly understood and efficiently managed.

Areas to Address

A. Concepts reviewed and approved by all departments before system design; simple; verified before implementation; followed.

6.4 Error Prevention 15 points

Describe how error prevention is emphasized in process and procedure design, and processes are controlled to be error free.

Areas to Address

A. Error prevention: stressed throughout organization; inherent in design of processes and procedures.
B. Process control: used to track and control processes; source of improvement; statistical methods utilized.

6.5 Technology and Innovation
15 points

Show how technology and innovation are planned and effectively utilized in processes and procedures.

Areas to Address

A. Technology and innovation: assess global competitors' innovation and technology; plan and utilize appropriate innovation for competitive advantage; computers, automation, and other technology used appropriately for quality improvement.
B. Capital equipment: Total Quality benefits quantified; used in justification; capable, reliable facilities exist.

6.6 Safety, Health and Environment
10 points

Describe goals and requirements to protect employees from hazards associated with products or services. Describe procedures for compliance with safety, health, and environmental standards.

Areas to Address

A. Formal employee safety program and standards. Evidence of compliance with OSHA, EPA or other mandatory standards.
B. Proper security and operation of hazardous materials, equipment or work areas.
C. Timeliness and effectiveness of corrective actions.

EVALUATION CRITERIA

7.0 INFORMATION   50 points

Required information is clear, complete, accurate, timely, useful, accessible and integrated with products, services, processes, and procedures.

7.1 Information Quality   20 points

Show how all information required to support Total Quality is complete, timely, accurate, useful, secure and clearly and appropriately communicated.

Areas to Address

A. Information: timely; accurate; updated; clear; complete; specific; meeting customer needs and used in decision processes; data converted to information.
B. Information system capability: provides measures of internal Total Quality; provides feedback on meeting customer requirements.

7.2 Information Improvement
                                        15 points

Describe how information quality is recognized as an essential element of Total Quality. Describe how information systems planning and implementation are done with the involvement of all departments to support process and organization requirements.

Areas to Address

A. Effective processes and procedures for identifying and correcting information quality problems.
B. Information System Plan: used; includes all departments; derived from process and organizational needs.
C. Support hardware system: reliable; backed up and secure. Software: monitored; evaluated; controlled. Users trained.

7.3 Customer and Process Requirements   15 points

Describe how external and internal customer product and process requirements are accurately communicated to all departments which must meet them.

Areas to Address

A. Customer requirements: communicated and promptly updated; interfaces to all departments; common base.
B. Product/service and process requirements: complete; integrated; communicated.

EVALUATION CRITERIA

8.0 SUPPLIERS   **50 points**

Supplied products and services, supplier contributions and supply processes meet all Total Quality requirements and enhance competitive advantage.

8.1 Requirements   **15 points**

Describe how supply requirements are mutually established with all involved internal groups actively participating.

Describe how early and continuous supplier involvement assures that requirements are mutually established, clearly understood, effectively communicated and consistently met.

Describe how total value is the primary basis for supply decisions.

Areas to Address

A.   Requirements: mutually established; clearly understood; effectively communicated.
B.   Supplier: early participation; continuously involved; understands needs; meets requirements.
C.   Supplier partnerships; all supplier contributions are considered; business impact, including strategic, is evaluated; superior performance is defined and expected; internal and external alternatives evaluated.

8.2 Product and Service Quality
                                    15 points

Describe how purchased products and/or services meet all Total Quality requirements.

Areas to Address

A.   Products and Services meet all Total Quality requirements: technical; supplier qualifications; reliability; safety; distribution; availability; responsiveness; quality; price; delivery.

8.3 Supply Processes   **10 points**

Show how processes involved in supply activities, from need identification to need satisfaction, are integrated with other processes and plans, and are achieving superior operating results.

Areas to Address

A.   Supply processes integrated: management involved in major decisions; internal and external communication effective; present in business plans.
B.   Processes effective: superior operating results achieved; process support resources available.

8.4 Supply Accountability   **10 points**

Describe how Total Quality of supplied Products and Services and the effectiveness of the supply processes are measured. Show how results are communicated to the organization and suppliers. Show how performance is continuously improved.

Areas to Address

A.   Measurement: supplier performance; product and/or service quality; process results; responsibility clearly defined; measures visible.
B.   Communication: data provided; analysis and conclusions developed; communicated.
C.   Improvement: plans exist; continuous improvement a way of life; suppliers involved; covers products and processes; success recognized.

EVALUATION CRITERIA

9.0 CULTURE   50 points

Management has established a value system in which individual and group actions reflect a 'Total Quality First' and appropriately innovative attitude and direction to meet established world-class requirements.

9.1 Organization Beliefs   15 points

Describe how the organization is bound together by the belief that Total Quality is the key to success. Show how 'Think Total Quality—all else will follow' describes the culture.

Show how Total Quality improvement is seen as a long-term process, not to be compromised by short-term conditions.

Areas to Address

A. Deeply held belief: held by all levels; not a fad; reflected in informal remarks and actions, speeches and bulletins.
B. Formal Total Quality policy exists. The organization's quality values are defined, communicated and understood.
C. Ownership: everyone's process; not just a management program; the way we do things.
D. Quality standards are not compromised to meet short-term objectives.

9.2 Change Leadership   15 points

Describe the right things which are being done to encourage and lead change toward world-class performance.

Areas to Address

A. Management of change: assess readiness for change; presence of a vision; reasons for change recognized; change accomplished through participation and involvement.
B. Innovation, risk-taking: appropriate; managed, encouraged and rewarded.

9.3 Total Quality System Description   10 points

Describe how the systems used to implement Total Quality are documented, implemented, regularly audited, updated and meet customer requirements. Describe how it is supported by procedures, manuals and other documentation which have been implemented by each department.

Areas to Address

A. Documented: can be found in policy; procedures; plans; manuals.
B. Requirements: published; implemented; regularly audited; updated.

9.4 Pride   10 points

Show that there is a sense of pride— individual and group.

Areas to Address

A. Pride: is shown in product or service; self; organization; Westinghouse.

EVALUATION CRITERIA

10.0 PLANNING   75 points

Strategic business and financial planning recogonize Total Quality as a primary business objective.

10.1 Strategic Imperative   30 points

Show that Total Quality improvement is seen as a strategic imperative, essential to long-term total business success. Show how Total Quality issues important to the business have been identified and are addressed in strategic plans.

Areas to Address

A.   Total Quality: seen as a strategic issue with management involvement; essential to long-term business success.
B.   Strategic plan: identifies and addresses Total Quality issues; translated into department objectives; communicated where applicable.
C.   Total organization provides for and involved in the planning process.

10.2 Total Quality Improvement Plan
30 points

Describe how annually revised quality improvement plans are used to detail formal Total Quality improvement projects with measurable goals for each department.

Areas to Address

A.   Total Quality Improvement Plan(s): exist; identify formal projects; contain measurable goals, each department involved; annually revised; responsibility assigned for development and implementation.

10.3 Organization Plan   15 points

Describe the dynamic organization plan which assures that structural changes and people capabilities accommodate changes in the business environment.

Areas to Address

A.   Organization plan: exists; routinely reviewed and modified; anticipates changes in people and business needs; applies planning tools; includes people development to meet future needs.
B.   Identification and selection processes; in place to support business plan.

EVALUATION CRITERIA

11.0 COMMUNICATIONS   50 points

Verbal and nonverbal communications are two-way, clear, consistent and forceful.

11.1 Policy and Requirement   15 points

Describe how Total Quality policy and requirements are clearly, consistently and forcefully communicated by management and understood by all employees.

Areas to Address

A. Communications plan: exists; emphasizes Total Quality; reaches audiences; is used; effective.
B. Employees show understanding; act on it.
C. Reinforcement: messages repeated more than once, in more than one way.

11.2 Two-Way   15 points

Show how two-way communications occur regularly.

Areas to Address

A. Feedback mechanisms: exist; are used; documented; management listens and actions are taken; communicated to all.
B. Results: shared.

11.3 Actions Versus Words   15 points

Describe how management actions and nonverbal signals promote Total Quality improvement and how they are consistent with verbal communications.

Areas to Address

A. Management actions seen as supporting expressed beliefs and expectations.
B. Formal and informal systems: goals of both systems seen as identical.

11.4 Public Responsibility   5 points

Describe the mechanisms used for external communications of information concerning Total Quality and support of quality improvement activities outside the company.

Areas to Address

A. Examples of quality improvement process and results being communicated to customers, the public, suppliers and distributors.
B. Management communication concerning the organization's quality improvement practices and results to outside audiences.
C. Evidence of management support of staff participation in outside activities aimed at quality improvement.

EVALUATION CRITERIA

12.0 ACCOUNTABILITY   100 points

Accountability measures for Total Quality are established, reported, analyzed and effectively used.

12.1 Performance Trends   35 points

Show how performance trends demonstrate steady progress towards meeting objectives.

Areas to Address

A. Business trends, i.e., profits, ROI, growth, market share, customer satisfaction, etc., are improving and are meeting objectives, compared to world-class competitors.
B. Total Quality indicators: exist; are improving; and are meeting objectives.

12.2 Reports and Diagnostic Techniques   20 points

Describe how managers use reports and diagnostic techniques which accurately reflect Total Quality performance and pinpoint improvement opportunities.

Areas to Address

A. Reports and diagnostic techniques: exist; are used; include summarizations; convert data to information; support the Total Quality improvement strategy; are credible; pinpoint improvement opportunities.

12.3 Progress Reviews   20 points

Describe how periodic, detailed, highly visible management progress reviews are used to monitor improvement.

Areas to Address

A. Management progress reviews: held frequently; are detailed and highly visible; respond effectively to measures/trends; external reviews used; capital and strategic programs are monitored.

12.4 Departmental Measures and Objectives   15 points

Describe how measures and improvement objectives are visible and used in each department.

Areas to Address

A. Total Quality performance indicators: exist; are understood; are visible.
B. Have goals: are used to improve.

12.5 Employee Objectives   10 points

Describe how evaluations of employees' performance include achievement of measurable Total Quality improvement Objectives.

Areas to Address

A. Evaluations of employees' performance: are conducted frequently.
B. Include measurable Total Quality performance objectives.
C. Merit increases and promotions are directly related to Total Quality performance.

SCORING INSTRUCTIONS

Since it takes a significant effort to reach high levels of Total Quality performance, the scoring system must allow discrimination between well-established Total Quality systems.

Consequently, the rating scale is non-linear with a 50% rating for a good Total Quality process and 100% for a world-class Total Quality process as shown in Table A.

Evaluation criteria for the self assessment process are the Westinghouse Conditions of Excellence for Total Quality.

The criteria and associated subcriteria are included in the self assessment scoresheet along with their weighted point scores.

Scoring for each Condition of Excellence has three major dimensions. i.e., the Applicant's:

- Approach to Total Quality Improvement
- Implementation of Total Quality
- Total Quality Improvement Results

These major dimensions expand into the following factors:

Approach

- Total Quality process-based
- Breadth of Integration across all functions
- Innovation evident in the approach

Implementation

- Breadth of Implementation (areas or functions)
- Depth of Implementation (ingrained in people)

Results

- Quality of Measurable Results
- Business Payoff of the Approach

Condensed Scoring Guidelines

100%
- World-class, effective, TQ-based approach
- Total Implementation and integration across all functions
- Ingrained in culture
- Exceptional, sustained business results
- Proven innovations

50%
- Superior to all competition

- Well planned, documented TQ approach
- Implemented in all major areas and functions
- Evident in culture of most groups
- Showing positive improvement results in most areas

- TQ awareness beginning
- Implementation beginning
- Not part of culture

0%
- Few or no results

Table A

Index